PERSPECTIVES

1

Lewis **LANSFORD**

Daniel **BARBER**

Amanda **JEFFRIES**

NATIONAL GEOGRAPHIC
LEARNING

Australia • Brazil • Mexico • Singapore • United Kingdom • United States

Perspectives 1a Combo Split
Lewis Lansford, Daniel Barber, Amanda Jeffries

Publisher: Sherrise Roehr

Executive Editor: Sarah Kenney

Publishing Consultant: Karen Spiller

Senior Development Editor: Brenden Layte

Development Editor: Lewis Thompson

Editorial Assistant: Gabe Feldstein

Director of Global Marketing: Ian Martin

Product Marketing Manager: Anders Bylund

Director of Content and Media Production: Michael Burggren

Production Manager: Daisy Sosa

Media Researcher: Leila Hishmeh

Manufacturing Customer Account Manager: Mary Beth Hennebury

Art Director: Brenda Carmichael

Production Management and Composition: Lumina Datamatics, Inc.

Cover Image: Bernardo Galmarini/ Alamy Stock Photo

© 2018 National Geographic Learning, a Cengage Learning Company

ALL RIGHTS RESERVED. No part of this work covered by the copyright herein may be reproduced or distributed in any form or by any means, except as permitted by U.S. copyright law, without the prior written permission of the copyright owner.

"National Geographic", "National Geographic Society" and the Yellow Border Design are registered trademarks of the National Geographic Society
® Marcas Registradas

For product information and technology assistance, contact us at
Cengage Learning Customer & Sales Support, cengage.com/contact

For permission to use material from this text or product,
submit all requests online at **cengage.com/permissions**
Further permissions questions can be emailed to
permissionrequest@cengage.com

Student Edition: Level 1 Combo Split A
ISBN: 978-1-337-29738-7

National Geographic Learning
20 Channel Center Street
Boston, MA 02210
USA

National Geographic Learning, a Cengage Learning Company, has a mission to bring the world to the classroom and the classroom to life. With our English language programs, students learn about their world by experiencing it. Through our partnerships with National Geographic and TED Talks, they develop the language and skills they need to be successful global citizens and leaders.

Locate your local office at **international.cengage.com/region**

Visit National Geographic Learning online at **NGL.Cengage.com/ELT**
Visit our corporate website at **www.cengage.com**

Printed in China
Print Number: 02 Print Year: 2023

ACKNOWLEDGMENTS

Paulo Rogerio Rodrigues
Escola Móbile, São Paulo, Brazil

Claudia Colla de Amorim
Escola Móbile, São Paulo, Brazil

Antonio Oliveira
Escola Móbile, São Paulo, Brazil

Rory Ruddock
Atlantic International Language Center, Hanoi, Vietnam

Carmen Virginia Pérez Cervantes
La Salle, Mexico City, Mexico

Rossana Patricia Zuleta
CIPRODE, Guatemala City, Guatemala

Gloria Stella Quintero Riveros
Universidad Católica de Colombia, Bogotá, Colombia

Mónica Rodriguez Salvo
MAR English Services, Buenos Aires, Argentina

Itana de Almeida Lins
Grupo Educacional Anchieta, Salvador, Brazil

Alma Loya Alma Loya
Colegio de Chihuahua, Chihuahua, Mexico

María Trapero Dávila
Colegio Teresiano, Ciudad Obregon, Mexico

Silvia Kosaruk
Modern School, Lanús, Argentina

Florencia Adami
Dámaso Centeno, Caba, Argentina

Natan Galed Gomez Cartagena
Global English Teaching, Rionegro, Colombia

James Ubriaco
Colégio Santo Agostinho, Belo Horizonte, Brazil

Ryan Manley
The Chinese University of Hong Kong, Shenzhen, China

Silvia Teles
Colégio Cândido Portinari, Salvador, Brazil

María Camila Azuero Gutiérrez
Fundación Centro Electrónico de Idiomas, Bogotá, Colombia

Martha Ramirez
Colegio San Mateo Apostol, Bogotá, Colombia

Beata Polit
XXIII LO Warszawa, Poland

Beata Tomaszewska
V LO Toruń, Poland

Michał Szkudlarek
I LO Brzeg, Poland

Anna Buchowska
I LO Białystok, Poland

Natalia Maćkowiak
one2one, Kosakowo, Poland

Agnieszka Dończyk
one2one, Kosakowo, Poland

Perspectives teaches learners to think critically and to develop the language skills they need to find their own voice in English. The carefully-guided language lessons, real-world stories, and TED Talks motivate learners to think creatively and communicate effectively.

In *Perspectives*, learners develop:

• AN OPEN MIND

Every unit explores one idea from different perspectives, giving learners opportunities for practicing language as they look at the world in new ways.

6 Do Your Best

The Selarón Steps in Rio de Janeiro, Brazil, are made from pieces of tile found in the city and donated from around the world.

IN THIS UNIT, YOU...
- discuss if perfection is good.
- read about someone who changed how he did things.
- learn about an unexpected artist.
- watch a TED Talk about teaching people bravery, not perfection.
- learn how to ask for and give advice.

6A The Best I Can Be

VOCABULARY Goals and expectations

1 MY PERSPECTIVE

Look at the photo. Many of the tiles used are broken or from the trash. Do you still think the stairs are beautiful?

2 Match the words in bold with the correct definitions.

1 ____ "I have not **failed**. I've just found several thousand ways that won't work." —Thomas Edison
2 ____ "The only place where **success** comes before work is in the dictionary." —Anonymous
3 ____ "Have no fear of **perfection**; you'll never reach it." —Salvador Dali
4 ____ "Beauty is about being comfortable in your own skin. It's about knowing and **accepting** who you are." —Ellen DeGeneres
5 ____ "Practice makes **perfect**." —Anonymous
6 ____ "Practice doesn't make perfect. Practice reduces the **imperfection**." —Toba Beta
7 ____ "True success is overcoming the fear of being **unsuccessful**." —Paul Sweeney

a (n) having no mistakes or problems
b (v, past) to finish without success
c (adj) without mistakes
d (n) the correct or wanted result
e (adj) not getting the correct or wanted result
f (n) not being exactly right
g (v) to feel that something is OK or normal

3 Choose the correct options to complete the meanings of the quotations in Activity 2.

1 When you find a way that doesn't work, you learn something new. When you learn nothing, you *fail / succeed*.
2 You *don't have to / have to* work before you can succeed.
3 Perfection is a nice idea, *and we should / but we shouldn't* expect to reach it.
4 Beauty isn't about how you look; it's about *how you feel / dressing comfortably*.
5 If you want to do something really well, *you won't fail / practice a lot*.
6 You can never be perfect, *but you can / and you can't* usually improve.
7 Success means not being afraid of *other people / failure*.

4 Match the opposites. Use your dictionary if necessary.

1 perfection ____ a unsuccessful
2 success ____ b fail
3 perfect ____ c imperfect
4 succeed ____ d imperfection
5 accept ____ e reject
6 successful ____ f failure

5 Work in pairs. Discuss the questions.

6D Teach Girls Bravery, Not Perfection

TED TALKS

"We have to show them that they will be loved and accepted not for being perfect but for being courageous."

RESHMA SAUJANI

Read about Reshma Saujani and get ready to watch her TED Talk. 6.0

AUTHENTIC LISTENING SKILLS

Contrast

A contrast is when a speaker shows that two ideas, facts, or situations are different. Words such as *but* and *however* often mark contrasts. A speaker may also change his or her tone to mark contrast.

1 Read the Authentic Listening Skills box. Match the contrasting ideas in the excerpts from the TED Talk.

1 "She tried, she came close, but ____
2 "She'll think that her student spent the past twenty minutes just staring at the screen. But ____
3 "Girls are really good at coding, but ____
4 "We have to begin to undo the socialization of perfection, but ____
5 "This was my way to make a difference. The polls, however, ____

a if she presses 'undo' a few times, she'll see that her student wrote code and then deleted it."
b we've got to combine it with building a sisterhood* that lets girls know that they are not alone."
c it's not enough just to teach them to code."
d she didn't get it exactly right."
e told a very different story."

sisterhood *a group of girls or women who work together and help each other*

2 Listen to the excerpts and check your answers to Activity 1.

WATCH

3 Work in pairs. Discuss the questions before you watch the talk.

1 Is perfection always better or more useful than imperfection? Why?
2 Is it more important to be perfect or to try new things? Why?
3 Can always wanting to be perfect make a person not try new things? Why? Has this ever happened to you?

4 Watch Part 1 of the talk. Choose the correct options to complete the sentences. 6.1

1 Reshma started her career working in ____.
a government
b banking
c marketing
2 She wanted to have a more active role in government to ____.
a make more money
b change things
c raise money for others
3 She tried for an elected job in government ____.
a and won
b but changed her mind
c and lost badly
4 She tells the story about running for government to show that ____.
a she was perfect
b she was brave for the first time
c she was always brave

5 Watch Part 2 of the talk. Answer the questions. 6.2

1 What does Reshma say that boys are rewarded for, but girls are taught to avoid?
2 What does she feel that girls lack?
3 What do teachers often learn about girls who are learning to code?
4 According to Reshma, why do girls often not answer questions?
5 According to Reshma, who should teach girls to be brave?

6 VOCABULARY IN CONTEXT

a Watch the clips from the TED Talk. Choose the correct meanings of the words. 6.3
b Work in pairs. Discuss the questions.
1 Think of a time when you had to be *courageous*. What happened?
2 Have you ever run for a position, for example, captain of a sports team? What was it? What would you like to run for?
3 What kind of things do you *negotiate* with your parents? With your teachers?
4 Have you ever seen a person's *supportive network* in action? What was the reason?
5 Do you think everyone has the *potential* to do something good or brave? What do you have the potential to do?
6 Is there anything that you have to *struggle* with to achieve? What?

7 Think of something you have learned to do—speak a language, play a musical instrument, play a sport, or something else. Make notes.

- What was the skill or activity?
- What challenges did you face? How did you have to be brave to continue learning?
- What kinds of mistakes did you make while learning it?
- What advice would you give to someone learning the activity?

8 Work in small groups. Discuss your activity from Activity 7.

CHALLENGE

Work in groups. Discuss the questions.

1 Writing code is a process of trial and error and requires perseverance. What other activities require trial and error and perseverance?
2 Reshma says in her talk that a supportive network is an important part of learning. Have you ever had a supportive network? Who was in it?
3 Can you think of a time when you did something—even something small or simple—that felt brave? What did you learn from it?
4 The journalist Arianna Huffington said, "Failure isn't the opposite of success, it's part of success." Do you agree or disagree? Why?
5 In your country, where are girls and women underrepresented and why?
6 Reshma talks about the ways that boys are socialized. Is this also harmful to society? Does it limit the opportunities for boys? If so, how?

76 Unit 6 Do Your Best

Unit 6 Do Your Best 77

• A CRITICAL EYE

Students learn the critical thinking skills and strategies they need to evaluate new information and develop their own opinions and ideas to share.

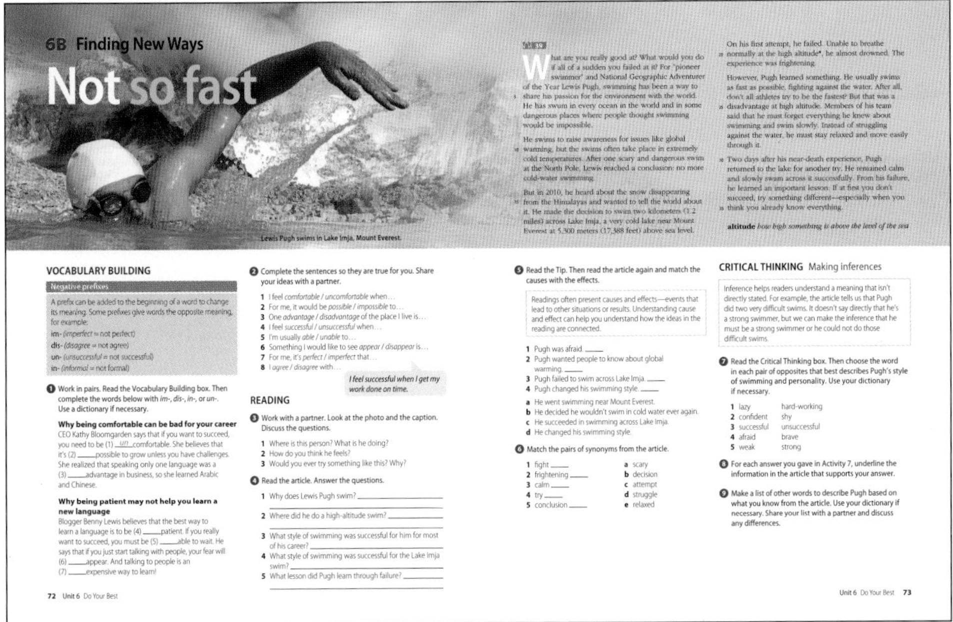

6B Finding New Ways

Not so fast

Lewis Pugh swims in Lake Imja, Mount Everest.

What are you really good at? What would you do if all of a sudden you failed at it? For "pioneer swimmer" and National Geographic Adventurer of the Year Lewis Pugh, swimming has been a way to share his passion for the environment with the world. He has swum in every ocean in the world and in some dangerous places where people thought swimming would be impossible.

He swims to raise awareness for issues like global warming, but the swims often take place in extremely cold temperatures. After one scary and dangerous swim at the North Pole, Lewis reached a conclusion: no more cold-water swimming.

But in 2010, he heard about the snow disappearing from the Himalayas and wanted to tell the world about it. He made the decision to swim two kilometers (1.2 miles) across Lake Imja, a very cold lake near Mount Everest at 5,300 meters (17,388 feet) above sea level.

On his first attempt, he failed. Unable to breathe normally at the high altitude*, he almost drowned. The experience was frightening.

However, Pugh learned something. He usually swims as fast as possible, fighting against the water. After all, don't all athletes try to be the fastest? But that was a disadvantage at high altitude. Members of his team said that he must forget everything he knew about swimming and swim slowly. Instead of struggling against the water, he must stay relaxed and move easily through it.

Two days after his near-death experience, Pugh returned to the lake for another try. He remained calm and slowly swam across it successfully. From his failure, he learned an important lesson: If at first you don't succeed, try something different—especially when you think you already know everything.

altitude *how high something is above the level of the sea*

VOCABULARY BUILDING

Negative prefixes

A prefix can be added to the beginning of a word to change its meaning. Some prefixes give words the opposite meaning, for example:
im- (*imperfect* = not perfect)
dis- (*disagree* = not agree)
un- (*unsuccessful* = not successful)
in- (*informal* = not formal)

1 Work in pairs. Read the Vocabulary Building box. Then complete the words below with *im-*, *dis-*, *in-*, or *un-*. Use a dictionary if necessary.

Why being comfortable can be bad for your career
CEO Kathy Bloomgarden says that if you want to succeed, you need to be (1) _un_ comfortable. She believes that it's (2) ____possible to grow unless you have challenges. She realized that speaking only one language was a (3) ____advantage in business, so she learned Arabic and Chinese.

Why being patient may not help you learn a new language
Blogger Benny Lewis believes that the best way to learn a language is to be (4) ____patient. If you really want to succeed, you must be (5) ____able to wait. He says that if you just start talking with people, your fear will (6) ____appear. And talking to people is an (7) ____expensive way to learn!

2 Complete the sentences so they are true for you. Share your ideas with a partner.

1 I feel *comfortable / uncomfortable* when…
2 For me, it would be *possible / impossible* to…
3 One *advantage / disadvantage* of the place I live is…
4 I feel *successful / unsuccessful* when…
5 I'm usually *able / unable* to…
6 Something I would like to see *appear / disappear* is…
7 For me, it's *perfect / imperfect* that…
8 I *agree / disagree* with…

I feel successful when I get my work done on time.

READING

3 Work with a partner. Look at the photo and the caption. Discuss the questions.

1 Where is this person? What is he doing?
2 How do you think he feels?
3 Would you ever try something like this? Why?

4 Read the article. Answer the questions.

1 Why does Lewis Pugh swim? ____
2 Where did he do a high-altitude swim? ____
3 What style of swimming was successful for him for most of his career? ____
4 What style of swimming was successful for the Lake Imja swim? ____
5 What lesson did Pugh learn through failure? ____

5 Read the Tip. Then read the article again and match the causes with the effects.

Readings often present causes and effects—events that lead to other situations or results. Understanding cause and effect can help you understand how the ideas in the reading are connected.

1 Pugh was afraid. ____
2 Pugh wanted people to know about global warming. ____
3 Pugh failed to swim across Lake Imja. ____
4 Pugh changed his swimming style. ____

a He went swimming near Mount Everest.
b He decided he wouldn't swim in cold water ever again.
c He succeeded in swimming across Lake Imja.
d He changed his swimming style.

6 Match the pairs of synonyms from the article.

1 fight ____ a scary
2 frightening ____ b decision
3 calm ____ c attempt
4 try ____ d struggle
5 conclusion ____ e relaxed

CRITICAL THINKING Making inferences

Inference helps readers understand a meaning that isn't directly stated. For example, the article tells us that Pugh did two very difficult swims. It doesn't say directly that he's a strong swimmer, but we can make the inference that he must be a strong swimmer or he could not do those difficult swims.

7 Read the Critical Thinking box. Then choose the word in each pair of opposites that best describes Pugh's style of swimming and personality. Use your dictionary if necessary.

1 lazy hard-working
2 confident shy
3 successful unsuccessful
4 afraid brave
5 weak strong

8 For each answer you gave in Activity 7, underline the information in the article that supports your answer.

9 Make a list of other words to describe Pugh based on what you know from the article. Use your dictionary if necessary. Share your list with a partner and discuss any differences.

72 Unit 6 Do Your Best

Unit 6 Do Your Best 73

• A CLEAR VOICE

Students respond to the unit theme and express their own ideas confidently in English.

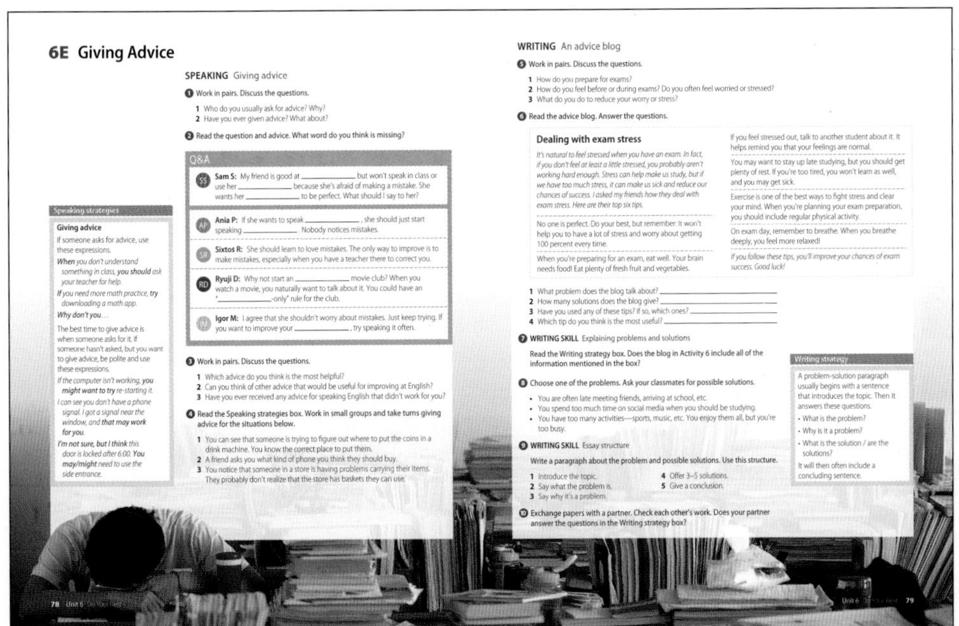

6E Giving Advice

SPEAKING Giving advice

1 Work in pairs. Discuss the questions.

1 Who do you usually ask for advice? Why?
2 Have you ever given advice? What about?

2 Read the question and advice. What word do you think is missing?

Q&A

Sam S: My friend is good at ____ but won't speak in class or use her ____ because she's afraid of making a mistake. She wants her ____ to be perfect. What should I say to her?

Ania P: If she wants to speak ____, she should just start speaking ____. Nobody notices mistakes.

Sixtos R: She should learn to love mistakes. The only way to improve is to make mistakes, especially when you have a teacher there to correct you.

Ryuji D: Why not start an ____ movie club? When you watch a movie, you naturally want to talk about it. You could have an "____-only" rule for the club.

Igor M: I agree that she shouldn't worry about mistakes. Just keep trying. If you want to improve your ____, try speaking it often.

Speaking strategies

Giving advice
If someone asks for advice, use these expressions.
When *you don't understand something in class,* ***you should*** *ask your teacher for help.*
If *you need more math practice,* ***try*** *downloading a math app.*
Why don't you…
The best time to give advice is when someone asks for it. If someone hasn't asked, but you want to give advice, be polite and use these expressions.
If the computer isn't working, ***you might want to try*** *re-starting it.*
I can see you don't have a phone signal. I got a signal near the window, and ***that may work for you.***
I'm not sure, but I think *this door is locked after 6:00.* ***You may/might*** *need to use the side entrance.*

3 Work in pairs. Discuss the questions.

1 Which advice do you think is the most helpful?
2 Can you think of other advice that would be useful for improving at English?
3 Have you ever received any advice for speaking English that didn't work for you?

4 Read the Speaking strategies box. Work in small groups and take turns giving advice for the situations below.

1 You can see that someone is trying to figure out where to put the coins in a drink machine. You know the correct place to put them.
2 A friend asks you what kind of phone you think they should buy.
3 You notice that someone in a store is having problems carrying their items. They probably don't realize that the store has baskets they can use.

WRITING An advice blog

5 Work in pairs. Discuss the questions.

1 How do you prepare for exams?
2 How do you feel before or during exams? Do you often feel worried or stressed?
3 What do you do to reduce your worry or stress?

6 Read the advice blog. Answer the questions.

Dealing with exam stress

It's natural to feel stressed when you have an exam. In fact, if you don't feel at least a little stressed, you probably aren't working hard enough. Stress can help make us study, but if we have too much stress, it can make us sick and reduce our chances of success. I asked my friends how they deal with exam stress. Here are their top six tips.

No one is perfect. Do your best, but remember: It won't help you to have a lot of stress and worry about getting 100 percent every time.

When you're preparing for an exam, eat well. Your brain needs food! Eat plenty of fresh fruit and vegetables.

If you feel stressed out, talk to another student about it. It helps remind you that your feelings are normal.

You may want to stay up late studying, but you should get plenty of rest. If you're too tired, you won't learn as well, and you may get sick.

Exercise is one of the best ways to fight stress and clear your mind. When you're planning your exam preparation, you should include regular physical activity.

On exam day, remember to breathe. When you breathe deeply, you feel more relaxed!

If you follow these tips, you'll improve your chances of exam success. Good luck!

1 What problem does the blog talk about? ____
2 How many solutions does the blog give? ____
3 Have you used any of these tips? If so, which ones? ____
4 Which tip do you think is the most useful? ____

7 **WRITING SKILL** Explaining problems and solutions

Read the Writing strategy box. Does the blog in Activity 6 include all of the information mentioned in the box?

Writing strategy

A problem-solution paragraph usually begins with a sentence that introduces the topic. Then it answers these questions.
• What is the problem?
• Why is it a problem?
• What is the solution / are the solutions?
It will then often include a concluding sentence.

8 Choose one of the problems. Ask your classmates for possible solutions.

• You are often late meeting friends, arriving at school, etc.
• You spend too much time on social media when you should be studying.
• You have too many activities—sports, music, etc. You enjoy them all, but you're too busy.

9 **WRITING SKILL** Essay structure

Write a paragraph about the problem and possible solutions. Use this structure.

1 Introduce the topic.
2 Say what the problem is.
3 Say why it's a problem.
4 Offer 3–5 solutions.
5 Give a conclusion.

10 Exchange papers with a partner. Check each other's work. Does your partner answer the questions in the Writing strategy box?

78 Unit 6

Unit 6 79

CONTENTS

GRAMMAR	TEDTALKS		SPEAKING	WRITING
Verb patterns: Verb + *-ing* or infinitive with *to*	Half a million secrets	**FRANK WARREN** Frank Warren's idea worth spreading is that sharing secrets can help us connect with others and know ourselves better. **Authentic Listening Skills** Word stress **Critical Thinking** Identifying the main idea	Talking about likes and dislikes	An introductory postcard **Writing Skill** Introducing yourself
Past continuous **Pronunciation** *-ing* in fast speech	Magical houses, made of bamboo	**ELORA HARDY** Elora Hardy's idea worth spreading is that bamboo is an incredibly adaptable and strong building material that pushes the boundaries of what we can create with sustainable materials. **Authentic Listening Skills** Listening for gist	Giving reasons	A travel review describing a house **Writing Skill** Answering *Wh*- questions
Phrasal verbs	The amazing story of the man who gave us modern pain relief	**LATIF NASSER** Latif Nasser's idea worth spreading is that pain is a testament to a fully lived life, an essential part of the human experience that all of us—including doctors—must acknowledge and deal with. **Authentic Listening Skills** Collaborative listening	Agreeing, disagreeing, and conceding a point	An opinion essay **Writing Skill** Hedging
Comparative forms	Don't eat the marshmallow!	**JOACHIM DE POSADA** Joachim de Posada's idea worth spreading is that children who pass the "marshmallow test" could potentially be more successful in life since the results show signs of patience and self-discipline. **Authentic Listening Skills** English speakers with accents	Asking about opinions; Making comparisons; Making a decision	An inquiry email **Writing Skill** Responding to an ad
Present perfect with *for*, *since*, *already*, *just*, and *yet*	Why we laugh	**SOPHIE SCOTT** Sophie Scott's idea worth spreading is that laughter is an ancient behavior that we use to benefit ourselves and others in complex and surprising ways. **Authentic Listening Skills** Dealing with fast speech **Critical Thinking** Recognize supporting evidence	Talking about availability; Accepting and denying an invitation	Informal invitations and replies **Writing Skill** Politely making and replying to invitations

1 Who are you?

IN THIS UNIT, YOU...

- learn about occupations, interests, and descriptions.
- talk about yourself and others.
- read about how people show emotions.
- watch a TED Talk about people's secrets.
- speak and write about what you like to do.

Many people use their physical appearance to say something about themselves.

1A He's really into music.

VOCABULARY Personality

1 MY PERSPECTIVE

Work in pairs. Discuss the questions.

1 Look at the photo. What words would you use to describe this person?
2 Circle two or three of the words below to describe yourself.

cool	friendly	funny	happy	honest	intelligent
kind	loud	mean	nice	popular	shy

3 Think of two or three words that other people might use to describe you.
4 Were your answers to questions 2 and 3 the same or different? Why?

2 Match the pairs of words that have a similar meaning. Use your dictionary if necessary. Then think of someone you know who you can describe with each pair of words.

1 smart ____	**a** relaxed
2 calm ____	**b** friendly
3 helpful ____	**c** intelligent
4 cheerful ____	**d** kind

3 Choose the correct option to complete each sentence.

1 I'm *active* / *lazy* on the weekends. I usually play sports and go out with my friends.
2 He's *confident* / *nervous* about giving presentations because he doesn't like making mistakes.
3 She's very *sociable* / *shy* and has a lot of friends.
4 Our coach is *serious* / *easygoing* and lets us listen to music before basketball practice.
5 Kenji is very *hard-working* / *talented*. He isn't the best, but he really wants to succeed.
6 Luis is really *loud* / *quiet*. You always know when he's in a room!

4 Work in pairs. Take turns describing people in your class, but don't say their names. Can your partner guess who you're talking about?

She's calm, helpful, and cheerful.

Is it Li?

No. She's also very active—but a little bit shy.

Oh, is it Ana?

5 Work in pairs. Think of a famous person together. Then, working separately, each make a list of words to describe this person. Use your dictionary if necessary. Then compare your lists. Did you use any of the same words? Do you agree with your partner's description? Why?

6 Work with the same partner. Make one list for your person from Activity 5 using all the words you agree on. Read your list to the class. Can the class guess your person?

LISTENING

7 Look at the picture and caption. Answer the questions.

1 What do you think DJ Spooky means by "We're all nature?"
  a We are made of trees. **b** We are part of the planet. **c** We are animals.

2 What type of music do you think DJ Spooky makes?
  a hip-hop **b** classical **c** rock

3 What types of music do you enjoy? Hip-hop? Rock? Pop? Jazz? Some other kind?

8 Listen to the conversation between two students meeting for the first time at a party. Complete the chart. 2

Who…	Bruno	Anna
1 listens to the school radio station?		
2 listens to DJ Spooky?		
3 plays an instrument?		
4 plays sports?		
5 is looking for new music?		

9 Are the sentences *true* or *false* or is the information not given? Listen again to check you answers. 2

1 Bruno and Anna like the music at the party.
2 Bruno and Anna both like hip-hop and rock.
3 Anna likes a lot of famous, popular music.
4 DJ Spooky mixes many styles of music.
5 DJ Spooky uses his art to make people think about the environment.
6 DJ Spooky has an easygoing personality.
7 Anna interviewed DJ Spooky.

10 Work in pairs. Practice asking and answering questions about interests. Use the models in the Useful language box to help you.

Useful language

Are you into (music / sports / art / books)?
Yes, I am. / No, not really.
What kind of (music / sports / art / books) do you like?
I'm into (rock / baseball / dance / science fiction).

National Geographic Explorer DJ Spooky uses music and art to make people think about the environment and the world around them. He says, "We're all nature."

GRAMMAR Simple present and present continuous

Simple present and present continuous

Simple present

a *They play really good music.*

Present continuous

b *They're playing really good music.*

11 Look at the Grammar box. Underline the verb in each sentence. Then answer the questions.

1 Which tense describes an activity happening right now?
2 Which tense describes something that happens all the time or is true right now?

12 Complete the information about DJ Spooky using the simple present of the verbs in parentheses.

DJ Spooky's real name (1) __________ (be) Paul D. Miller. He (2) __________ (live) in New York, but he (3) __________ (have) fans all over the world. They (4) __________ (love) his shows—especially the way he (5) __________ (use) music and pictures together. "I (6) __________ (like) to think of music not just as music, but as information," he says. "Art and music and science and technology (7) __________ (not be) separate things." At his concerts, people (8) __________ (hear) music, (9) __________ (see) pictures of the natural world, and most of all, (10) __________ (learn).

Check page 128 for more information and practice.

13 Complete the sentences with the simple present or present continuous of the verbs in parentheses.

1 My sister usually __________ (watch) TV at night.
2 David __________ (be) from Mexico City.
3 Marta isn't here because she __________ (study) in the library.
4 Our football team __________ (practice) on Saturdays.
5 Be quiet, please. I __________ (try) to use the phone.

14 Complete the conversation with the simple present or present continuous of the verbs. Some words are used more than once.

be do go play wait want work

A What (1) __________ you (2) __________ right now?
B I (3) __________ to Ella's house.
A Who (4) __________ Ella?
B She (5) __________ a friend from my basketball team. We (6) __________ basketball after school on Tuesdays. (7) __________ you (8) __________ to come?
A Sorry, I can't. I (9) __________ for Tony because we (10) __________ together on a science project.

15 **PRONUNCIATION** *-s* verb endings

Read the Pronunciation box. Then listen and write each word in the correct list. Listen again to check your answers. 3

There are three ways to pronounce *-s* at the end of a verb: /s/ as in *gets*, /z/ as in *sings*, or /ɪz/ as in *washes*.

goes likes plays practices studies uses wants watches writes

/s/ works, __________
/z/ sings, __________
/ɪz/ dances, __________

16 **MY PERSPECTIVE**

Work in pairs. Find five things that you and your partner like that are different. Make sentences about them to share with the class. Use these verbs or your own ideas.

- like (music, sports, books)
- watch (TV shows, movies)
- want (a pet, a new phone)
- play (guitar, video games)
- go (to the park, shopping)

She plays the guitar, but I play the piano.

1B How are you feeling?

VOCABULARY BUILDING

Collocations

Collocations are words that are often used together. Certain verb collocations are often used to describe emotions.

*She **looks nervous**.* *I'**m bored**.* *You **seem angry**.*

1 **Read the collocations. Then choose the best words to complete the sentences below.**

Start to experience an emotion: *become / get*	*afraid* *bored* *frightened* *nervous*	*angry* *excited* *upset* *worried*
Experience an emotion: *feel / be*		
Appear to experience an emotion: *look / seem*		

1 Are you __________? Don't worry. The test won't be that bad.
2 I'm getting __________ about my vacation next week.
3 They feel __________ about their exams next month.
4 Dan __________ like he is upset about something, but I don't know what the problem is.
5 The teacher __________ angry when everyone was late.
6 You __________ nervous about the test, but I'm sure you'll do well.

2 **Work in pairs. Pick three of the emotions in Activity 1. Tell a partner about a time you felt each one.**

READING

3 **Read the tip. Preview the article and answer the questions.**

Before you read a text, preview it. This will help you understand what it's about before you read it carefully.

- Look at the title. What is the text probably about?
- Look at any pictures. What do they tell you about the text?
- Read the first and last paragraph. What are the main ideas?

4 **Read the article. Which paragraph discusses each idea?**

a There are four types of feelings.
b Animals experience emotions.
c Some animals understand human feelings.
d Seeing people is an important part of communication.
e Humans experience many different feelings.

5 **Read the article again. Choose the correct option to complete each sentence.**

1 Recent scientific research ___*b*___ the idea that we experience many very different feelings.
a proves **b** disagrees with **c** says nothing about

2 According to researchers, feeling nervous is basically the same as being _____ .
a sad **b** angry **c** afraid

3 People everywhere show their emotions _____ .
a on their face **b** in their voice **c** through their words

4 Researchers found that horses recognize _____ emotions on people's faces.
a four **b** three **c** two

5 Horses understand people's feelings because _____ .
a horses' brains are like people's brains
b they work closely with people
c people teach them to understand

6 Carl Safina believes that human and animal emotions are _____ .
a very different **b** similar **c** impossible to compare

7 According to the article, animals _____ with each other.
a share their emotions
b communicate in "animal language"
c often feel angry

8 Understanding feelings helps us _____ .
a stop feeling angry
b control animals
c communicate

6 **Which of these statements is true according to the article? Underline the information that explains your answer.**

a Some animals can understand human language.
b Email isn't a good way to discuss important things.
c We should try to hide our feelings from animals.

7 **MY PERSPECTIVE**

Work in pairs. Discuss the questions.

1 What did you learn from the article?
2 Did the article change your thinking about animals and emotions?
3 Do you think it's true that some discussions should be had face to face? Why? Give examples.

IT'S WRITTEN ALL OVER YOUR FACE

4 _______ **How are you feeling right now?** Excited? Bored? Worried? Upset? How many possible answers are there? Interested, nervous, relaxed, angry, lonely… the list goes on. We feel so many different things, so feelings can seem very complicated. But recent scientific research actually says this might not be completely true.

_______ **Basic feelings**

A group of scientists at the University of Glasgow in Scotland say that people only experience four basic feelings: sad, happy, angry, and afraid. All of the other feelings we describe are really part of one of the basic four. So if you feel worried or nervous, that's fear. If you're relaxed or excited, that's happiness. If you're bored or lonely, that's sadness. Many scientists also say that people all over the world can see these feelings in the faces of the people around them. In fact, we're so good at it, we can easily understand the feelings on the face of a cartoon.

Try it! Look at the pictures and match each one with a basic feeling—*sad, happy, angry, afraid.*

THE FOUR BASIC FEELINGS

_______ **Not just for humans**

Our faces show our feelings so clearly that even some animals know how we feel. Scientists at the University of Essex in the UK say that horses can identify happy or angry faces and can even recognize these feelings on the faces of strangers. This makes sense because horses live and work closely with humans in many places. They enjoy being with happy people. They also learn to avoid angry people whenever possible. Scientists want to know more. Can we expect animals to recognize other feelings, too? The research continues.

_______ **What do animals feel?**

It's not just horses that recognize human emotions. Animal expert Carl Safina believes that other animals experience many of the same feelings people have. "They play. They act frightened when there's danger. They relax when things are good," he says. In his book *Beyond Words: What Animals Think and Feel*, Safina explains that dogs, elephants, and even whales* show their feelings and understand the feelings of other animals. He tells the story of a whale who rescued a seal* from danger and says that elephants love meeting their friends and become very sad when a friend or family member dies. Scientists say that emotions help animals to survive. For example, research shows that animals who don't feel fear don't live for very long.

_______ **Face time**

Understanding feelings is important. In fact, it's so important that people's faces usually tell others exactly how they feel, and these feelings are often obvious to us. We can use this information to make communication easier, or sometimes to know what other people are thinking or feeling, even when they don't tell us. So when you need to talk about something important, try to have a face-to-face conversation—or at least a video chat.

whale *a large sea mammal that breathes through the top of its head*
seal *a sea mammal with thick fur and flippers*

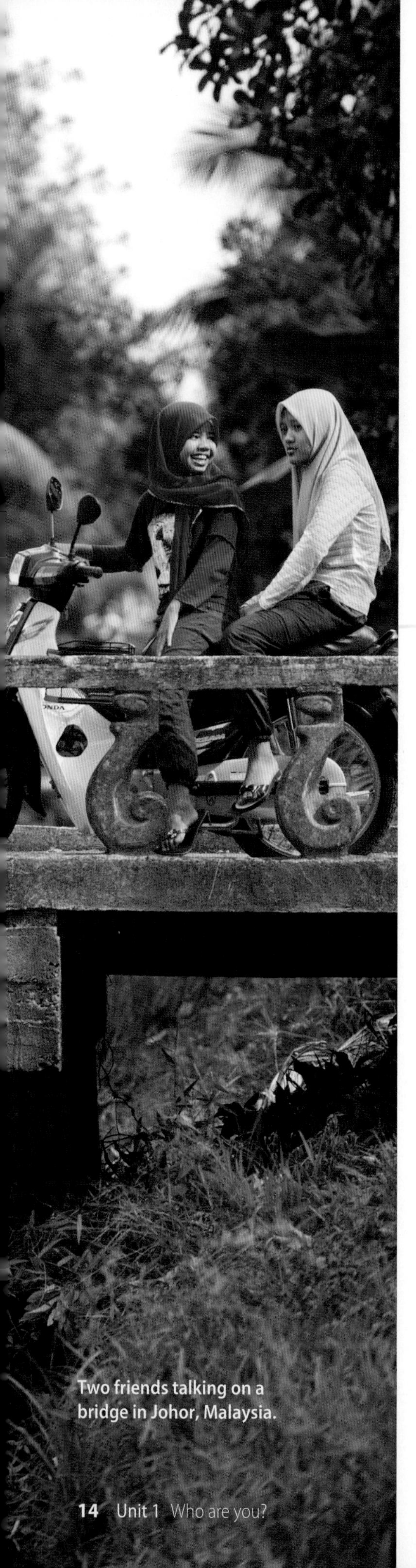
Two friends talking on a bridge in Johor, Malaysia.

1C I expect my friends to understand.

GRAMMAR Verb patterns: Verb + *-ing* or infinitive with *to*

1 Work in pairs. Discuss the questions.

1 Name two or three things you love doing.
2 Name two or three things you hate doing.

2 Look at the Grammar box. Underline the main verbs in each sentence. Circle the verb that follows the main verb.

Verb + *-ing* or infinitive with *to*

a *They enjoy being with happy people.*
b *They also learn to avoid angry people whenever possible.*
c *Scientists want to know more.*
d *Elephants love meeting their friends.*

3 Look again at the sentences in the Grammar box. Complete the table with the verbs in Activity 2.

Verbs followed by…

-ing form	*to* + infinitive
enjoy	

Check page 128 for more information and practice.

4 Choose the correct options to complete the sentences below. Are any of the sentences true for you?

1 I suggest *talking / to talk* to someone when you feel lonely.
2 Whenever I feel happy, I want *sharing / to share* it with my friends!
3 I always manage *making / to make* myself feel better when I discuss my problems with someone.
4 I can't help *feeling / to feel* closer to my friends when I share how I feel with them.
5 My friends and I don't mind *telling / to tell* each other about our feelings. It's free entertainment!

5 Complete the text with the verb + *-ing* or the infinitive with *to*. Sometimes both options are possible.

We can't help (1) ___________ (smile) when the people around us smile. And when we see our friends laugh, it makes us want (2) ___________ (laugh), too. It's almost impossible to avoid (3) ___________ (share) the feelings of the people around us. But this doesn't stop with being happy, sad, angry, or afraid. It affects us physically, too! Our own body temperature actually begins (4) ___________ (drop) when we watch someone put their hand in ice water.

Why are we able to feel the emotions of the people around us? Humans need (5) ___________ (understand) each other well because we spend a lot of time working together. When we don't manage (6) ___________ (get along), we may start (7) ___________ (fight)—and that's bad for everyone.

6 Complete the exchanges using the correct forms of the verbs. Sometimes more than one option is possible.

bother	help	receive	send
share	talk	not tell	write

1 A I hate __________ you, but can I ask for some advice?
B I don't mind __________ you, but I can't talk right now. I'm late for class!

2 A Do you promise __________ my secret?
B I'm not sure! Sometimes I can't keep myself from __________ secrets!

3 A I like __________ about my feelings in a notebook.
B I don't do that. I prefer __________ to someone face-to-face.

4 A I plan __________ you a postcard from my vacation.
B Oh, thanks. I love __________ postcards.

7 Complete the sentences with true information about yourself. Use verb + *-ing* and infinitive with *to*.

I like *riding my bike* on the weekend.

1 I like __________ on the weekend.
2 I want __________ next summer.
3 I usually avoid __________ .
4 I hope __________ before I'm 20 years old.
5 I need __________ for school.

8 Work in pairs. Take turns asking and answering questions about Activity 7. Use the correct form of *do* in the questions.

A *What do you like to do on the weekend?*
B *I like…*
A *What do you want to do next summer?*
B *I want…*

9 **CHOOSE**

Choose one of the following activities.

- Ask questions to find other people in the class who are similar to you.

Do you like riding your bike on the weekend?

Yes, I do.

Do you avoid being late for school?

Of course! But I'm sometimes late anyway.

- Report back to the class about what you learned about your partner in Activity 8.

Majid likes watching movies on the weekend.

- Write a paragraph comparing you and your partner using the information you learned in Activity 8.

A family laughs on a roller coaster. What activities do you do with your friends and family that make you laugh?

1D Half a Million Secrets

> "Secrets can take many forms. They can be shocking or silly or soulful. They can connect us to our deepest humanity or with people we'll never meet again."

FRANK WARREN

Read about Frank Warren and get ready to watch his TED Talk. ▶ 1.0

AUTHENTIC LISTENING SKILLS

Word stress

In English, words with two or more syllables have the main stress on one of the syllables. Learning the pronunciation of words and where the stress is will help you recognize them when you hear them.

1 Read the Authentic Listening Skills box. Listen to the words from the TED Talk and underline the syllables that are stressed. 🎧 5

1 collect	**3** girlfriend	**5** advertisement	**7** instructions
2 received	**4** stranger	**6** memory	**8** collection

2 Now listen to two extracts from the talk. Notice the stressed syllables in the first extract. Underline the stressed syllables in the second extract. 🎧 6

1. Hi, my name is Frank, and I collect secrets. It all started with a crazy idea in November of two thousand and four.
2. I printed up three thousand self-addressed postcards, just like this. They were blank on one side, and on the other side I listed some simple instructions.

WATCH

3 Watch Part 1 of the talk. Choose the correct options to complete the sentences. ▶ 1.1

1. Frank gave the postcards to *strangers / friends*.
2. The idea *made people angry / became very popular*.
3. People from *the US / many different countries* sent postcards to Frank.
4. The green postcard was *a little sad / very funny*.

4 Complete the sentences. Then watch Part 2 of the talk and check your answers. ▶ 1.2

cat	email	ending
postcard	ring	website

1. The man's postcard had a picture of a __________ and a ring.
2. The man said he wanted to give the __________ to the woman.
3. Frank put the __________ on his website.
4. A little while later, Frank received a very happy __________ from the man.
5. The man and the woman looked at Frank's __________ together.
6. The story had a happy __________ because the woman said yes.

5 Watch Part 3 of the talk. Which ideas does Frank Warren discuss? Check the ones he mentions. ▶ 1.3

1. The website IFoundYourCamera helps people find lost cameras.
2. Many people feel unhappy when they see their pictures on the website.
3. IFoundYourCamera shows that people want to help other people.
4. The woman in the picture found another person's camera.
5. The man, woman, and child in the picture are very happy now.

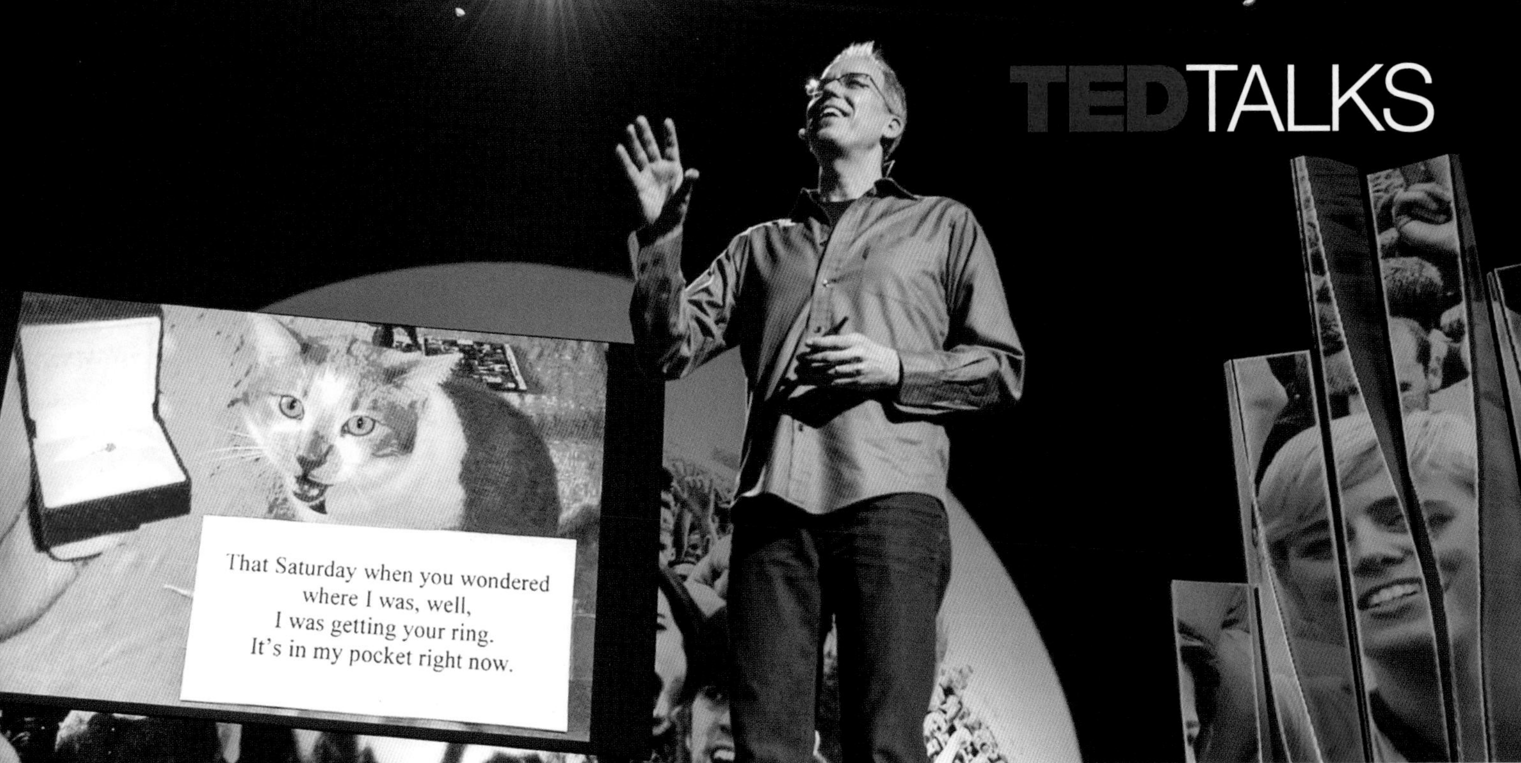

TED TALKS
That Saturday when you wondered
where I was, well,
I was getting your ring.
It's in my pocket right now.

6 VOCABULARY IN CONTEXT

a Watch the clips from the talk. Choose the correct meaning of the words and phrases. ▶ 1.4

b Complete the sentences with your own ideas. Then discuss with a partner.

1 I sometimes *struggle* when ________ .
2 My favorite *image* is ________ .
3 When I need to feel *calm*, I ________ .
4 One time I experienced a *language barrier* when ________ .

7 Frank says that secrets can be shocking or silly or soulful. Write a couple of sentences sharing a silly secret about yourself. Choose something that you don't mind telling the whole class.

I always cry at the end of Stars Wars *movies. I try to hide it from my friends and family, but every time I watch one, I cry.*

8 Work in groups. Share your answers to Activity 7.

CRITICAL THINKING Identifying the main idea

9 Read the Critical Thinking box. Then work in pairs. Say what you think the main idea of the talk is.

Usually a talk contains one main idea, but it isn't always stated directly. You have to think about how all the parts of the talk work together to create a message.

10 Read the statements below. Which one correctly identifies the talk's main idea? Why? How are the ones you didn't choose wrong?

a Frank is showing us that we should have secrets that we never tell. Telling too much information about ourselves can cause real problems.

b Frank is saying that when we see other people's secrets, we understand that everyone is human—everyone feels the same feelings. This can help us be kind to ourselves and to other people.

c Frank thinks that writing postcards is a good way to share information. He says that people are honest when they send postcards.

11 MY PERSPECTIVE

Frank talks about the kindness of strangers. Does he think people are generally kind or generally unkind? How do you know? Do you agree with him?

CHALLENGE

Matty's website uses the kindness of strangers to help people find lost cameras and photographs. Can you think of other ways that people help strangers? Write down three ideas and share them with a partner.

People sometimes give directions to strangers who visit their city.

1E What are you into?

SPEAKING Talking about likes and dislikes

Useful language

Talking about likes and dislikes	
Are you into...	*sports / music / gaming / cycling?*
I play... *I love to watch...* *I'm not that interested in...* *I don't mind...* *I can't stand...*	*baseball / basketball / soccer.*
Do you have a favorite...	*team / kind of music / place to go hiking?*
I'm really into...	*Real Madrid / hip-hop / going to the mountains.*
That's cool. / Really? / Wow!	

1 MY PERSPECTIVE

Work in pairs. Discuss the questions.

1 When you meet someone new, what information do you usually learn about them?
2 What are you interested in knowing about other people?
3 What do you want them to know or not know about you?

2 Listen to the conversation. Check (√) the topics they talk about. 7

☐ baseball ☐ hiking ☐ soccer ☐ tennis ☐ running

3 Listen again. Write the missing information in the profiles. 7

Name: Juan	Name: Beata
Doesn't like: (1) *playing team sports*	Loves: (4) ________
Doesn't mind: (2) ________	Best thing about it: (5) ________
Likes: (3) ________	Doesn't like: (6) ________
Favorite place: The Rincon Mountains	Doesn't mind: (7) ________

4 Make notes about your own interests. Think about sports, music, hobbies, or anything else you like doing.

I like: ________

Best thing about it: ________

I don't mind: ________

I can't stand: ________

5 Read the Useful language box. Use your notes from Activity 4 and the words and expressions in the box to ask and answer questions with a partner about likes and dislikes.

People express themselves in many ways, including with mailboxes! What do you think these mailboxes say about the people they belong to?

WRITING An introductory postcard

6 Work in pairs. Imagine you are going to write a postcard to a student your age in another country. Think of five pieces of information you would give or topics you would write about to introduce yourself.

7 Read the postcard from a student in Mexico to a student in Vietnam. Do you think the boys already know each other? Explain your answer.

> Dear Thanh,
>
> My name is Jayro. My friends call me Jay. I'm from Tabasco, Mexico. I'm a student in 9th grade.
>
> My favorite subjects are art and music. I love drawing superhero comics, and I play the drums. I'm also really into soccer. I think I'm a great player, but my friends don't always agree! One thing that a lot of people don't know about me is that I speak three languages: Spanish, English, and Mayan, my family's language.
>
> What about you? Are you into sports? What are your favorite subjects?
>
> I look forward to hearing from you.
>
> Best regards,
>
> Jayro

Useful language

Introducing yourself

I'm from…

I'm a student in… grade at…

My favorite subjects are…

I'm also really into…

Asking questions

What about you? Are you into…?
What are your favorite…?

8 What information does the card give about the sender?

- ☐ an interesting personal fact
- ☐ hobbies and interests
- ☐ description of personality
- ☐ favorite music
- ☐ favorite school subjects
- ☐ name
- ☐ home town
- ☐ favorite foods
- ☐ something his friends don't think
- ☐ things he would like to know about Thanh

9 **WRITING SKILL** Introducing yourself

Using your notes from Activity 6 and the expressions in the Useful language box, write a postcard introducing yourself and asking a couple of questions.

10 Exchange postcards with a partner. Check each other's work. Does it use the language from the Useful language box correctly?

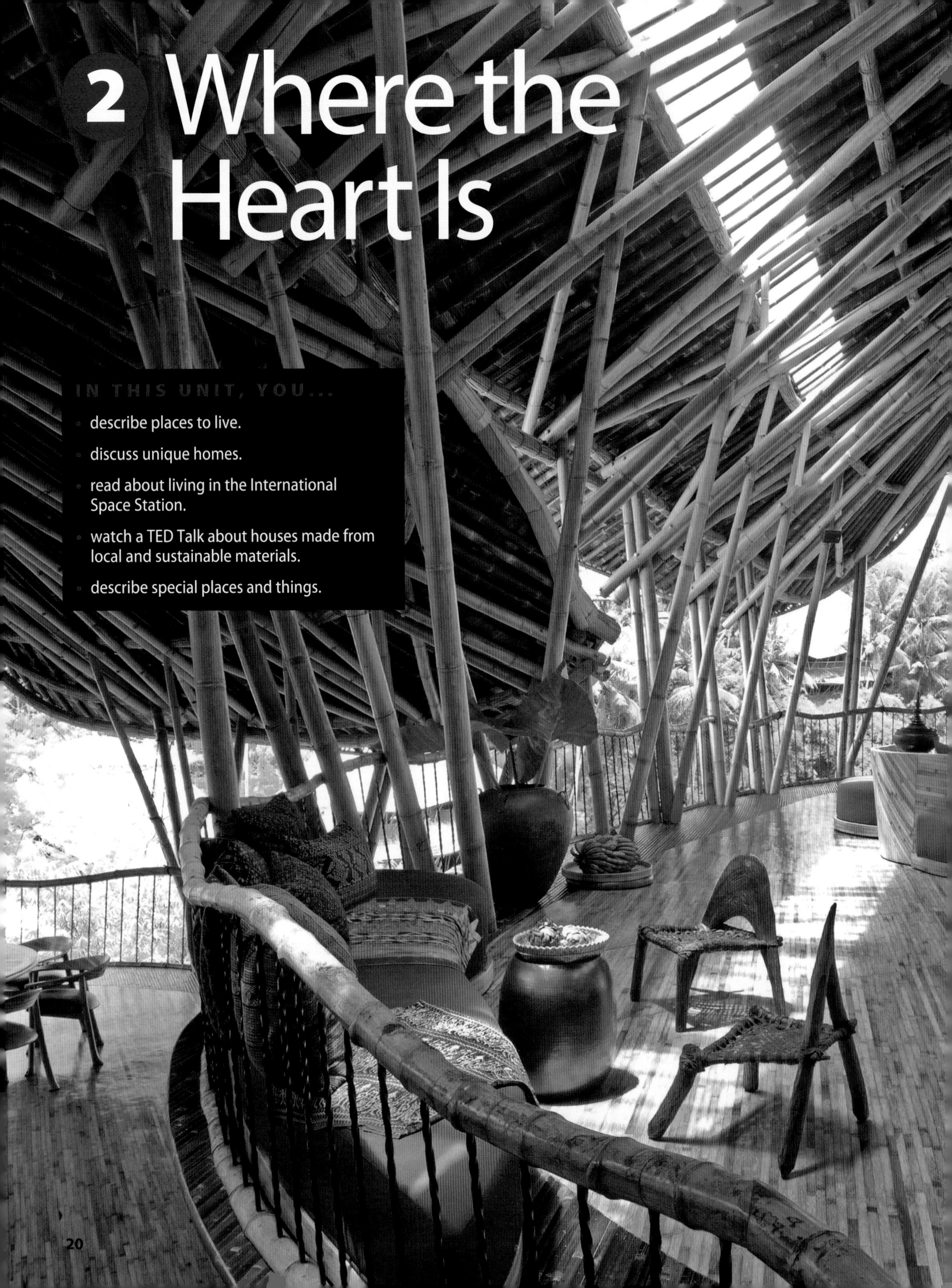

2 Where the Heart Is

IN THIS UNIT, YOU...

- describe places to live.
- discuss unique homes.
- read about living in the International Space Station.
- watch a TED Talk about houses made from local and sustainable materials.
- describe special places and things.

TED speaker, Elora Hardy, designs houses using local bamboo in Bali, Indonesia.

2A Different Places

VOCABULARY Describing where you live

1 Look at the inside of the house. What things do you see?

☐ stairs	☐ a refrigerator	☐ a couch
☐ a window	☐ a table	☐ a door
☐ a chair	☐ art/decorations	☐ a light

2 **MY PERSPECTIVE**

Work in pairs. Look at the photo. Answer the questions.

1 What do you think living in a house like this is like?
2 Would you like to live in this house? Why?

3 Complete the city descriptions with the words in the boxes.

business lively old-fashioned residential shopping district walkable

A new city: Songdo, South Korea

Songdo International Business District is a "planned" city in South Korea. It includes a (1) ______________ area where companies like Samsung have offices, a (2) ______________ with stores and restaurants, and also (3) ______________ areas where people live. This includes a skate park and a lake with boats to rent. There's also a (4) ______________ and exciting entertainment area with a concert hall, an arts center, and movie theaters. The city is (5) ______________, so people don't need to use their cars much. Bikes are very popular, too. None of the buildings in the city are (6) ______________ because the city is only a few years old.

crowded ~~historic~~ modern rural suburban traditional ~~urban~~

An ancient city: Mexico City

Mexico City is about seven hundred years old. The city center is very busy and (7) ___*urban*___, with busy shopping streets which sometimes feel (8) ______________. However, Chapultepec Park, in the middle of the city, is the largest city park in Latin America. It has an amusement park, a swimming pool, and an old castle. There aren't many (9) ______________ buildings in the (10) ___*historic*___ city center. Construction began in the 1500s, so many buildings are old and (11) ______________. There are, however, modern office buildings in Santa Fe, the city's business district. And there are homes and apartment buildings in the more quiet (12) ______________ areas, which grew around the city center in recent times. There are also many beautiful (13) ______________ areas—areas without many buildings—near Mexico City, like Desierto de los Leones National Park, which is actually within the city limits.

4 Work in pairs. Answer the questions.

1 Are there cities like Songdo or Mexico City in your country? How are they similar?
2 Would you prefer to live in an urban, suburban, or rural area? Why? Consider:

- shops and restaurants
- entertainment (movie theaters, arts, parks)
- green spaces / parks
- living in a house or an apartment
- transportation

LISTENING

5 Listen to the news report about living in Vienna, Austria. Choose the correct words to complete the sentences. 8

1 Vienna is one of the world's most *pleasant* / *expensive* cities.
2 The boy lives in a(n) *rural* / *urban* area near the city center.
3 He says that people in New York pay *more* / *less* to go out with friends.
4 The girl says that the *subway is* / *restaurants are* open 24 hours.
5 She *lives* / *works* in the suburbs*.
6 She says the city *is* / *isn't* boring.

suburb *a quiet area just outside of a city*

6 Work in pairs. Discuss the questions.

1 Would you rather live in Vienna, Songdo, or Mexico City? Why?
2 Nearly half of the world lives in rural areas. What are the pros (good things) about living in a rural area?
3 What are the cons (bad things) about living in a rural area?
4 Look at the photo of the container house. Do you think the people you listened to would like to live there? Would a house like this fit in your town or city?

GRAMMAR Simple past

7 Work in pairs. Answer the questions from the news report about Vienna. Listen again to check your answers. 8

1 When did the boy's family move to Vienna? ______________
2 Why did they move to Vienna? ______________
3 Where did they stay when they first arrived? ______________
4 Why did the girl's family move to the suburbs? ______________

In some places, like London, England, entire neighborhoods are made of shipping containers.

8 Look at the Grammar box. Match the sentence halves to make rules about the simple past.

Simple past

Use the simple past to talk about an action that was completed before now.

*We **moved** here five years ago.*

*I **didn't like** it at first.*

***Did** you **meet** new friends? Yes, I **did**. I **met** a lot of people.*

*Where **did** you **live** when you were a child? I **lived** in Madrid.*

1 For affirmative statements about the past, ______
2 For negative statements about the past, ______
3 For questions about the past, ______

a we use the past form of *do* and the simple present verb.
b the verb shows the past tense.

Check page 130 for more information and practice.

9 **Use the simple past to complete the article about an interesting living situation.**

When did Brenda Kelly (1) ______ (become) interested in very small houses? When she was just thirteen years old. She (2) ______ (draw) plans and pictures and (3) ______ (dream) of building her own small house.

A few years later, she (4) ______ (be) ready for a house, but she (5) ______ (not have) a lot of money to spend on it. One day, she (6) ______ (see) some shipping containers at a container terminal*, and she (7) ______ (think) it would be cool to live in one.

Brenda (8) ______ (not be) sure it was possible to make a house from a container. She did research and found people who (9) ______ (make) houses with materials that used to be something else. It (10) ______ (not take) long for her to find help and start building.

terminal *a dock or port where ships load and offload goods*

10 Work in pairs. Answer the questions.

1 Is Brenda's house made from new materials?
2 What did the house use to be?
3 What are some changes you think she made?

11 Look at the Grammar box. Answer the questions.

used to

Use *used to* to talk about past habits, routines, or states.

*My dad **used to** work in a bank.*

*We **didn't use to** live in a container house; we lived in an apartment.*

***Did** you **use to** visit the city center a lot? No, we **didn't**.*

1 Do the sentences say exactly when the habits, routines, or states happened? ______
2 How is the past tense shown in questions and negatives? ______
3 Can we use the simple past to talk about past habits, routines, or states as well? ______

Check page 130 for more information and practice.

12 Choose the correct options to complete the text.

Brenda Kelly's house (1) *travels / used to travel* the world on trucks, trains, and boats carrying products from place to place. But shipping containers (2) *aren't / didn't use to be* the only building material that (3) *are / used to be* something else.

In the mountains of Chile, there's a house that (4) *flies / used to fly*—because (5) *it's / it used to be* an old airplane. And at a farm in the Netherlands, you can stay in a train-car hotel that (6) *carries / used to carry* passengers every day—and it has a kitchen sink (7) *that's / that used to be* a car tire!

13 **PRONUNCIATION** /zd/ and /st/ in *used*

a Look at the Pronunciation box and listen to the examples. 9

When we say the simple past of *use*, we say /juzd/, with a /z/ and /d/ sound:

*Some people in Chile **used** an old airplane as a house.*

When we use *used to* to describe a habit or situation in the past, we say /just/ with an /s/ and /t/ sound.

*Brenda Kelly's house **used to** travel the world.*

b Listen to the sentences and check the sound you hear. 10

	/juzd/	/just/		/juzd/	/just/
1	☐	☐	**4**	☐	☐
2	☐	☐	**5**	☐	☐
3	☐	☐	**6**	☐	☐

14 Have there been any changes in your house or neighborhood? Describe them to a partner with *used to*. Use the correct pronunciation.

2B MySpace

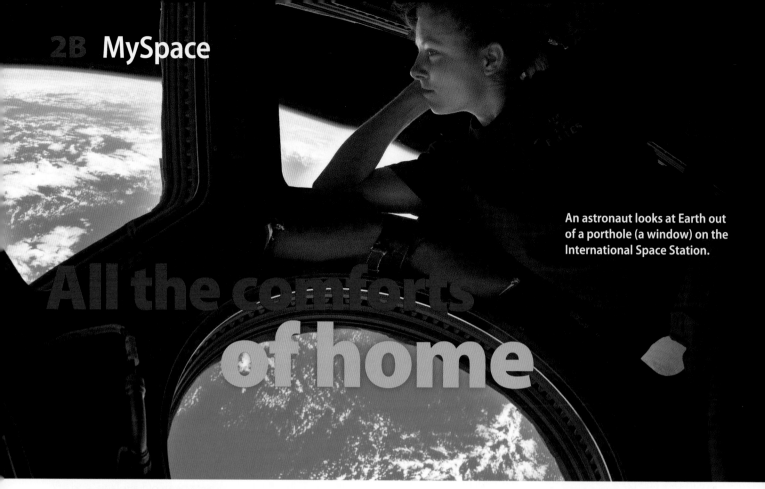

All the comforts of home

An astronaut looks at Earth out of a porthole (a window) on the International Space Station.

VOCABULARY BUILDING

Suffix: *-ion*

We can use the suffix *-ion* to make the noun form of many common verbs. There are several ways to do this:

-ion: communicate → communication

-ation: imagine → imagination

Add *-ion* to the end of the word: direct → direction

1 Read the Vocabulary Building box. Then complete the table. Use a dictionary if necessary. Listen and check your answers. Listen a second time and underline the stressed syllable in each word. Which words have a different stress in the verb form and noun form? 11

Verb	Noun
accommodate	(1) ________
construct	(2) ________
direct	(3) ________
educate	(4) ________
(5) ________	exploration
locate	(6) ________
(7) ________	transportation

2 Complete the text with words from Activity 1.

The International Space Station is a base for space (1) ________ and research. It travels 400 kilometers (249 miles) above the Earth, always moving in an east-to-west (2) ________. Moving at 28,000 kilometers (17, 398 miles) per hour, it passes over the same (3) ________ on Earth every four minutes. Rockets (4) ________ astronauts to and from the ISS, which can (5) ________ six astronauts at one time.

READING

3 Work in pairs. Look at the photo. Discuss the questions.

1 What in the photo do you have in your own bedroom?
2 What do you think these rooms are like in the space station: bathroom, kitchen, living room, dining room?

12 "The size is similar to an old telephone box*," said Japanese engineer Koichi Wakata as he was giving a video tour of his bedroom in the International Space Station (ISS). "It's a little taller than my height. There's a sleeping bag here, which is very comfortable. It's fixed* to the wall so I don't float away." Wakata, who lived on the ISS three different times, had two computers in his room; one for official ISS business and a second for Internet access. He also had a camera and earphones for communication with family and friends back home on Earth. His room also had a small lamp for reading in bed, but instead of a dresser for his clothes, he kept them in a small storage locker. There simply wasn't room for a table or chair.

The ISS accommodations didn't offer Wakata many luxuries, but it provided a lot of the basic comforts of a usual home. He and the other astronauts ate packaged food in a small kitchen and dining area, which had an oven but no refrigerator. Wakata couldn't have a shower in the ISS, but Italian astronaut Samantha Cristoforetti, who spent 199 days on the space station, explained that when she was living there, every astronaut had an area where they washed, brushed their teeth, and so on. "But you don't have a sink," she explains. When she was washing, she used very small amounts of water from small containers and a special "no-rinse" soap and shampoo.

As astronaut Scott Kelly tweeted, "All the comforts of home. Well, most of them."

telephone box *a small booth where people could use public phones*
fixed *stuck; fastened*

The International Space Station (ISS) timeline

1984 The US government decided to build a space station for scientific research, education, and space exploration.

1990s The Russian, Canadian, Japanese, and European space programs agreed to help with the construction.

1998 The Russian space agency sent the first part of the ISS into space, working with the other countries.

1998 to 2009 Astronauts added to the ISS to improve the accommodations on it.

4 Read the tip and then skim the article. Choose the best description of the article.

> To skim, read a text quickly without focusing on all of the words. Only look for main ideas. Read the title and the first sentence of each paragraph; notice familiar and repeated words throughout the text.

a It explains how engineers designed the living areas of the International Space Station.
b It gives examples of problems that astronauts have living in the International Space Station.
c It gives a description of the living areas in the International Space Station.
d It talks about how people will build homes on Mars.

5 Read the article and timeline. Choose the correct words to complete the sentences.

1 Koichi Wakata's *bedroom / bed* is the size of an old telephone booth.
2 The bed is on the *floor / wall.*
3 His bedroom *does / doesn't* have a chair.
4 There *isn't / is* a refrigerator in the kitchen area.
5 There isn't *water / a sink* for washing.
6 In 1984, the US government decided *to construct / construction* the ISS.
7 *Australia / Japan* helped build the ISS.
8 The first part went to space in *1998 / 2009.*

CRITICAL THINKING Analyze fact and opinion

> A fact is something that is true for everyone, for example, *Tokyo is in Japan*. An opinion is something you believe, but you can't prove, for example, *Tokyo is the world's most exciting city*. We often mix fact and opinion when we communicate, so it's important to think about what is fact and what is opinion.

6 Look at the Critical Thinking box. Are the sentences fact (F) or opinion (O)?

1 The bedroom is small. _____
2 The sleeping bag is very comfortable. _____
3 A computer provides Internet access. _____
4 Working in space, away from family, is very difficult. _____
5 The food in space isn't very tasty. _____
6 There's no shower on the ISS. _____

7 Work in pairs. Discuss the questions.

1 Scott Kelly thinks that the ISS has most of the comforts of home. Do you agree or disagree? Why?
2 **a** Make a list of eight things to take with you to live on the ISS. You will have basic food and water, but you may choose to bring special foods or drinks.
b Now cut four things from your list.
c What is the most important item on your list?

Rows of canal boats and houseboats

2C A Unique Style

GRAMMAR Past continuous

1 Can you remember who did what, according to the article in Lesson 2B? Match the sentence halves.

1 When he was living on the ISS, Koichi Wakata _____
2 When Samantha Cristoforetti was working in space, she _____
3 When Scott Kelly was doing his research, he _____

a washed with "no-rinse" soap.
b sometimes stopped to send tweets back to Earth.
c often spoke with friends and family at home.

2 Look at the Grammar box. Choose the correct options to make rules about the past continuous.

Past continuous

The past continuous is used to talk about ongoing actions or events in the past.

*I **was taking** a shower when the water stopped.*

*We **weren't expecting** a call when the phone rang.*

***Was** she **living** on the ISS when she received the award?*

1 The bold words describe *single actions or events / general situations* in the past.
2 All of them are formed with the simple past of *be / have* and a verb in the *-ed / -ing* form.

3 Read the article. For each statement below, write S (ongoing past situation) or A (past action or event).

The perfect home

When Charlotte Tindle (1) **was preparing** to move to London to study music, her college (2) **suggested** student housing at a price of £1,000 per month. That's £36,000 for three years! The Tindles (3) **were making** plans to pay for Charlotte's housing when Mr. Tindle (4) **had** an idea: Why not spend the money on a houseboat and then sell it after his daughter finished school? And so the family (5) **bought** one. While they (6) **were cleaning** and (7) **repairing** the boat, friends (8) **joined** in and helped. Charlotte says that living in her unusual house is an adventure, but she says "It is my home."

1 _____ **3** _____ **5** _____ **7** _____
2 _____ **4** _____ **6** _____ **8** _____

Check page 130 for more information and practice.

4 Read the article again. Disagree with the statements below.

1 Charlotte wasn't expecting to leave home.
Yes, she was. She was preparing to move to London to study music.
2 Before she went to school, Charlotte was living with a roommate.
_____
3 For years, Charlotte was planning to live on a boat when she went to school.
_____
4 The Tindles were relaxing while Charlotte's friends cleaned the boat.
_____

5 Complete the text with the simple past or past continuous of the verbs in parentheses.

Coming together and mixing

When Yinka Ilori (1) ________________ (grow up), his parents often (2) ________________ (advise) him to think about becoming an engineer. Instead, when he finished high school, he (3) ________________ (choose) to study furniture design. Three years after he (4) ________________ (graduate), while he (5) ________________ (try) to develop his own style, he (6) ________________ (do) a project where he took two old chairs and made them into one new one. He then (7) ________________ (realize) that his work was about storytelling and different cultures coming together and mixing. He (8) ________________ (develop) these ideas when an art expert (9) ________________ (find) his work online and invited him to show it at Milan Design Week—the world's largest design fair.

6 Use the words to make questions. Then ask and answer the questions with a partner.

1 parents / when / Ilori's / advise / to think / did / him / engineering / about / ?
When did Ilori's parents advise him to think about engineering?

2 Ilori / study / what / choose / did / to / ?
____

3 two / Ilori / did / realized / chairs / when / made / into / he / what / one / ?
____
____

4 found / Ilori's / when he / work / was developing his / who / about / online / cultures and / ideas / storytelling / ?
____
____

7 **PRONUNCIATION** *-ing* in fast speech

Read the Pronunciation box. Then listen and check the sentences you hear. 13

Often, especially in fast speech, *-ing* in continuous verb forms is spoken as /ɪn/

1 I didn't find what I wanted.
☐ I was looking for the furniture store.
☐ I'll look in the furniture store.

2 I saw you at the art competition.
☐ Did you put in a painting?
☐ Were you putting up paintings?

Yinka Ilori "upcycles" old tables and chairs. He says, "The UK is a very multicultural place: there are so many cultures here…, and it's nice to try and put that into furniture."

3 Are you hungry?
☐ We were going to eat at four.
☐ We go in to eat at four.

8 **CHOOSE**

Choose one of the following activities.

- When Charlotte Tindle was looking for a home, she found an amazing way to live. Think of three important events in your life related to your home. In pairs, explain the ongoing situation and each single action or event.

My family was living in Athens when my little brother was born.

- When Yinka Ilori was working on an art project, he discovered his interest in different cultures coming together. Think about something you love doing or are very interested in. Write about what was happening in your life when you discovered it. Explain how you have learned more about it.

I was watching a music video when a thought hit me: I want to learn the guitar. I didn't have a hobby at the time, so I asked my parents for guitar lessons.

- Instead of writing about your hobby or other interest, prepare a presentation about it.

2D Magical Houses, Made of Bamboo

“With creativity and commitment, you can create beauty and comfort and safety, and even luxury, out of a material that will grow back.”

ELORA HARDY

Read about Elora Hardy and get ready to watch her TED Talk. ▶ 2.0

AUTHENTIC LISTENING SKILLS

Listening for gist

When you listen, don't try to understand every word. Try to relax and focus on what you do understand, not what you don't understand. Notice words that the speaker repeats or stresses and the types of words that are used a lot, for example, adjectives. Try to figure out the connections between the words you understand.

1 Read the Authentic Listening Skills box. Listen to the extract from the TED Talk. Circle the topics Elora talks about. 🎧 14

a doors
b windows
c shapes
d construction materials

2 What is the general idea of what she is talking about? Write a sentence.

____

____

3 Share your idea with a partner.

WATCH

4 Look at the photo on page 20 and read the caption. Why do you think it might it be important to use local materials, like bamboo in Bali, to build houses?

5 Watch Part 1 of the talk. Choose the correct options to complete these sentences. ▶ 2.1

1 _____ designed a fairy mushroom house.
a When Elora was a child, her mother
b Last year, Elora
c When she was a child, Elora

2 The curved roof helps keep the house _____.
a dry
b cool
c warm

3 It's easy to _____ a person who is using the bathroom.
a hear
b see
c avoid

6 Watch Part 2 of the talk. Are the sentences *true* or *false*? ▶ 2.2

1 Bamboo is a grass. _____
2 Bamboo grows very slowly. _____
3 Bamboo is light and strong. _____
4 Hardy plans to build a school from bamboo. _____
5 The Green School used sustainable materials. _____

7 **Watch Part 3 of the talk. Choose the correct options to complete the sentences.** ▶ 2.3

1 Elora says it is important to *make the bamboo do what you want / design for the bamboo's strengths*.
2 Elora builds models of her houses to *help sell houses to her customers / test the design*.
3 She prefers to build doors that are *balanced / not shaped like teardrops*.
4 Bamboo grows back quickly, so it is *a safe / an environmentally friendly* material.

8 **VOCABULARY IN CONTEXT**

a **Watch the clips from the TED Talk. Choose the correct meanings of the words.** ▶ 2.4

b **Answer the questions.**

1 What is one thing that just *doesn't feel right* in your town or city?
2 Has someone ever had to *just tell you something*? What was it?
3 Who is one person who has *treated you well*?
4 In your city, what material *makes perfect sense* to build with?

9 **Work in small groups. Discuss the questions.**

1 As a child, Hardy's dream house looked like a mushroom. What is your idea of a dream house?
2 Hardy designs her houses to be comfortable in hot weather. What is the weather like where you live? How do you make your house comfortable?
3 How are Hardy's houses similar to your house? How are they different?

10 **Work in pairs. Read the extract from the talk. Discuss the questions.**

The floor that you walk on, can it affect the way that you walk? Can it change the footprint that you'll ultimately leave on the world?

1 Is Hardy talking about an actual floor?
2 How can the floor we walk on change our *footprint*?
3 We can't all build bamboo houses. What else can we do in our homes to change the footprint we leave?

CHALLENGE

Think of the dream house you described in Activity 9, item 1. Do the following:

1 Decide what material you would build with: wood, brick, bamboo, something else?
2 Decide how it will work with the environment. How will it stay comfortable in hot or cold weather?
3 Draw a plan for the house and label the rooms and other details in the house. Include as many rooms as you would like—a music room, a movie room, etc.

2E Special Things, Special Places

SPEAKING Giving reasons

1 **Work in pairs. Answer the questions.**

1 For you, is the idea of living alone on a tropical island an exciting or scary idea?
2 Think back to your answers on page 25, Activity 7 about what you would like to take with you to live on the ISS. Would your answers be different for life on a tropical island? For example, what clothes would you take? How would you protect yourself from the sun? How would you get food?
3 What parts of civilization would you miss the most?

2 **Listen to the conversation. Are the sentences *true* or *false*?** 15

1 David became rich and as a result, he bought the island.
2 There was a small community of people already living on the island, so David joined them.
3 Denika left because she wasn't completely comfortable on the island.
4 The reason David has electricity on the island is that he set up a solar power system.
5 David says that moving to the island was a big mistake because he's not happy living alone.

Useful language

Giving reasons

Use *The reason…*, *because*, *so*, and *since* to give reasons.

The reason *he went there was to get away from his money problems.*

He went **because** *his business failed.*

She thought life was too hard, **so** *she left.*

Since *he loved living a simple life in a tiny house, he didn't want to leave.*

3 **Read the Useful language box. Then, in small groups, take turns giving the reasons for the items you talked about taking to a tropical island in Activity 1. Try to use all of the expressions in the box.**

I'd want a computer because…

I'd need a cell phone so…

The reason I'd want a music system is…

I'd need a swimsuit since…

4 **Think of five things that you use every day. Explain why they are important to you using the useful language.**

I need my backpack every day because…

5 **Do you think your items would still be useful on a tropical island? With a group of three, plan a list of ten items to take. Give reasons for each item.**

Shuri Castle in Naha, Japan

WRITING

6 WRITING SKILL Answering *Wh-* questions

Think of a home that you really like. It can be a place you have seen or visited—a friend's house, a family home, or a famous place such as a castle. Answer the questions.

1 Where is it?
2 When did you go there?
3 How old is it?
4 Why is it special? The location? The way it looks?
5 Who lives there (or used to live there)?
6 What did you see or do there?

7 Read the paragraph. Answer the questions below.

> Shuri Castle is a beautiful castle in the city I'm from—Naha, Japan. I went there last year when my cousin was visiting from Tokyo because the castle is famous in our area. The oldest part is about seven hundred years old. It has many beautiful buildings, gardens, and huge gates. That's the reason I like it. It's unlike any other place I've ever seen. A king used to live there, but now it is like a museum. When we were taking the tour, the tour guide showed us the inside of the castle and told us about its history. It's definitely the coolest house I've ever seen.
> —Kana

1 Where is Shuri castle?
2 When did Kana go there?
3 How old is it?
4 Why is it special?
5 Who used to live there?
6 What did Kana do there?

8 Look at the Writing skill box. Does the paragraph in Activity 7 answer all of the questions?

9 Write a paragraph that describes the home you talked about in Activity 6.

10 Exchange papers with a partner. Check each other's work. Does your partner's paragraph answer all of the questions from Activity 6?

Writing strategy

Describing a visit to a place

You can describe a visit to a place by answering the questions *Who?, What?, When?, Where?, Why?* and *How?*

3 Health and Happiness

This teen in Tokyo, Japan, shows that good food can make people both healthy and happy.

IN THIS UNIT, YOU...

- talk about staying healthy.
- read about a girl who doesn't feel pain.
- learn about what makes people happy.
- watch a TED Talk about a doctor who changed the way people think about health.
- write about staying healthy.

3A Treating the Whole Person

VOCABULARY Being healthy

1 Discuss in pairs. Look at the photo. What is he happy about? What things do people need to be happy?

2 Check (√) the parts of the body that you can see in the photo.

☐ arm	☐ shoulder	☐ chest	☐ ear
☐ elbow	☐ finger	☐ foot	☐ hand
☐ head	☐ knee	☐ leg	☐ mouth
☐ neck	☐ nose	☐ stomach	☐ throat

3 Look at the photo. What parts of the body can tell you if a person is happy?

4 Read the article. Match the words in bold with the definitions.

A doctor in the jungle

In Cameroon, it isn't always easy to find a (1) **hospital** when you're (2) **sick**. But if you're lucky, a doctor may find you. Almost every weekend, Dr. Georges Bwelle and his assistants take care of the (3) **health** needs of about 500 people in small villages in the jungle. They see (4) **patients** with a variety of (5) **illnesses** and (6) **injuries** and give people (7) **medicine**. Dr. Bwelle also provides items that people need to make their lives better, like (8) **eyeglasses**. Why does he do it? Helping people to be (9) **healthy** brings a lot of (10) **happiness** to Dr. Bwelle. "To make people laugh, to reduce the (11) **pain**, that's why I'm doing this," he says.

a _____ a problem with the body or the mind
b _____ the condition of someone's body and mind
c _____ a bad feeling
d _____ glasses worn over the eyes to help you see
e _____ something the doctor gives you when you are sick
f _____ people who are sick and need help from a doctor
g _____ the condition of feeling good and not sad
h _____ a place where sick and injured people get treatment
i _____ not healthy; unwell
j _____ well; not sick
k _____ when a part of the body is hurt

5 Are these words illnesses (IL), injuries (IN), or symptoms* (S)? Use a dictionary if needed. Check your answers with a partner.

_____ a broken arm	_____ a virus
_____ the flu	_____ pain
_____ a headache	_____ seasickness
_____ a stomachache	_____ a high temperature
_____ a broken leg	_____ a backache

*symptom *a change in the body that shows you are sick or injured*

6 **MY PERSPECTIVE**

Work in pairs. Answer the questions.

1 Do you do anything to stay healthy? Eat certain foods? Exercise? Something else?
2 When you're sick or hurt, do you take medicine? Why or why not? If so, what kind? Do you try anything else to fix the problem?

LISTENING

7 Complete the questionnaire about your experience going to the doctor. You may check (√) more than one answer for each question.

1 When or why do you go to the doctor?

☐ because of an illness ☐ for a check-up (a routine health check) ☐ for school

☐ other reasons ____________________

2 What does the doctor usually do?

☐ check my height and weight ☐ check my eyes and ears ☐ give me medicine
☐ ask questions about my health and happiness (*Have you been sick? Do you feel any pain?*)
☐ ask about symptoms

3 What other things does the doctor talk to you about?

☐ family ☐ food ☐ staying healthy (exercise, getting enough sleep, etc.)

☐ sleep ☐ school ☐ staying safe (wearing a seatbelt, not smoking, using sunscreen)

☐ other things ____________________

8 **Read the sentences. Then listen to a lecture about "whole-person" healthcare. Check (√) the ideas that the speaker discusses.** 16

1 ☐ Today, finding new medicines is the world's biggest problem.
2 ☐ Many doctors look after a person's health and happiness, not only a patient's illness.
3 ☐ Sometimes people think they are sick, but really, the problem is just in their mind.
4 ☐ The World Health Organization says that many hospitals need to think more about people and the world they live in.
5 ☐ Dr. Paul Tournier believed that only medicine could make people healthy.

9 **Work in pairs. Listen to the lecture again. Answer the questions.** 16

1 What examples of common health problems does the speaker give?
2 What did Dr. Tournier mean by "the whole person"?
3 What does the World Health Organization say that health is connected to?
4 What do "whole-person" doctors talk about with their patients?

10 **MY PERSPECTIVE**

Work in a small group. Discuss the questions.

1 Is your doctor an "illness" doctor or a "whole-person" doctor? Which type of doctor do you prefer? Why?
2 Is there anything you would like your doctor to do differently?

GRAMMAR Quantifiers

11 Read the information in the Grammar box. Then look at the sentences. Underline the word or words that tell about a quantity.

Quantifiers

With countable nouns:

A few / Some / A lot of / Many doctors are good listeners.

How many doctors work here?

With uncountable nouns:

*The doctor gave me **a little** / **some** / **a lot of** medicine.*

How much water do you drink every day?

1 Some doctors still think about illnesses, not about people.
2 Many doctors and hospitals still need to change.
3 Do you eat a lot of fruit?
4 Do you have much stress in your life?

12 Which words in Activity 11 are countable? Which are uncountable?

Check page 132 for more information and practice.

13 Choose the correct options to complete the text.

Nature's pharmacy

(1) *A lot of / Many of* the medicine we use today comes from plants. For example, aspirin, a common pain medicine, used to come from (2) *some / a* tree. An important cancer drug comes from (3) *many / the* Pacific yew tree, but after years of cutting them down, there weren't (4) *some / many* trees left. Then in the 1990s, scientists learned how to make the medicine without killing the trees or even causing it (5) *many / much* damage. A (6) *few / little* health products also come from animals. For example, (7) *many / much* people take (8) *a few / a little* fish oil in their diet to stay healthy.

How much / How many?

14 Complete the questions with *How much* or *How many*. Listen to the interview and check your answers. 17

1 ________ plants in Tanzania can you use as medicine?
2 ________ traditional doctors did you interview?
3 ________ time did you spend on the project?
4 ________ information did you collect?

15 Listen again. How does Amy answer the questions? 17

16 Work in pairs. Think of six *How much* and two *How many* questions to ask each other.

17 **PRONUNCIATION** Nuclear stress

Read the Pronunciation box. Then listen and match each sentence with the correct meaning (a–d). 18

How many different plants are there in Tanzania?
(I want to know the number.)
*How many different **plants** are there in Tanzania?*
(I'm interested in plants, not animals.)
*How many different plants are there in **Tanzania**?*
(I'm interested in Tanzania, not Kenya.)

I drink a little milk every day.

1 ____ **2** ____ **3** ____ **4** ____

a I never miss a day.
b I don't drink a lot.
c I don't drink a little soda.
d My brother doesn't drink any.

Services like the Royal Flying Doctor Service in Australia work to provide medical care to people in remote areas.

3B Painless

VOCABULARY BUILDING

Synonyms

A synonym is a word that has a similar meaning to another word. Writers often use synonyms to add variety to a text. Synonyms should be the same part of speech. One way to check if two words are synonyms is to use the words in the same place in a sentence. If the sentences have the same meaning, the words are synonyms.

1 For each pair, read the first sentence from an article about a girl who doesn't feel pain. Then complete the second sentence with a synonym of the word in bold.

block	calm	frightening	realize	sore

1 Ashlyn Blocker was a **quiet** baby.
Her parents felt lucky to have such a ________ child.
2 It was red and looked **painful**.
The doctor carefully touched her ________ eye.
3 At first, he didn't **understand**.
After checking, he began to ________ that Ashlyn wasn't like most other kids.
4 "It was **scary**," says her mother.
That idea was very ________.
5 Now doctors are studying Ashlyn to understand how her body can **stop** pain.
It may help them to develop new medicines to ________ pain.

READING

2 Read the tip. Then read the article. Number the events from the article in the correct order.

Understanding the time and order of events can help you understand the whole text. Look for dates, ages, and time expressions such as *When…* and adverbs of order such as *then*, *after that*, and *next*.

a ____ Ashlyn has something wrong with her eye.
b ____ Ashlyn's doctors discover other people with the same illness.
c ____ The doctor discovers that Ashlyn doesn't feel pain.
d ____ Doctors study Ashlyn to learn more.
e ____ Ashlyn's parents feel lucky.

3 Choose the correct options to complete the sentences.

1 As a baby, Ashlyn Blocker didn't cry because ____.
a she was never hungry **b** she didn't feel pain
c she was a quiet child
2 Ashlyn is taken to the doctor because she ____.
a didn't cry **b** was upset
c had an eye problem
3 Feeling no pain is dangerous because you can easily ____.
a hurt yourself **b** hurt someone else
c become ill
4 Ashlyn's illness is ____.
a common in some places **b** very unusual
c often seen in young babies
5 Doctors may use Ashlyn's case to help people who ____.
a can't feel or smell anything **b** have a lot of pain
c have eye problems
6 For Ashlyn, feeling no pain is ____.
a very strange **b** normal
c something she loves

4 MY PERSPECTIVE

Work in pairs. Discuss the questions.

1 When might Ashlyn's condition be good or helpful?
2 What skills or habits do you think Ashlyn developed to deal with her condition?
3 What does the photo tell you about Ashlyn?

CRITICAL THINKING Making ideas clear

To make sure their ideas are clear, writers often:
- report what someone said.
- give examples.
- say the same thing using different words.

5 Read the Critical Thinking box. Then find the ideas below in the article. How is each idea made clear?

1 As a small baby, Ashlyn Blocker seemed very happy.
2 Pain is necessary.
3 Pain keeps us from danger.
4 Mr. and Mrs. Blocker were afraid for their daughter.
5 Ashlyn isn't the only person with her condition.
6 Ashlyn is comfortable with her condition.

6 Work in pairs. Discuss the questions. Which ideas in the text would you like to know more about? What questions would you like to ask Ashlyn, her parents, or her doctors?

Feeling NO PAIN

19 Ashlyn Blocker was a quiet baby. She didn't cry even when she was hungry. At first, her parents felt lucky to have such a calm child. But then when Ashlyn was eight months old, Mr. and Mrs. Blocker noticed a problem with her eye. It was red and looked painful, so they took her to the doctor. As he checked Ashlyn, the doctor carefully touched her sore eye. Patients—especially babies and children—usually don't like this, and they try to move away. Ashlyn didn't do this. The doctor was surprised and, at first, he didn't understand. But after checking, he began to realize that Ashlyn wasn't like most other kids because Ashlyn didn't feel pain.

You may think this sounds like a good thing—no pain means never getting hurt, right? But we feel pain for a reason. It has an important purpose: it tells us that our body has an injury or illness. Pain also helps to keep us safe. When a child touches a hot stove, the pain says "Danger!" and stops a more serious injury.

After discovering that their daughter couldn't feel pain, the Blockers no longer felt lucky. "It was scary," says her mother, Tara Blocker, because Ashlyn could easily injure herself and not know it. That idea was very frightening. As Ashlyn began to move around more and to walk, keeping her safe every day became more and more of a challenge.

No one had ever come to Ashlyn's doctors with this condition*, and at first they thought she might be the only case in the world. But they found out that there were others with the condition—a whole family in Pakistan and eight other kids who lived nearer to Ashlyn in the US.

"It's just me. It's all I've ever known."

Ashlyn Blocker

Now doctors are studying Ashlyn and other people who don't feel pain. They want to understand the condition and help people who have it. But they also want to understand how the body can stop pain. It may help them to develop new medicines to block pain—good news for anyone who experiences a lot of it.

What's it like to feel no pain? Ashlyn deals with the condition well and has a happy life. She says, "It's just me. It's all I've ever known."

condition *health problem*

3C What makes us happy?

GRAMMAR Phrasal verbs

1 Read the sentences. Answer the questions.

Ashlyn's body **turns** pain **off**.

They **found out** that there were others with the same condition.

Ashlyn **deals with** the condition well and has a happy life.

1 What parts of speech are the words in bold? ___________
2 What do they all have in common? ___________
3 What's different about the first one? ___________

2 Look at the Grammar box. Then check the Grammar Reference. Are the verbs below separable (write S) or inseparable (write I).

Phrasal verbs

Phrasal verbs are a verb and preposition combination which gives them a special meaning. For example, *find out* means *discover* and *put off* means *delay*.

Some phrasal verbs can be separated with a noun or a pronoun:

Her body ***turns off*** *pain. Her body* ***turns*** *pain* ***off***.

Some must always stay together:

She ***deals with*** *her condition.* ~~*She* ***deals*** *her condition* ***with***~~.

1 put on _____
2 turn on _____
3 get along (with) _____
4 give up _____
5 hang out _____
6 hand in _____
7 look into _____
8 find out _____
9 work out (at the gym) _____
10 take out _____

See page 132 for more information and practice.

WHAT MAKES TEENS HAPPY?

- Good health
- Exercise
- Good diet (a lot of fresh fruit, eating breakfast)
- Enjoying school
- Friendly classmates

Source: World Health Organization

3 Read the information about research carried out by the World Health Organization. Write a reason for happiness from above for each statement below.

1 My school friends and I **get along** well—they're nice. ___________
2 I go to the gym and **work out** once or twice a week. ___________
3 I **gave up** sugary foods. I also have a bowl of cereal every morning. ___________
4 I almost always **hand in** my homework on time. I don't mind doing it. ___________
5 I'm not sick very often because I **look after** myself. ___________

4 Rewrite the two sentences in Activity 3 with phrasal verbs that can have the preposition after the object.

____

____

5 Complete the sentences using phrasal verbs from Activities 1 and 2. Then listen to the conversation and check your answers. 20

1 Some scientists __________ teenagers' happiness.
2 Did they __________ what makes us happy?
3 I feel happy when I __________ my headphones __________ and listen to some music.
4 For me, it's TV. I always feel happy when I __________ it __________ .
5 Happy teenagers __________ with their friends a lot.
6 I __________ the rubbish* __________ every day!

rubbish *British English for* trash

6 Listen to the conversation again. What things do the speakers say make teenagers unhappy? 20

7 Look at the facts about what makes teens unhappy. Then complete the advice with verbs and prepositions from the chart below. One preposition is used twice.

WHAT MAKES TEENS UNHAPPY?

- Poor health
- No exercise, a lot of TV
- Poor diet (a lot of sugary foods, no breakfast)
- School stress/not having time to do schoolwork
- Bullying

Source: World Health Organization

Verbs						Prepositions				
deal	give	hand	look	put	take	after	in	off	up	with

Advice

- __________ yourself so you don't become ill.
- __________ a sport or another physical activity.
- __________ drinking sweet drinks, like soda, every day. Save them as a weekend treat.
- Don't __________ your homework __________ . __________ it __________ on time.
- __________ bullying by telling an adult about it. Ask for help.

8 MY PERSPECTIVE

What do *you* think helps make people happy? Use the verbs below or your own ideas. Write five sentences. Then discuss your sentences with a partner.

Belonging to…	Dealing with…	Giving up…	Looking after…
Putting on…	Speaking with friends about…		Taking up…

A teen jumps from the U Bein Bridge into Taungthaman Lake, Myanmar.

3D The Amazing Story of the Man Who Gave Us Modern Pain Relief

"Bonica saw pain close up. He felt it. He lived it. And it made it impossible for him to ignore in others."

LATIF NASSER

Read about Latif Nasser and get ready to watch his TED Talk. ▶ 3.0

AUTHENTIC LISTENING SKILLS

Collaborative listening

When you listen to authentic speech, you usually won't understand everything you hear, and you often can't go back and listen again. However, different people often understand different parts of a message. You can increase your understanding by comparing listening notes with others.

1 Read the Authentic Listening Skills box. Then listen to the extract from the TED Talk and write down the words you remember. 21

2 Work in small groups. Compare notes on what you heard. Did you write the same words? Write a summary of what you heard as a group. Do you have more information now?

3 Listen to the extract again. Did you understand more this time? Tell a partner what the extract means. 21

WATCH

4 Think of a time when you saw something that changed the way you thought about something. What happened? How did it change you? Make some notes. Share your ideas with a partner.

5 Watch Part 1 of the talk. Choose the correct options to complete the sentences. ▶ 3.1

1 The lion tamer's main problem was that ______ .
- **a** the lion bit him
- **b** he couldn't breathe with his head in the lion's mouth
- **c** he was scared

2 The strongman gave the lion tamer ______ to save his life.
- **a** mouth to mouth
- **b** medicine
- **c** an operation

3 The strongman worked at the circus to help pay for ______ .
- **a** a new car
- **b** healthcare
- **c** medical school

4 At the army hospital, Bonica's job was ______ .
- **a** helping patients with pain
- **b** doing amputations
- **c** looking after the whole hospital

5 Pain is a signal for ______ .
- **a** fear
- **b** an injury
- **c** being tired

6 He was surprised that many patients felt ______ when the injury was better.
- **a** very angry
- **b** a lot of pain
- **c** ready to go home

6 Watch Part 2 of the talk. Choose the correct options. ▶ 3.2

1 Bonica often discussed pain with *other doctors / patients' families.*
2 Bonica read medical books and found that they gave *a lot of / only a little* information about pain.
3 To get more people talking about pain, Bonica *tried to get experts to write about it / wrote about it himself.*
4 Bonica didn't want to just make his patients healthier, he wanted to *be famous / make them feel better.*
5 Now there are *only a few / hundreds of* pain clinics around the world.
6 Bonica understood pain well because he *felt a lot of / read a lot about* pain.

7 Think about Parts 1 and 2 of the talk. What evidence does Latif give to support these statements?

1 Bonica "inflicted (caused) pain, and he treated it." ________
____
2 "Bonica saw pain close up. He felt it. He lived it." ________
____
3 Bonica's "goal wasn't to make patients better; it was to make patients feel better." ________________
____

8 **VOCABULARY IN CONTEXT**

a Watch the clips from the talk. Choose the correct meaning of the words and phrases. ▶ 3.3

b Answers the questions. Share your answers with a partner.

1 Have you ever had a problem and tried to *ignore* it? What happened?
2 When do you usually *hit the books*? Where do you do it?
3 Have you or a friend or family member ever *passed out*? What happened?
4 Is there anyone in your family who is a *specialist* in a subject? Who? Which subject?
5 How many *institutions* can you name in your area? What kinds of *institutions* are they?
6 When was the last time you felt like someone *didn't take you seriously*? Who? How did you feel?

CHALLENGE

Bonica did a lot of good in the world, making life better for people in pain. Think of a teacher, doctor, nurse, scientist, politician, athlete, or someone else you know about who has helped people feel better. Make some notes about what they did.

Cristiano Ronaldo
- *soccer star*
- *gave money to a ten-year-old fan who needed medical help*
- *paid for a cancer center in Portugal*

9 Write a paragraph describing the person you made notes about in CHALLENGE. Then share your ideas with a partner. What things are similar about the people? What things are different?

3E Opinions About Health and Happiness

SPEAKING Agreeing, disagreeing, and conceding a point

1 Do you agree or disagree with the statements? Why? Tell a partner.

1. People should be free to smoke cigarettes anywhere.
2. People should not be allowed to smoke in restaurants, cafes, movie theaters, or other public places.
3. The government should ban (completely stop) smoking because it is bad for everyone's health and well-being.

2 Listen to the conversation. Who makes or agrees with each statement—Al (A), Marta (M), or both (B)? 22

1. Smoking should be completely forbidden. _____
2. Smoking should be allowed. _____
3. Smoking is bad for smokers' health. _____
4. Smoking is bad for everyone. _____
5. Everyone does something dangerous every day. _____

3 Work in small groups. For each topic below, think of 3–5 arguments *for* the statement and 3–5 arguments *against* the statement.

- The government should ban junk food.
- Schools should make students get more exercise.
- Using a phone while walking or cycling should be illegal.

4 Look at the phrases in the Useful language box. Working with another small group, take turns arguing for and against the points in Activity 3.

Useful language

Saying what you think:
I think... / I believe...
In my opinion...

Disagreeing:
Really / Are you kidding? I'm not sure about that.
I don't agree.
Sorry, but I don't think so.

Asking follow-up questions:
Why do you say that?
Could you explain that a bit more?

Conceding a point:
You're right that...
Well, that's true...

WRITING An opinion essay

5 Rank the ways to stay healthy in order from 1 (the most important) to 8 (the least important). Discuss your answers with a partner.

_____ exercise every day
_____ don't smoke cigarettes
_____ see a doctor every six months
_____ see friends and family
_____ finish schoolwork on time
_____ have a healthy diet
_____ get plenty of sleep
_____ wear a seatbelt

People ride their bikes through Bonsecours Basin Park in Montreal, Canada.

6 Read the essay. Answer the questions below.

Agree or disagree: Exercising every day is the best way to stay healthy.

While it's true that doing a little exercise every day is good for you, I think eating well is more important than exercise.

One reason I think this is that exercise can make people eat too much. Everyone knows someone who exercises and then eats a lot of junk food as a reward. This doesn't improve their health. I believe that for the best health, everyone should first make sure they have a healthy diet.

Second, in my opinion no one should smoke, because cigarettes are bad for you. They're also bad for people around you.

For me, exercise is the third most important thing. It isn't necessary to go to the gym, but you should try to walk to school instead of going by car or bus.

Not smoking and getting exercise are important, but the best way to stay healthy is to have a good diet.

1 Does the writer agree or disagree with the statement "Exercising every day is the best way to stay healthy"?
2 According to the writer, what does exercise sometimes make people do?
3 In addition to good food and exercise, what does the writer advise?

Useful language

Acknowledging other ideas:
While it's true that…, I think…

Giving your opinion:
I believe…
In my opinion, …
For me, …

Giving reasons for your opinion:
One reason I think this is…
… because…

7 **Read the Useful language box. Then read the essay again. Underline the expressions from the box that you find in the essay.**

8 **WRITING SKILL** Hedging

When hedging an opinion, phrases are used to slightly weaken what is being said.

Read the expressions. In which category in the box do these phrases belong?

I think this because… *My view is that…* *I accept that…, but…*

9 **Work in pairs. Say if you agree or disagree with each statement and why.**

1 Happiness is more important than health.
2 The best way to stay healthy is to stay happy.
3 It's more important to *feel* OK than to be healthy.

10 **Choose one of the statements in Activity 9 and write an essay about whether you agree or disagree. Use the Useful language.**

11 **Exchange papers with a partner. Check each other's work. Does it use the Useful language correctly? Do you agree with your partner?**

4 Learning

IN THIS UNIT, YOU...

- talk about schools, classes, and education.
- read about an outdoor skills course.
- learn about the education and skills needed for life.
- watch a TED Talk about an important skill for success.
- ask about and compare summer programs.

Students stand on their desks during a classroom activity in Maryland in the United States.

4A How We Learn

VOCABULARY Education

1 Work in pairs. Look at the photo. Point to the items below.

a blackboard | a desk | a notebook | a pen | a student | a teacher

2 Match the words that go together. Use your dictionary if necessary.

1 develop ____ | **a** geography / math / science / art
2 study ____ | **b** (good / bad) grades / an education
3 get ____ | **c** (elementary / high / private / public) school
4 take ____ | **d** (new) skills
5 attend ____ | **e** creative / hard-working
6 be ____ | **f** a test / exams

3 Choose the correct options to complete the descriptions of three unique schools.

- The Indian government provides (1) *public / private* schools for all children. But when students don't live near a school and can't afford to travel, it's difficult for them to get (2) *bad grades / an education*. The solution? Teachers travel to the students! (3) *Elementary / High* school students (up to age 12) and students in the first two years of (4) *elementary / high* school (ages 13 and 14) can attend "train platform schools." The students are very (5) *creative / hard-working*. Some older students are even already at the station because they have jobs there!
- Students of the Khan Academy (6) *attend / study* geography, math, science, and other subjects online by watching videos. After watching, they can take short (7) *grades / tests* to check their progress. Most Khan Academy students are teens taking classes in addition to their usual studies. They want extra work to develop (8) *skills / studies* in certain subjects and do better on exams. Since the videos are online, students from around the world can (9) *take / get* the classes.
- Students who (10) *attend / get* the Zip Zap Circus School in Cape Town, South Africa, don't study math and science; they (11) *take / learn* entertainment skills. Zip Zap is a private (12) *education / school*, but it isn't expensive. In fact, unlike most private schools, it's free. The main purpose of the school is to help students learn to live and work together—and to have fun.

4 Answer the questions. Take notes. Share your answers with a partner.

Which school...

1 doesn't teach traditional school subjects? What does it teach?
2 is the most like your school? Why?
3 helps students trying to get very good grades or prepare for an exam? Why?

5 **MY PERSPECTIVE**

Work in pairs. Discuss the questions.

1 Is your school a public school or a private school? What are the differences between the two? Think about cost, class size, teachers, building(s), etc.
2 Which subjects from this list are you taking? Which classes are your favorites? Why?

arts (music, drama)	computers	history	language
literature	math (algebra, geometry)	science (biology, chemistry)	

3 Do any of your classes include online learning? Which one(s)?

LISTENING

6 Have you ever talked to a student from another country? If yes, what was it like? If not, would you like to? What are the benefits of talking to people from other countries?

7 Listen to two students talking about a project at school. Are the sentences *true* or *false*? 23

1. Karina's class is video chatting with students around the world.
2. They are watching movies to learn about each other's countries.
3. They learned about the school week in Japan.
4. They discussed school clothes in England.
5. Maria, in Brazil, is going to take an important examination soon.
6. Karina says that teenagers in other countries are very different.

8 Listen again. Complete the notes. 23

Karina's favorite class: (1) ____________
Project: video chatting with students in Brazil, (2) ____________, Japan, England, and (3) ____________
People usually learn about America from (4) ____________
Some Japanese kids go to school on Saturday for sports or to (5) ____________
Kids in the UK start school at the age of (6) ____________
Maria is taking extra classes in (7) ____________ and (8) ____________
Teenagers everywhere have a lot in (9) ____________

9 Work in pairs. Discuss the questions.

1. Do you like the idea of video chatting with students in other countries? Why?
2. Say two or three things you know about another country—about food, sports, weather, products they make, and so on. Where did you learn the information?
3. What questions would you ask a student from another country? Think of one question about school and one question about another topic.

New communication technologies, like video chatting, are helping students around the world connect and learn about each other.

GRAMMAR Comparatives and superlatives

10 Look at the Grammar box. Answer the questions.

Comparative and superlative adjectives

Use the comparative form to compare two things.

Learning from a person is ***more interesting than*** *learning from a book.*

Talking to someone is ***easier than*** *reading.*

Use the superlative form to compare three or more things.

Doing projects is ***the best*** *way to learn.*

1 Which form uses *than* after an adjective? ______
2 Which form uses *the* before an adjective? ______
3 Write the plain adjective forms for these items.

a more interesting *interesting*
b easier ______
c the best ______

Check page 134 for more information and practice.

11 Work in pairs. Complete the sentences with the correct forms of the adjectives. Then discuss if you agree with the sentences.

1 Studying for a short time every day is ______ (useful) than studying all night the night before a test.
2 Breakfast is the ______ (important) meal.
3 A light lunch is ______ (good) than a big one because a big lunch can make you sleepy.
4 Studying is important, but the ______ (good) way to learn a new skill is by using it.

12 Look at the Grammar box. Then answer the questions.

Comparative and superlative adverbs

Use comparative and superlative adverbs to describe actions.

a *I learn* ***better*** *by talking to people than by reading.*

b *I worked* ***the hardest*** *in the two weeks before my exams.*

1 Which sentence is comparative? Which is superlative?
2 What is the superlative adverb form of *good*?
3 What is the comparative adverb form of *hard*?

Check page 134 for more information and practice.

13 Complete the sentences with the comparative or superlative adverb forms of these words. One word is extra.

careful good hard often quiet recent

Students in a UN school talk to other students around the world.

1 I work ______ in history than I do in English.
2 Yusuf speaks ______ in class, so it's hard to hear him.
3 Ella graduated from high school ______ than Jim. She just finished last year.
4 My grades are improving. I did ______ on my final exam than on the mid-term exam.
5 I checked the essay section of the test ______ because that's where I usually make a lot of mistakes.

14 **PRONUNCIATION** Linking and elision

Which two words in the example are connected by linking? Which two are connected by elision? 24

Fluent speakers often join words together either by linking sounds or leaving out sounds (elision).

I work harder in history than I do in English because it's more difficult to remember dates than words.

15 Say the sentences. Do the bold words connect with linking or elision? Listen to check your answers. 25

1 Yusuf spoke the **most quietly**.
2 Ella graduated from school **more recently** than Jim.
3 I did **better on** my final exam than on the mid-term.
4 I checked the essay section the **most carefully**.

16 Make true sentences about you. Use comparatives and superlatives of the words in parentheses. Then, share your ideas with a partner.

1 Compare two school subjects (difficult).
2 Compare one school subject to the others (easy).
3 Compare the way two friends speak (quiet).
4 Compare how you work at two things (hard).

4B Outdoor Classroom

Nothing's Impossible

VOCABULARY BUILDING

Adjectives with *-ful* and *-less*

We can create adjectives by adding a suffix to some nouns. The suffix *-ful* means *with*, and *-less* means *without*. But be careful—you can't always make opposites using *-ful* and *-less*.

thankful – ~~thankless~~ not thankful

1 Read the Vocabulary Building box. Choose the correct options to complete the sentences from the article. Use your dictionary if necessary.

1 The trip was *stressful* / *stress-free* because of stormy weather.
2 I am *thankful* / *not thankful* for this amazing opportunity.
3 One *careful* / *careless* mistake could really hurt someone.
4 Working closely with students from other cultures is a great way to learn this *useful* / *useless* lesson.
5 There were moments when she felt afraid and *hopeful* / *hopeless*.

2 PRONUNCIATION Adjective stress

Listen to the sentences from Activity 1. Underline the stressed syllable in each adjective. 26

3 Make two or three sentences about yourself using the words from Activity 1. Practice saying them with the correct stress.

For me, taking exams is stressful.

READING

4 Read the tip and the sentences about the article. Scan the article to see if the sentences are *true* or *false*.

When you answer questions about a text, you need to find specific information. Looking through a text just for this information is called *scanning*. When you scan:

- focus on the information you are looking for.
- think about the type of information it is: a name, a date, a number, etc.
- let your eyes go over the text a few lines at a time. When you see useful information, stop and read closely.

1 Students in Singapore have a three- or five-day outdoor-skills course as part of their education.
2 Students learn outdoor skills as a reward for their hard work on more important school subjects like math.

"The rocks were *really* hard to grab. Then something magic happened. I climbed over the rock wall and made it! I didn't know I could make it that high."

—A blogger named Singapore Student

27 In Singapore, elementary and high school students take outdoor-skills courses as part of their studies. They're usually three or five days long and include rope and rock climbing, going to sea in a small boat called a kayak, sleeping in a tent each night, taking long walks in the jungle, and learning to start a fire. It's real life. One careless mistake could really hurt someone. So should outdoor skills really be taught at school? Why does the Singapore government think this should be part of every student's education?

Minister for Education Ng Chee Meng says that the challenge of the outdoor course helps students develop skills like critical thinking, working together, and good communication—abilities that are necessary for work and life. He believes that these skills are as important as traditional subjects like math, science, literature, and so on. Students need to learn from books, but for some lessons, reading isn't as useful as doing.

What do the students think? "It was so good!" said one teenager after the course. According to blogger Singapore Student, "It makes you a more independent and caring person." Angelique, another student in Singapore, had such a good experience that she went back for a twenty-one-day course. "It helped me to grow stronger," she says. The kayak trip was stressful because of stormy weather. She says there were moments when she felt afraid and hopeless—she thought the trip was too hard. But she remembered that "smooth seas never made a skilled sailor" and felt brave enough to continue against the storm. "I am thankful for this amazing opportunity, and I would do it again," she says.

Right now, students attend courses with groups from their own school. After 2020, however, all students will do the course in groups from several different schools. Why does this matter? People from China, Malaysia, India, and other cultures live closely together in Singapore. Good communication skills are more important now than ever in order for people to live and work together. Working closely with students from other cultures is a great way to learn this useful lesson.

One student said it this way: "There is nothing to be afraid of, and nothing's impossible." And that's a great lesson to learn.

3 A student named Angelique said the course was a terrible experience and she would never do it again.
4 In the future, students will take the outdoor-skills course with people from other schools.
5 According to the article, one student described the course as "impossible."

5 Work in pairs. Discuss the questions.

1 The article asks if outdoor skills should be taught at school. What do you think? Why?
2 Angelique says she felt afraid and hopeless at times, but that she would do it again. What difficult experience have you had that you learned something from?
3 In the future, students from different communities and schools will take the course together. How will difficult experiences outdoors help them learn to communicate?
4 What outdoor skills does the article mention? Which of them would you be afraid to try? Which of them do you think you would enjoy?
5 What skills does Ng Chee Meng believe students learn outdoors? Do you agree with him that they are as important as the traditional subjects? Why?

CRITICAL THINKING Analyzing quotations

6 Read the Critical Thinking box. Work in pairs. Discuss the questions.

> Quotations (quotes) are the original words of real people and are marked with quotation marks (Example: "It was good," she said). Writers use quotes to clearly show people's ideas or opinions. Writers may agree with the quotes and use them as supporting evidence, or they may argue against them. Writers sometimes use quotes from different people to show two sides of an argument.

1 How many separate quotes are used in the text?
2 What does each quote show about the outdoor-skills course?
3 Why do you think the author used quotes instead of just explaining the ideas in his own words?
4 Does the article include different points of view? Why do you think the author used the quotes that are used?

7 MY PERSPECTIVE

1 Would you like to learn skills like this at school? Why?
2 What do you think this kind of class could teach you about life?

Skills for Life

Adults say kids today need these skills

FROM **Very Important** TO **Not Very Important**

Very Important/Useful
Communication
Reading

Important/Useful
Math
Working together
Writing
Logic (clear thinking)
Science

Not Very Important/ Useful
Sports
Music
Art

4C Skills for Life

GRAMMAR Comparative forms

1 What can you remember about the outdoor-skills course in Singapore?

- activities: *rock climbing,* ______
- skills developed: ______
- challenges faced by students: ______

Comparative forms

Use (*not*) *as… as* to compare two things and say how they are similar or different.

1 *Outdoor skills are* ***as important as*** *the traditional subjects.*
2 *For some lessons, reading is****n't as useful as*** *doing.*

Use *too* + adjective to say that the quality described by an adjective is more than wanted or needed.

3 *She thought the trip was* ***too hard.***

Use adjective + *enough* to say that the quality described by an adjective is the right amount.

4 *She felt* ***brave enough*** *to continue against the storm.*

Use *not* + adjective + *enough* to say that the quality described by an adjective is less than the right amount.

5 *I was****n't brave enough****, so I gave up.*

Use *so* and *such* to make adjectives stronger. *So* comes before an adjective. *Such* comes before an adjective + noun.

6 *It was* ***so*** *good!*
7 *Angelique had* ***such*** *a good experience.*

2 Look at the Grammar box. Then choose the correct options to complete the information about the sentences in the box.

1 Outdoor skills and traditional subjects *have / don't have* the same importance.
2 For some lessons, reading and doing are *equal / not equal.*
3 This sentence is about something being *more than is needed / the right amount.*
4 This sentence is about something being *more than is needed / the right amount.*
5 This sentence is about something being *less than is needed / the right amount.*
6 The expression ***It was so good*** is *stronger than / not as strong as* ***It was good***.
7 ***Such*** *comes / doesn't come* directly before the noun.

Check page 134 for more information and practice.

3 Look at the information to the left. Then complete the sentences with (*not*) *as… as* and the adjective in parentheses.

According to the research…

1 writing and math skills are ______ (important) communication and reading skills.
2 science is ______ (useful) math.

3 sports are ________________ (useful) science.
4 communication is ________________ (important) reading.
5 art is ________________ (useful) working together.

4 Work in small groups. Discuss the questions.

1 What do you think *useful* means? To whom? For what?
2 Do you agree with the research? Why? Make your own comparisons of the skills using (*not*) *as*… *as* sentences.

5 Choose the correct options to complete the paragraph.

Some people feel that high school students shouldn't study art because it (1) *is too serious / isn't serious enough* to be a real school subject. But research shows that art education is (2) *too powerful / powerful enough* to improve students' grades in their other classes. This is especially true for students who find traditional subjects (3) *too challenging / not challenging enough* to do well in. Art classes also help students connect with each other, work together, and express themselves. Those benefits are (4) *too important / important enough* to support art in high schools.

6 Work in pairs. Discuss the questions.

1 Do you agree with the paragraph in Activity 5? Why?
2 Make sentences giving your opinion about art and your other classes using *too*… and (*not*)… *enough* sentences. Use the words below and other adjectives you know.

serious   challenging   useful   interesting   important

7 Complete each sentence with *such* or *so*.

1 Music is ________________ an important part of my life.
2 His experience with team sports was ________________ important to him.
3 Their art class was ________________ good—it made them look forward to school.
4 I had ________________ a good math teacher last year that I've decided I'd like to study math in college.
5 Working together is ________________ a useful skill that I think everyone should learn it and practice it at school.
6 The reading skills I learned made me do ________________ much better on my exams.

8 Make two sentences that are true for you for each item. Share your ideas with a partner.

1 (School subject) is / isn't as (adjective) as (school subject).

Math is as hard as science.

2 (School subject) is too (adjective).
3 (School subject) isn't (adjective) enough.
4 My (school subject) class is so (adjective)!
5 I had such a(n) (adjective) (school subject) class that I (result).

9 **CHOOSE**

Choose one of the following activities.

- List ten skills you think students need to learn, from most to least important. Compare your list in a group. Present your group's results to the class.
- Write a paragraph like the one in Activity 5, saying why a skill that some people think is less important is useful.
- Make notes about what you think the most useful skill is. Compare your skill to a partner's.

Students practice in a music class.

principle for success, which is the ability to delay gratification. ”

JOACHIM DE POSADA

Read about Joachim de Posada and get ready to watch his TED Talk. ▶ 4.0

AUTHENTIC LISTENING SKILLS

English speakers with accents

About 75% of the English spoken in the world is spoken by people who are speaking it as a second language. This means that you will hear many different pronunciations of both vowels and consonants. Identifying features of different accents can help you understand them more easily.

1 Read the Authentic Listening Skills box. Then listen to two people speaking the sentence below. Notice the pronunciation of *the*. Which sentence is spoken by a Spanish speaker? Which sentence is spoken by an American English speaker? 🎧 28

I think we have found **the** *most important factor for success.*

2 Listen to the sentences. Notice the words in bold. What's the difference between Joachim's pronunciation and the American speaker's pronunciation? 🎧 29

1 Johnny, I am going to leave you here with a marshmallow for fifteen **minutes**.
2 As soon as **the** door closed… two out of three ate **the** marshmallow.
3 Five **seconds**, ten **seconds**, forty **seconds**, fifty **seconds**…
4 And **they** found **that** 100 percent of the children that had not eaten the marshmallow were successful.

WATCH

3 Have you ever waited to do something? Why? What happened? Tell a partner.

4 Watch Part 1 of the talk. Complete the sentences. ▶ 4.1

1 The researcher told the children to wait for ________________ minutes.
2 Children who did not eat the marshmallow would have ________________ marshmallows.
3 This is the same as an adult waiting for ________________ for coffee.
4 ________________ out of ________________ children looked at the marshmallow and then put it back.

5 Watch Part 2 of the talk. Answer the questions. ▶ 4.2

1 How old were the kids when the researchers met with them again?
2 How does Joachim describe the successful kids?
3 How does he describe the unsuccessful kids?
4 What country did Joachim do his next experiment in?

6 Watch Part 3 of the talk. Correct the sentences. ▶ 4.3

1 One girl in Colombia ate only the outside of the marshmallow.

2 Joachim says that she should work in a bank.
3 Joachim says that a bad salesperson asks the customer questions.
4 Joachim says that the marshmallow principle should be taught in Korea.

7 Work in pairs. Discuss the questions.

1 You could say that the students who didn't eat the marshmallow followed the rules. Do you think following the rules is important? Why?
2 Delaying gratification means not doing something right away. Is it sometimes necessary to do something right away and not wait? Can you give an example?

8 VOCABULARY IN CONTEXT

a **Watch the clips from the talk. Choose the correct meaning of the words.** ▶ 4.4

b **Complete the sentences so they are true for you.**

1 *One hundred percent* of my friends are ________________ .
2 *I was in trouble* when ________________ .
3 I hope I can *make it to* ________________ .
4 When I finish my education, I'd like to *go into* ________________ .
5 One thing my country *produces is* ________________ .

9 Work in pairs. Discuss the questions.

1 Why does the ability to delay gratification mean you might get better grades?
2 Joachim says the ability to delay gratification is the key to success. Can you think of other factors that might be important to success?
3 Younger people often have to wait to do things such as drive or vote. Why is it important for people to reach a certain age before they can do these things?

CHALLENGE

Design your own experiment to test the ideas in the TED Talk. Follow these steps.

- Think about how you will ask people to delay gratification. For example, by telling them not to check their phones or not to watch a TV show right away.
- Think about how long you will ask people to delay gratification for.
- Think about what people will get if they can delay gratification for this long. For example, if students can go a whole class without checking their phones, they get a prize or don't have to do homework for one day.
- Share your ideas with the class and vote for the best experiment.

4E It's such a cool subject.

SPEAKING Making a decision

1 MY PERSPECTIVE

Work in pairs. Discuss the questions.

1 What do you think of taking classes during school vacation? Have you done this, or would you consider it?
2 What are the pros and cons of studying during vacations?

2 Work in pairs. Look at the list of courses. Which three look the most interesting?

- Computer skills: Create a website and learn how to write code for apps and games
- Indoor climbing: Learn climbing skills on a 15-meter climbing wall
- Science lab: Do fun and exciting experiments in the laboratory
- Art camp: Drawing, painting, photography—anything you're interested in
- Team sports: Play soccer, baseball, basketball, and other sports
- Video making: Write and produce short films

3 Listen to two students talking about choosing a summer school course. What three courses do they mention? 30

4 Complete the sentences. Then listen again and check your answers. 30

better choice	fun enough	more interesting
most interesting	such a cool	too much like school

1 Which ones look the ________________?
2 I'm not sure about computer skills—________________!
3 The sports classes look ________________.
4 Do you think it's ________________ for a two-week course?
5 Video making is ________________ subject.
6 That's a ________________ than indoor climbing!

5 What course do the students decide to take?

6 Read the Useful language box. In pairs, discuss the six courses in Activity 2 and choose one.

Useful language

Asking about opinions

Which ones look the most interesting / useful / exciting?
Is it too boring / long / expensive?
Do you think it's fun / useful / exciting enough?

Making comparisons

(The sports classes) look more interesting.
(Science lab) isn't as interesting / useful / exciting as (art camp).
(Computer skills) looks the most interesting / useful / exciting.

Making a decision

I think (art camp) is the best choice.
(Indoor climbing) is the most interesting.

WRITING An inquiry email

7 Read the email asking for information about a course. Match each part with the best description.

> [1]Dear City Summer School,
>
> [2]I saw your ad for the two-week course in video making on vacationcourses.com. [3]I'm writing because I have a couple of questions.
>
> [4]First, does each student make a video, or do students work in groups to produce projects? Second, do students have to choose to make a story or a documentary, or is it possible to do both?
>
> [5]Thanks in advance for any information you can give me. [6]I look forward to hearing from you.
>
> [7]Yours sincerely,
>
> [8]Alfonso Alongi

a 3 the reason for the email
b ____ the main message of the email
c ____ greeting
d ____ thanking the person for helping you
e ____ where you saw the advertisement
f ____ the writer's name
g ____ closing statement asking for a reply
h ____ polite closing expression

8 **WRITING SKILL** Responding to an ad

Read the Writing strategy box. Use the expressions to write an email asking questions about a course you'd be interested in finding out about. Use the email in Activity 7 as a model.

9 Exchange emails with a partner. Check each other's work. Does it use the structure from Activity 7 and the language from the Writing strategy box?

Writing strategy

Saying how you know about the person or company you're writing to

I saw your ad / website / poster.

Saying why you're writing

I'm writing because I'd like more information / I have a couple of questions / I'd like to ask about…

Saying thank you

Thanks (in advance) for…

High school students work on a robot that they invented in a robotics club.

5 Family and Friends

IN THIS UNIT, YOU...

- talk about friends and family members.
- learn how we greet the people in our lives.
- read about how people celebrate life's changes.
- watch a TED Talk about why we laugh.
- make and describe plans for a party.

A group of friends performs on a subway car in New York City, US.

5A The People in My Life

VOCABULARY How's it going?

1 Look at the photo. Answer the questions.

1 How would you describe these people? Do you know anyone like this?
2 Why do you think they're doing this?

2 MY PERSPECTIVE

Which of your friends and family are important if you want to talk about difficult things? Need advice? Want to have fun? Want to learn about something? Share your ideas with a partner.

When I need help with my homework, I usually ask my dad.

3 Copy the chart below. Write the words in the correct column. Use your dictionary if necessary. Add one or two words of your own to each column.

aunt	best friend	bow	brother	classmate
cousin	friend of a friend	grandfather	grandmother	hug
kiss	partner	say hello	shake hands	sister
stranger	teammate (sports)	uncle	wave	

Family	Other people	Greetings

4 Follow the steps below. Then share your ideas with a partner.

1 Choose three words from the "Family" column. Then write a definition for each family member.

Your aunt is the sister of your mother or father.

2 Put the "Other people" in order from 1 (the closest to you) to 5 (the least close).
3 Which greeting do you use for each person? Are there any greetings that you use that aren't on the list?

I usually greet my best friend with a hug. When I meet a stranger for the first time, we usually just say hello.

5 Describe a person in your life using the following information. Can your partner guess who it is?

- Male or female?
- Age
- How you greet them
- Something you usually do together
- Where they live

A *He's 45 years old. He lives in a town two hours from here. I usually greet him with a hug. When I see him, we usually play soccer.*
B *Is he your cousin?*
A *No, he isn't. My cousins are all my age.*
B *Is he your uncle?*
A *Yes, that's right!*

LISTENING

6 The chart shows how people greet the people around them. Listen to the podcast and match each column of the chart with a speaker. Write the number of the speaker at the bottom. 31

People	Types of greetings		
Strangers	kiss	shake hands	bow, wave
People I've met	kiss	shake hands	bow, wave
Friends	kiss and hug	wave	bow, wave
Best friends	kiss and hug	hug	bow, wave, say hello
Family	kiss and hug	shake hands, hug, kiss	show respect
	______	______	______

7 Listen again. Choose the correct words. 31

1 In Chen's family, respect *is more important than / isn't as important as* hugs and kisses.
2 Chen's parents *talk about / show* their love with their actions.
3 Bowing is a way of showing *respect / agreement.*
4 Luiza doesn't kiss her friends when *she says hello / she's in a hurry.*
5 Luiza *kisses / doesn't kiss* her sister.
6 Hugh *hugs / doesn't hug* his cousins.
7 Hugh always shakes hands with his *teachers at school / tennis coach.*

8 Which speaker is the most like you? Complete the chart with people you know and your ways of greeting them. Use the chart in Activity 6 as an example.

People	Types of greetings

GRAMMAR Present perfect and simple past

9 Look at the Grammar box. Read the sentences from the podcast. Match each with the best description below.

Present perfect and simple past: statements

a *I've never hugged my dad.*
b *She's learned to hug and kiss like a Brazilian, so she feels at home now.*
c *I've met people from other countries.*

The sentences refer to...
1 ______ an action in the past with a result in the present.
2 ______ a situation that started in the past and continues to the present.
3 ______ an experience or experiences that happened at an unspecified time.

Check page 136 for more information and practice.

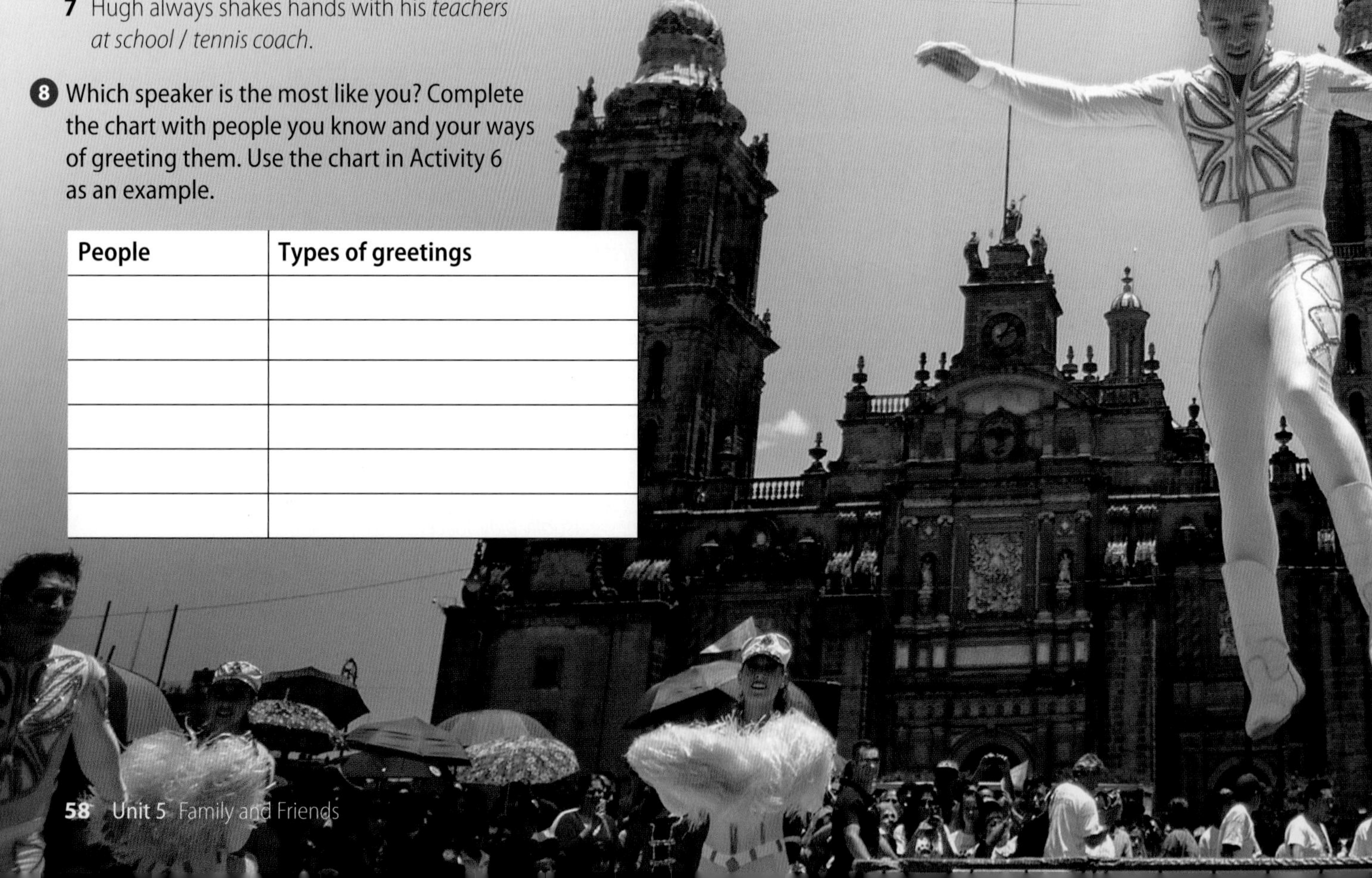

10 Complete the article with the present perfect form of the verbs.

Photographer and anthropologist Emily Ainsworth (1) __________ (travel) the world because she wants to learn about other cultures. She (2) __________ (have) amazing experiences in many different countries, but she says Mexico is very special. "I (3) __________ (return), and returned again," she says, adding, "it (4) __________ (be) my second home." And the people (5) __________ (welcome) her—at celebrations, family events, and even in a circus, where she (6) __________ (perform) as a dancer many times.

11 Circle the verbs in each sentence. Then answer the questions.

Present perfect and simple past: questions and short responses

a *Have you ever visited Mexico?*
b *Yes, once. I went there last year.*

1 Which sentence is about a certain time in the past? _____
2 Which is about an unspecified time in the past? _____

12 Choose the correct options to complete the text.

Emily was sixteen when she first (1) *went / has been* to Mexico, and she (2) *went / has been* back to the country many times. Now she has a lot of friends there. During her visits, she (3) *took / has taken* pictures of Day of the Dead celebrations and many other important cultural events. At first, she just (4) *wanted / has wanted* to have photos to remember her trip. But over time, she says, she (5) *has built / built*—and continues to build—"relationships with some really interesting people," and wants to tell their stories. As a result, she (6) *won / has won* several awards for her work.

13 **PRONUNCIATION** /d/, /t/, /ɪd/ verb endings

Read the Pronunciation box. Check (√) the *-ed* pronunciation for the words in bold. Listen and check your answers. 32

There are three ways to pronounce *-ed* when it comes at the end of a verb: /d/ as in *tried*, /t/ as in *wished*, or /ɪd/ as in *wanted*.

	/d/	/t/	/ɪd/
1 We **celebrated** my sister's fifteenth birthday last year.			
2 My dad has **photographed** our most important family events.			
3 I've never **stayed** awake all night during the new year celebration.			
4 When my cousin **turned** twenty, he had a huge party.			
5 I've never **invited** more than two or three friends to a birthday celebration.			
6 My friends and I have always **laughed** a lot at our village *fiestas*.			

14 Use the words to make questions about experiences. Use the simple past or present perfect.

1 you meet anyone from another country?
2 you celebrate on the last day of elementary school?
3 when the last time you laugh a lot with your friends?
4 what events you celebrate with friends?
5 what you do last weekend?

15 Work in pairs. Ask and answer the questions in Activity 14.

Events like this circus in Mexico City can show what is important to a culture. When Emily joined the circus in Mexico, she learned about the people in it, as well as herself. Is there anything like this in your country?

5B Coming of Age

VOCABULARY BUILDING

Adjectives ending in *-al*

The suffix *-al* usually means *related to*. For example, *national* means *related to a nation*.

1 **Read the sentences from the article. Match the words in bold with the correct meaning below.**

1 A girl's fifteenth birthday is a huge **social** occasion for many Latin American families.
2 The tradition has become **international**, spreading through Central and South America.
3 It marks a time of important **personal** change.
4 The event has both personal and **historical** importance.

Connected with...

a _____ many countries
b _____ the past
c _____ a person
d __1__ groups of people

2 **Complete the sentences with these adjectives.**

cultural emotional traditional typical

1 The *fiesta de quince años* is hundreds of years old. It's a __________ Mexican celebration.
2 Certain things are expected at most parties. At a __________ party, the girl's father removes her shoes.
3 The party brings out strong feelings. The shoe-changing can be a very __________ moment.
4 It's part of the Mexican way of life, but many countries don't have a __________ tradition like this.

3 **What adjectives can you make from these nouns? Be careful. You need to delete a letter from some nouns.**

center music nature politics profession

READING

4 **MY PERSPECTIVE**

Work in pairs. Discuss the questions.

1 What are the most important celebrations in your family?
2 What do you think is the most important birthday in a person's life? Why?
3 Are there any unique social celebrations in your city or country?

5 **Read the tip and the article. Then choose the topic and main idea of the article.**

The topic of a text is a word or phrase that answers the question "What is the text about?" The main idea of a text answers the question "What is the writer's most important point about the topic?" This is usually expressed as a sentence.

1 Topic:
  a Latin American celebrations
  b The *fiesta de quince años*
  c Becoming an adult
2 Main idea:
  a The culture of ancient Mexico has affected all of Latin America.
  b The *fiesta de quince años* shouldn't be more important than a wedding.
  c A girl's fifteenth birthday is one of the most important celebrations for Latin American families.

6 **Read the article again. Is the information *true*, *false*, or *not given*?**

1 According to the article, the biggest *fiestas de quince años* are held in Spain.
2 In the US, the *fiestas* usually aren't as big as weddings.
3 The history of the *fiesta* goes back more than 500 years.
4 There are over 500,000 *fiestas* in the US a year.
5 Some *fiestas* in the US last for a week.
6 New shoes show that the girl has become a young woman.

7 **Find information in the article to support each sentence.**

1 The *fiesta de quince años* is an international celebration.
2 The girl is seen as a different person after the celebration.
3 The celebrations have become bigger over time.
4 People spend a lot of money on a *fiesta de quince años*.
5 The celebration is a very old tradition.

8 **Read the comments. Write one of your own, making some connection with your own life or culture.**

Comments

BeijingGuy Interesting post! I'm Chinese, and I've just celebrated my "Guan Li"—a twentieth birthday celebration for boys. We also celebrate a girl's fifteenth birthday. We call it "Ji Li." Both of these are like the *fiesta de quince años*—we celebrate becoming men and women.

Agnieska In Poland, we don't have a cultural tradition like this, but for us, 18 is a big birthday. We usually have a party with friends. You can vote and drive a car when you're 18. I haven't had my eighteenth birthday yet—one more year!

9 **Design your perfect party. Where is it held? Who do you invite? What do you do?**

A father and daughter celebrate at a *fiesta de quince años*.

From **child** to **adult**—in one day

33 Delilah Bermejo, a New Yorker with family history in Puerto Rico and Colombia, says that "it's the most important day" of a girl's life. The *fiesta de quince años*—a girl's fifteenth birthday celebration—is a huge social occasion for Latin American families and is one of life's biggest celebrations. Friends and relatives come together to celebrate a girl's passing from childhood into the adult world. It marks a time of important personal change. According to Ed Hassel, manager of a company that provides food for parties in New York, the celebrations are now "bigger than the weddings I do. We're talking 125, 150, 175 people. And they're taking Saturday night, my most expensive night."

The event has both personal and historical importance. Families have held special celebrations for fifteen-year-olds for at least 500 years—since the time of the Aztecs in Mexico. At age 15, Aztec boys became warriors—men old enough to fight in a war—and girls became women with adult rights and duties.

In the past, parties were usually small, with a few friends and family members. It was a chance for the young woman to meet young men. Only very rich families had big *fiestas*. Since the arrival of Europeans in the Americas, the tradition has become international, spreading through Central and South America and into North America. Nowadays, big celebrations are popular with the nearly 60 million Latinos in the US and Canada.

Friends and family take an active part in a traditional Mexican *fiesta de quince años*. A "man of honor," usually a member of the girl's family, accompanies the *quinceañera* throughout the celebration. She also chooses a "court," often fourteen girls and fourteen boys, one for each year of her life. They stay near the *quinceañera*, join all of the dances, and look after her on her special day. The celebration often begins with a formal ceremony before it becomes a more usual birthday party with food and dancing. Families with more money usually have bigger parties. A typical ceremony ends with the girl's father removing the flat shoes that she wore to the party and replacing them with a pair of more grown-up shoes with a high heel. This can be an emotional moment. It means that the person who walked into the party as a girl leaves the party as a young woman.

Many young people celebrate Coming of Age Day in Japan when they turn 20.

5C Stop me if you've already heard this one.

GRAMMAR Present perfect with *for*, *since*, *already*, *just*, and *yet*

1 Look at the Grammar box. Choose the correct option to complete each explanation for the sentences below.

Present perfect with *for, since, already, just,* and *yet*

1 *Families* ***have celebrated*** *the fiesta de quince años* ***for*** *about 500 years.*
2 ***Since*** *the arrival of Europeans in the Americas, the tradition* ***has become*** *international.*
3 *I'm Chinese, and I****'ve just celebrated*** *my "Guan Li."*
4 *I* ***haven't had*** *my eighteenth birthday* ***yet****—one more year.*
5 *My sister* ***has already celebrated*** *her eighteenth birthday.*

1 This sentence refers to *a period of time / a certain time in the past.*
2 This sentence refers to a certain event in the *past / present* and the situation afterward.
3 This event happened *in the recent past / a long time ago.*
4 This *has / has not* happened.
5 This happened, *but we don't know / and we know* when.

Check page 136 for more information and practice.

2 Complete the exchanges with *for* and *since.*

1 **A** I haven't seen my cousins ________ last month.
B Really? I haven't seen mine ________ almost three years.
2 **A** We've been friends ________ ten years.
B Yeah, I guess you're right. We've known each other ________ we were five years old.
3 **A** Has your brother been in the running club ________ long?
B Not really. He's been a member ________ January.

3 Complete the questions with *you* and the correct form of verbs in parentheses. Then work in pairs to answer each question with *for* and *since*.

1 How long ________ (know) your best friend?
2 How long ________ (live) in the home you now live in?
3 How long ________ (study) English?
4 How long ________ (attend) the school you go to now?

4 Complete the text with *just, already,* or *yet.*

"Comedy is kind of a language, so you're connected and relating." — Gad Elmaleh

Moroccan-born comedian Gad Elmaleh has taken a lot of English lessons in his life but jokes that he doesn't really speak English (1) ________. However, that hasn't stopped him from performing comedy for American audiences. Although he arrived in the US fairly recently, he's (2) ________ done shows in New York, Los Angeles, and lots of cities in between. He's (3) ________ completed a tour of more than ten US cities and plans to continue performing.

Although Gad has (4) ________ started his comedy career in America, he's (5) ________ a superstar in Europe—especially France. In the US, he hasn't (6) ________ become that popular. His career, like his English, is a work in progress.

5 Put the words in the correct place in each sentence. Some words can go in more than one place.

A I've heard a really funny joke. (1. just)
Why is *U* the happiest letter?
B Because it's in the middle of *fun*.
Sorry, but I've heard that one! (2. already)
A OK, here's one you probably haven't heard. (3. yet)
Why is six afraid of seven?
B Because seven ate nine! My brother has told me that one! (4. already)

6 Answer the questions. Use the present perfect.

1 What have you done recently that you're proud of?

My paper is due next week, and I've already finished writing it.
I've just passed my piano test.

2 What have you done for a long time that you're proud of?

I've been on the soccer team for five years.
I've taken art classes on Saturdays since I was eleven years old.

3 What haven't you done yet but would like to do?

I haven't learned to play a musical instrument yet, but I'd like to.
I haven't read a novel in English yet, but I want to read one.

7 **CHOOSE**

Choose one of the following activities.

- Work in pairs. Tell your partner about the things you wrote about in Activity 6. Ask and answer questions.

  A *How long have you played the piano?*
  B *Since I was about five years old.*
  A *Does anyone else in your family play?*
  B *Yes, my mother plays, and my brother does, too.*
- Write a paragraph about one of the things you wrote about in Activity 6. Give more information about it.
- Prepare a short presentation about one of the things you wrote about in Activity 6. Tell the class about it.

Birthday celebrations are important get-togethers for many families around the world. This family is celebrating in Brazil.

5D Why We Laugh

“You are laughing to show people that you understand them, that you agree with them, that you're part of the same group as them.”

SOPHIE SCOTT

Read about Sophie Scott and get ready to watch her TED Talk. ▶ 5.0

AUTHENTIC LISTENING SKILLS

Dealing with fast speech

Some people speak very quickly, often because they are excited about a topic or they are nervous. Here are some ways to deal with fast speech:

- Listen for words or ideas that the speaker repeats.
- Try to identify the main idea and then connect it with what you hear.
- Focus on what you *do* understand and try not to worry too much about what you don't understand.

1 Read the Authentic Listening Skills box. Then listen to the first part of the TED Talk and answer the questions. 🎧 34

1 What words or ideas does the speaker repeat?
2 What words tell us that she's talking about her childhood?
3 In your own words, say what you think she's describing.

2 Listen again. What is the point of Sophie's story? 🎧 34

a When she was a child, she usually didn't understand her parents' jokes.
b When we hear people laughing, we want to laugh with them.
c Sometimes, laughing can make the people around you feel bad.

WATCH

3 Watch Part 1 of the talk. Are the sentences *true* or *false*? ▶ 5.1

1 Sophie's parents were laughing at a song.
2 The first recording includes both a man and an animal.
3 Sophie is worried that the second person laughing doesn't breathe in.
4 The third recording is an example of a monkey laughing, which is very similar to a human.

4 Watch Part 2 of the talk. Choose the correct options to complete the sentences. ▶ 5.2

1 People laugh mostly when _____ .
a they hear a joke **c** they're with friends
b they watch a comedy

2 When we hear other people laugh, we usually _____ .
a start laughing **c** think they're laughing at us
b ask why they're laughing

3 Laughter that we cannot control is called _____ laughter.
a voluntary **c** vocal
b involuntary

4 We can choose to laugh when we want to be _____ to another person.
a horrible **c** polite
b funny

5 The first recording is _____ laughter.
a polite **c** not really
b involuntary

6 The second recording is _____ laughter.
a polite **c** not really
b involuntary

5 Complete the summary of Part 3 of the talk before you watch it. Then watch it and check your answers. ▶ 5.3

animals bonds emotions humans laughs sounds

(1) __________ are not the only (2) __________ that laugh—many mammals laugh to feel better. And animals also have both real and fake (3) __________ with very different (4) __________. Laughter helps us maintain social (5) __________ and control our (6) __________.

6 **VOCABULARY IN CONTEXT**

a Watch the clips from the talk. Choose the correct meaning of the words and phrases. ▶ 5.4

b Complete the sentences with your own words. Then discuss with a partner.

1 I think __________ is *weird.*
2 I had an *odd* experience when __________.
3 I think __________ is *silly.*
4 I would like to know more about the *origins* of __________.
5 I would like to know the *roots* of __________.

CRITICAL THINKING Recognize supporting evidence

Speakers often give evidence to support their theory or idea. Evidence may include images, recordings, demonstrations, or quotations from experts or other reliable people.

7 Read the Critical Thinking box. Work in pairs. How does this evidence from the talk support Sophie Scott's message that "laughter is an ancient behavior that we use to benefit ourselves and others in complex and surprising ways."

1 She plays examples of real human beings laughing and asks us to think about how primitive laughter is as a sound.
2 She points out that the audience laughed when listening to others laugh.
3 She plays recordings of voluntary and involuntary laughter.

8 Work in pairs. Discuss the questions.

1 Which part of Sophie's talk was the most interesting to you? Why?
2 Have your ideas about laughter changed? How?

CHALLENGE

For a couple of days, listen for people laughing. Try to notice examples of both real and polite laughter. Make notes. Present your results to the class, explaining the situations where you heard each type of laughter.

9 Work in groups. Discuss the questions.

1 Sophie says that we laugh "to show people that [we] understand them, that [we] agree with them, that [we]'re part of the same group as them." What other ways do we show that we are part of the group?
2 Most people are part of more than one group. How many groups are people in at your school?
3 How do the people in the groups you named in Question 2 show that they are part of that group?

5E Invitations

SPEAKING Taking about availability

1 MY PERSPECTIVE

How do you think the students in the photo feel? Why?

2 Listen to the conversation. What important life event is mentioned? 35

3 Listen again. Write down the days and times mentioned. 35

4 You're having a party to welcome a new student, Delia, to your school. Decide on a day, time, location, and type of food for it.

5 Work in pairs. Take turns inviting each other and saying whether you can or can't go. Use phrases from the Useful language box.

Useful language

Asking if someone is available

Are you busy next Saturday?
Are you around / free on Sunday?
Are you doing anything on Tuesday night?

Saying if you are available or not

I (don't) think so.
It depends.
I'm not sure.
I'll have to ask my parents.
I need to check my schedule.

Accepting an invitation

Sure, I'd love to.
That sounds great!

Saying *no* to an invitation

Thanks for inviting me, but I'm afraid I'm busy.
Sorry, I can't make it. But thank you for inviting me.

WRITING Informal invitations and replies

6 Read the three notes. Match each one to the correct purpose.

1 _____ Making an invitation
2 _____ Accepting an invitation
3 _____ Saying no to an invitation

a

Hi Davina,

Thanks for inviting me to your graduation party. It sounds like a lot of fun. I'd love to come. What should I wear? Should I bring anything? Let me know A.S.A.P.!

Lena

b

Anders,

Thank you for the invitation to your New Year's party. I'm sorry, but I can't make it. I've already made other plans that night. I'm going to be with my family.

Lucas

P.S. I hope you have a great time! Let's catch up soon!

c

Hey Sylvia,

I'm having a birthday party on Saturday the 25th from 5:00 to 10:00 at my house. We're going to have pizza and cake and then watch a movie and play some games. Can you make it? R.S.V.P.

Joanna

7 In each note, underline the expressions used for making, accepting, or saying *no* to an invitation.

8 In informal notes, we sometimes use abbreviations. Find an abbreviation in each note. Which one means:

1 *Let me know if you can come?*
2 *As soon as possible?*
3 *I also want to say...*

9 **WRITING SKILL** Politely making and replying to invitations

Work in pairs. Read the Writing strategy box. Think of a celebration you would like to have. Write an informal invitation to your partner. Use two abbreviations.

10 Exchange invitations. Then write a reply to your partner's invitation.

11 Check each other's work. Do the notes use abbreviations and the Writing strategies correctly?

Writing strategy

Politely making and replying to invitations

- When you write an invitation, give the time, date, location, and type of event. Remember to ask the person to let you know if they can come.
- When you accept an invitation, begin by saying *thank you*. If you have any questions about the event, ask them. It can be polite to offer to bring something (food or drinks, for example).
- When you say *no* to an invitation, begin by saying *thank you*. Apologize that you can't make it and say why—without giving too many details if you don't want to. It can be polite to end by saying you hope they enjoy the event and offering to make plans another time.

Students in Punjab, India, celebrate their graduation.

SIMPLE PRESENT AND PRESENT CONTINUOUS

Simple Present

The simple present is used to talk about permanent states and regular habits in the present and things that are always true.

*I'm 13 years old. I **live** in Istanbul. I **have** two sisters.*
*My school day **starts** at 8:00. I **play** soccer every Saturday.*

Affirmative	Negative
I / You / We / They **drink** milk.	I / You / We / They **don't drink** milk.
He / She / It **drinks** milk.	He / She / It **doesn't drink** milk.

Question	Short answer
Do you / we / they **drink** milk?	Yes, I / we / they **do**. No, I / we / they **don't**.
Does he / she / it / **drink** milk?	Yes, he / she / it **does**. No, he / she / it **doesn't**.

The third person singular is formed by adding *-s* to the verb.

*He **lives** in Rome.*

When verbs end in *-o*, *-s*, *-sh*, *-ch*, *-x*, and *-z*, add *-es*.

*She **watches** soccer every Saturday.*

When verbs end in a consonant + *-y*, replace the *-y* with *-i* and add *-es*. *He **studies** English.*

Negatives and questions are formed with *do / don't / does / doesn't* and the main verb.

Present continuous

The present continuous is used to talk about things that are happening at the moment of speaking.

*I'**m** not **playing** soccer today because it'**s raining**.*

The present continuous is also used to talk about things that are happening around the time of speaking.

*I'**m reading** a good book right now.*

When a verb has one syllable and ends in a consonant, *-ing* is added: *work* ⟶ *working*.

When a verb has one syllable and ends in a vowel followed by *-b*, *-d*, *-f*, *-l*, *-m*, *-n*, *-p*, or *-t*, the final letter is usually doubled.

stop ⟶ *stopping*, *sit* ⟶ *sitting*, *plan* ⟶ *planning*
Exceptions: *failing, feeling, seeming, sleeping, waiting*

When a verb ends in *-e*, it is usually deleted when *-ing* is added. *make* ⟶ *making*

Affirmative	Negative
I'**m studying**. You / We / They **are studying**.	I'**m not studying**. You / We / They **aren't studying**.
He / She **is studying**. It **is raining**.	He / She **isn't studying**. It **isn't raining**.

Question	Short answer
Am I **playing**?	Yes, I **am**. No, I'm **not**.
Are you / we / they **playing**?	Yes, you / we / they **are**. No, you / we / they **aren't**.
Is he / she / it **playing**?	Yes, he / she / it **is**. No, he / she / it **isn't**.

VERB PATTERNS: VERB + *-ING* OR INFINITIVE WITH *TO*

Verb + infinitive	agree, decide, expect, hope, learn, need, offer, plan, promise, seem, want, like
Verb + *-ing*	can't help, consider, enjoy, finish, not mind, suggest, tell
Verb + *-ing* OR to + infinitive	begin, continue, hate, like, love, prefer, start

Verb + infinitive

After some verbs, the infinitive form of another verb is used.

*I **want to be** more active.*

The second verb is made negative by putting *not* before it:

*She tells her parents **not to worry** about her.*

Verb + *-ing*

After some verbs, the *-ing* form of another verb is used.

*I **enjoy being** sociable.*

Verb + *-ing* OR *to* + infinitive

After some verbs, either can be used with no change in meaning.

*They **like sharing** / **like to share** information.*

Questions

Form questions like this:

*What do you **want to do**? What does he **enjoy doing**?*
*Does she **need to talk** to someone?*

1 Complete the exchanges. Use the notes to write simple present questions and answers.

1 **A** you / live in Argentina? *Do you live in Argentina?*
B yes *Yes, I do.*
2 **A** he / play soccer? __________
B no __________
3 **A** they / know Beatriz? __________
B yes __________
4 **A** we ready? __________
B yes __________
5 **A** I / late? __________
B no __________
6 **A** you / like school? __________
B yes __________

2 Complete the sentences using the present continuous forms of the verbs.

expect get have stay study take talk try

1 I __________ for my final exams.
2 My brother __________ to find a part-time job.
3 They __________ in a hotel.
4 We __________ a lot of fun!
5 You __________ a German class, right?
6 She __________ an email from her teacher.
7 I think he __________ to the new student. He's very outgoing.
8 It's pretty loud in here. I __________ a headache.

3 Are the underlined present continuous verbs and phrases used correctly? If not, re-write the sentences using the simple present.

1 I'm knowing his first name but not his last name.
2 Are you owning a bicycle?
3 We're staying with friends this week.
4 They're preferring soccer to basketball.
5 You're learning the guitar very quickly.
6 Is she learning Spanish?
7 She's thinking about the test.
8 He's thinking about the answer to the question.

4 Choose the two options that can complete each sentence.

1 She _____ to tell me a secret.
a didn't mind **b** started **c** promised
2 They _____ talking to each other.
a enjoy **b** like **c** want
3 I _____ to learn to talk about my feelings.
a can't help **b** want **c** need
4 We _____ asking our mother for advice.
a were **b** suggest **c** agree
5 Can you _____ to write about your experience?
a consider **b** begin **c** manage
6 He _____ to believe his brother is telling the truth.
a seems **b** enjoys **c** wants

5 Put the words in the correct order to make sentences.

1 sister / I / my / to / hope / talk / to
__________.
2 wants / to / my / explain / feelings / me / She
__________.
3 We / emotions / mind / don't / about / talking
__________.
4 hate / You / your / sharing / feelings
__________.
5 know / would / He / to / it / like / about / more
__________.
6 My / still / get / easygoing / she / seems / to / good / is / friend / grades / but
__________.

6 Complete the sentences with the verb in parentheses. Use one gerund and one infinitive form.

1 (read) I really enjoy __________. I want __________ a new book every week.
2 (meet) I suggest __________ some new people. You can expect __________ new people by joining a club.
3 (enjoy) They seem __________ painting. Even when they're in a bad mood, they can't help __________ it.
4 (go) He agreed __________ to the movies with us. He didn't consider __________ out for dinner afterwards, though.
5 (wait) Do you mind __________ for Ella? We need __________ about ten minutes.

SIMPLE PAST

The simple past is used:

- for completed actions and events in the past.
  We ***built*** *the house last year.*
- for actions and events in a story or series of events in the past.
  We ***bought*** *the container on eBay, and the company* ***delivered*** *it to us. We* ***worked*** *on it for six months.*
- for repeated past actions and past states.
  I ***went*** *to the office every day.*
- for past actions or events over a long period of time.
  I ***grew up*** *in Tu Son, near Hanoi.*

There are some spelling rules for regular verbs.

- verbs ending in *-e*: add *-d*: *like* ⟶ *liked*
- verbs ending in *-y*: change *-y* to *-i* and add *-ed*: *try* ⟶ *tried*
- do not change the *-y* to *-i* if the verb ends in vowel + *-y*: *play* ⟶ *played*
- verbs ending in consonant + vowel + consonant: double the final consonant and add *-ed*: *stop* ⟶ *stopped*
- do not double the consonant if it is a *-w* or *-x*: *fix* ⟶ *fixed*

Some verbs are irregular in the affirmative form:

build ⟶ built, come ⟶ came, find ⟶ found, go ⟶ went, have ⟶ had, take ⟶ took, think ⟶ thought

The simple past of *be* is *I/he/she/it* was and *we/you/they* were.

It ***was*** *a beautiful traditional house.*
We ***were*** *very happy there.*

Time expressions are often used to say when things happened in the past.

this (*morning / afternoon / evening*), *yesterday, last* (*Friday*), *last* (*week / month / year*), *in* (*2000*), (*two*) *weeks ago, when I was* (*a child*)

Negative and questions

Negatives in the simple past are formed with *didn't* and the base form.

They ***didn't pay*** *for the shipping container.*

Questions in the simple past are formed with *did / didn't* and the base form.

Did *they* ***move*** *to the city? Yes, they did.*
Didn't *she* ***buy*** *an old house? No, she didn't.*
Where *did you* ***live****?*

Negatives are formed by adding *not* (*n't*) to the past affirmative.

It ***wasn't*** *his house; it was hers.*
They ***weren't*** *chairs; they were old boxes.*

used to

To talk about situations, habits, and routines in the past use *used to* + the base form.

They ***used to live*** *in Mexico.*

Form the negative using *didn't use to* + the base form.

I didn't use to go *to work every day.*

Form questions with *did / didn't use to* + the base form.

Did *you* ***use to live*** *in an apartment?*

PAST CONTINUOUS

The past continuous is used:

- for ongoing actions and ongoing events in the past.
  We ***were walking*** *to school.*
- for continuing situations, actions, and activities in the past, especially when a single action or event happens during them.
  They ***were looking*** *for an apartment when they discovered a houseboat.*
- for past situations that continued for a long period of time.
  In 2014, he ***was living*** *in Abu Dhabi.*

The past continuous is formed with the past tense of be and the present participle.

search ⟶ *was/were searching, live* ⟶ *was/were living, work* ⟶ *was/were working*

They ***were searching*** *for a place to live.*
We ***were living*** *in a new house.*
He ***was working*** *downtown.*

There are some spelling rules for forming the present participle.

- verbs ending in a consonant: add *-ing*: *think* ⟶ *thinking*
- verbs ending in *-e*: change *-e* to *-ing*: *take* ⟶ *taking*
- verbs ending in consonant + vowel + consonant: double the final consonant and add *-ing*: *hit* ⟶ *hitting*

Negative sentences are formed with *wasn't / weren't* and the present participle.

They ***weren't looking*** *for a house.*
I ***wasn't living*** *in Singapore.*

Questions are formed with *was / were* and the present participle.

Were *your parents* ***working*** *in Jakarta?*
Wasn't *she* ***trying*** *to find a new apartment?*

1 Choose the correct option to complete the sentences.

1 Did you *see* / *saw* Beata's new house?
2 We *weren't* / *didn't* live in an apartment.
3 The company *was recycled* / *recycled* old shipping containers.
4 Where did you live when you *were* / *was* a child?
5 Why did your family *move* / *moved* to Prague?
6 Last year my brother *find* / *found* a really good apartment.

2 Complete the conversation with the simple past of the verbs in parentheses.

A (1) __________ (you see) the documentary on TV last night about small houses?
B No, (2) I __________ (not). (3) __________ (be) it good?
A Yes, it (4) __________ (be). It (5) __________ (show) people around the world living in tiny spaces—houseboats, tiny apartments. They (6) __________ (interview) a guy who (7) __________ (live) in his van at the beach.
B Why? (8) __________ (he not have) a job?
A Yes, he (9) __________ (do). But he (10) __________ (want) to save money. And he (11) __________ (go) surfing every day, before or after work!

3 Put the words in the correct order to make questions. Capitalize the first word of the sentences.

1 you / did / the house / by yourself? / build
____
2 free? / was / container / the shipping
____
3 a shipping container? / easy / was it / to find
____
4 expensive? / the container / was
____
5 electricity supply? / to the / you connect / did / the house
____

4 Complete the conversations with *used* or *use*.

A Didn't you (1) __________ to live in Argentina?
B No, I didn't, but my grandparents (2) __________ to live there. They lived in an apartment in Buenos Aires, and I (3) __________ to visit every summer for a few weeks.
A We didn't (4) __________ to live in the suburbs, but now we do.
B Where did you (5) __________ to live?
A We (6) __________ to live in the country.

5 Look at the photos. Answer the questions.

1 What are these home furnishings now?
2 What did they use to be?

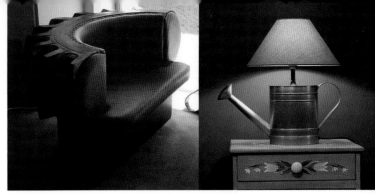

6 Write sentences in the past continuous.

1 My parents / live in Jakarta
My parents were living in Jakarta.
2 We / stay in a hotel and look for a house
____
3 I / walk to school and think about my homework
____
4 They / not look for a new house
____
5 You / not try to sell your houseboat
____

7 Choose the correct option.

1 My dad was working in Dubai when he *met* / *was meeting* my mother.
2 I *prepared* / *was preparing* to move away for college when I changed my plans.
3 When I was looking through some old photos, I *found* / *was finding* a photo of our old house.
4 While we *stayed* / *were staying* at my grandmother's house, my uncle visited every afternoon.

8 Complete the conversation with the simple past or past continuous of the verbs in parentheses.

A How (1) __________ (your parents find) your new apartment?
B My dad (2) __________ (drive) to work when he (3) __________ (see) a man putting up a "for rent" sign. He (4) __________ (stop) the car right away. The man (5) __________ (drive) away, but my dad (6) __________ (yell), "Hey, wait!", and the man (7) __________ (stop).
A Was the man surprised?
B Yes, but then my dad (8) __________ (ask) to see the apartment. While he (9) __________ (look) around, he (10) __________ (call) my mom and (11) __________ (tell) her to come see it. She (12) __________ (love) it, too. So they (13) __________ (rent) it!

QUANTIFIERS

some and *any*

Use *some* and *any* with plural countable and uncountable nouns.

	Countable nouns	Uncountable nouns
Affirmative	*He took **some** vitamins.*	*They drank **some** tea.*
Negative	*She didn't have **any** vitamins.*	*We didn't take **any** fish oil.*
Question	*Do you have **any** ideas?*	*Did you take **any** medicine?*

much, many, a lot of, a little, a few

Countable nouns

Use *a lot of* and *a few* in affirmative sentences with plural countable nouns.

__A lot of__ doctors treat the whole person.
*There are **a few** types of tea that are like medicine.*

Use *many* and *a lot of* in negative sentences and questions.

*I don't know **many** / **a lot of** natural medicines.*
*Did your doctor give you **many** / **a lot of** pills?*

Uncountable nouns

Use *a lot of* and *a little* in affirmative sentences.

*I have **a lot of** information about natural medicines.*
*There's **a little** tea in the pot.*

Use *much* and *a lot of* in negative sentences and questions.

*There isn't **much** / **a lot of** time.*
*Do you have **much** / **a lot of** work to do?*

How much? How many?

Use *How much* to ask about the amount of uncountable nouns.

__How much__ information do you want?

Use *How many* to ask about the quantity of countable nouns.

__How many__ doctors work here?

Indefinite pronouns and adverbs: *some-, any-, no-, every-*

Use words with *some-*, *any-*, *no-*, and *every-* to talk about people and things when not sure who or what is being talked about.

	People	Things
Affirmative	*I can see **someone**.*	*He's holding **something**.* *Let's go **somewhere** quiet.*
Negative	*I can't see **anyone**.* *There's **no one** there.*	*She doesn't have **anything**.* *There's **nothing** to do.*
Question	*Do you see **anyone**?*	*Did you take **anything**?*

PHRASAL VERBS

Phrasal verbs are made up of a verb and a particle (a preposition or an adverb).

Many phrasal verbs can't be separated.

*Can you **wait for** me?*
~~*Can you **wait** me **for**?*~~

*Will you **look after** my bag?*
~~*Will you **look** my bag **after**?*~~

*His car **broke down** on the way to work.*
***Did** her car **break down** yesterday?*
*Their car **didn't break down**.*

Notice that *down* in the expressions above doesn't refer to the direction. Often, the particle doesn't have its usual meaning.

Some phrasal verbs can be separated by a noun or pronoun. A noun can be placed before or after the particle, but a pronoun must come between the verb and the particle.

*Did you **write down** the information?*
*Did you **write** the information **down**?*

*His friend **picked** him **up** at six o'clock.*
~~*His friend **picked up** him at six o'clock.*~~

Common phrasal verbs

Inseparable
belong to, come in, complain about, deal with, eat out, get along (with someone), go in, grow up, hand in, lie down, look after, look around, look into, sit down, speak about, take off (fly), wake up

Separable
bring back, call back, carry out (do), fill in, find out, give up, hang out, keep up, pass on, pick up, put on (clothes, music, a movie), put off, take off (clothing), take out, take up, turn down, turn on, work out, write down

1 Write the number for each noun on the correct line.

a singular countable nouns: 5, ____
b plural countable nouns: ____
c uncountable nouns: ____

Before there were [1]doctors

Before modern **[2]science**, people used natural materials like **[3]plants** to cure **[4]sickness**. Older generations passed down information about the best **[5]method** for treating each **[6]illness**.

2 Choose the correct option.

1 A Do you have (1) *any* / *many* information about going to the doctor for our school check-up?
B No, I don't. I'm expecting to get a letter with (2) *much* / *some* instructions.
2 A Did the doctor give you (3) *some* / *many* medicine?
B No, she didn't give me (4) *some* / *any*.
3 A How (5) *much* / *many* nurses work at your school?
B There are a (6) *little* / *few*. Three or four, I think.

3 Complete the sentences with the words in the box.

a little | any | many | much | not any | some

1 I don't have ____ aspirin.
2 Sorry, but do you have ____ time to help me?
3 There are ____ flowers growing in the garden.
4 We have some milk, but not ____ .
5 How ____ plants did she write about?
6 There is ____ food in the fridge—it's empty.

4 Complete the questions with *How much* or *How many*.

1 A ____ doctors work in this hospital?
B About 30.
2 A ____ days were you sick?
B Three.
3 A ____ schoolwork did you miss?
B A lot! I missed two tests!
4 A ____ money do you have?
B Sorry, I don't have any.
5 A ____ brothers does she have?
B Two.

5 Correct the mistakes. Cross out the incorrect word and write the correct one on the line.

1 I'm not taking ~~some~~ medicine. any
2 Hurry up. We don't have many time. ____
3 Doctors earn much money. ____
4 Can you give me a few advice? ____
5 I need a few information. ____
6 How much days was your vacation? ____

6 Complete the text with the phrasal verbs.

eat out | lie down | pick up | put on | take off | turn down

1 When I ____ , I try to order healthy food.
2 I need to stop at the pharmacy to ____ some medicine.
3 Are you feeling OK? Maybe you should ____ .
4 Could you ____ the music? I have a headache.
5 I'm tired, so I just want to ____ a movie and relax.
6 You look hot. Would you like to ____ your coat?

7 Rewrite four sentences in Activity 6 with the verbs separated. Two sentences have inseparable phrasal verbs.

____
____
____
____

8 Put the words in order to make sentences. For separable phrasal verbs, write two answers.

1 pain / deal / do / with / How / you
____ ?
2 down / name / this / of / medicine / Write / the
____ .
3 carried / Who / out / research / the
____ ?
4 He / headache / of / complained / a
____ .

9 Choose the correct particle to complete each sentence.

1 My dad looked *around* / *after* me when I was sick.
2 Everyone wants their kids to be healthy when they grow *up* / *over*.
3 It's cold. Would you like to put a sweater *on* / *off*?
4 Who does this medicine belong *for* / *to*?
5 I don't feel well. Can I lie *down* / *off*?
6 The helicopter bringing the doctor just took *up* / *off*.

10 Complete each exchange with a verb or particle.

1 A May I speak with Dr. Chu, please?
B He isn't here now. I'll ask him to ____ you back.
2 A I'm really tired every day. I don't sleep well.
B What time do you wake ____ in the morning?
A About 4:30.
3 A Excuse me. May I go ____ now?
B Yes, please do. The doctor is ready to see you.
4 A Did you find ____ what the problem was?
B The doctor said it was a cold.

COMPARATIVES AND SUPERLATIVES

Comparative adjectives

Comparative adjectives are followed by *than* to compare two things.

My grandfather is ***older than*** *my father.*

Superlative adjectives follow *the* and compare one thing with two or more similar things.

Raul is ***the oldest*** *of my cousins.*

To form comparatives for most short adjectives, add *-er*. To form superlatives for most short adjectives, add *-est*.

Adjective	Comparative	Superlative
old	older	the oldest
big	bigger	the biggest
easy	easier	the easiest

Spelling rules:

- for regular, short adjectives, add *-er / -est*.
  short → *shorter* → *the shortest*
- for short adjectives ending in *-e*, add *-r / -st*.
  safe → *safer* → *the safest*
- for short adjectives ending in *-y*, change the *-y* to *-i* and add *-er / -est. noisy* → *noisier* → *the noisiest*
- for short adjectives ending in consonant-vowel-consonant, double the final consonant and add *-er / -est*.
  big → *bigger* → *the biggest*

To form comparatives for most longer adjectives, use *more*. To form superlatives for most longer adjectives, use *the most*.

Adjective	Comparative	Superlative
fun*	more fun	the most fun
important	more important	the most important
interesting	more interesting	the most interesting

*Even though *fun* is a short adjective, we don't say ~~funner~~ or the ~~funnest~~.

Some adjectives have irregular forms.

Adjective	Comparative	Superlative
good	better	the best
bad	worse	the worst

Comparative adverbs

Comparative adverb + verb is used to compare two actions.

To form comparatives for most short adverbs, use *-er*.

Adverb	Comparative	Superlative
fast	faster	the fastest
late	later	the latest
quickly	more quickly	the most quickly
slowly	more slowly	the most slowly

Some adverbs have irregular comparative and superlative forms.

Adverb	Comparative	Superlative
well	better	the best
badly	worse	the worst

COMPARATIVE FORMS

(not) as… as

To say how two things are similar or equal, use *as* + adjective + *as*.

Math is ***as difficult as*** *science.*

To say how one thing has less of a quality than another, use *not as* + adjective + *as*.

*The elementary school is****n't as big as*** *the high school.*

too and *(not) enough*

Use *too* + adjective to say that the quality described is more than you want or need.

I didn't finish my homework. It was ***too difficult****.*

To make it negative, put *not* in front of *too*.

*I finished my homework. It was****n't too difficult****.*

Use adjective + *enough* to say that the quality described is the right amount.

Were the teacher's instructions ***clear enough****?*
*We didn't finish the project. The class was****n't long enough****.*

Expressions with *too* and *enough* often have a clause after them that gives more information about the situation.

*The weather was****n't good enough to use*** *the kayak.*

so and *such*

Use *so* before an adjective to make the adjective stronger.

My outdoor-skills class was ***so exciting****.*

Use *such* before an adjective + noun to make the combination stronger.

I had ***such a good science teacher*** *last year.*

So and *such* can also have a clause after them which shows the result of the action in the first clause. This clause starts with *that*.

My outdoor-skills class was ***so exciting that*** *I decided to stay for another hour.*

1 Write sentences with comparatives that give your opinion.

1 studying / watching TV (fun)
I think *studying is more fun than watching TV* .
2 languages / science (important)
I think ______ .
3 reading / writing (hard)
I think ______ .
4 information on the Internet / information in books (interesting)
I think ______ .
5 speaking / listening (easy)
I think ______ .
6 studying late at night / studying early in the morning (good)
I think ______ .

2 Complete the sentences with the superlative form of the adjectives in parentheses.

1 ______ (hard) part of the school year is final exams.
2 For me, ______ (bad) part of PE is running.
3 ______ (important) subject in elementary school these days is information technology.
4 Friday is ______ (good) day of the week.
5 English is ______ (popular) foreign language.
6 In my school, ______ (big) class has eighty students in it.

3 Put the words in the correct order to make sentences.

1 than at night / I study / in the morning / better
______ .
2 more quickly than / Davina finished / I did / the science exam
______ .
3 than the other / on the project / harder / groups / Our group worked
______ .
4 his math test / than on / He did worse / on his science test
______ .
5 learned French / faster than / They learned German / they
______ .
6 more slowly / the teacher / I asked / to speak
______ .

4 Complete the exchanges with the correct form of the words in the box.

bad	fast	good	hard	late	slow

1 A I have a test tomorrow. How can I learn a list of vocabulary words *the fastest* ?
B You should try flash cards. But you learn ______ by studying a little bit every day for several weeks.
2 A The heavy rain caused a lot of traffic delays. Who arrived at school ______ ?
B I did. I think my bus driver drove ______ .
3 A I work ______ in math, because it's my most difficult subject.
B Me, too. I always do ______ on math tests. I never get good grades.

5 Write sentences with (*not*) *as… as* that are true for you.

1 playing sports / watching TV (relaxing)
2 taking a test / writing an essay (stressful)
3 school lunch / lunch at home (tasty)
4 the weekend / weekdays (busy)
5 walking / taking the bus (enjoyable)
6 speaking English / reading English (easy)

6 Complete the rewritten sentences with the words in parentheses.

1 I don't have the right amount of time to do my homework. (enough)
I don't have ______ time to do my homework.
2 The weather wasn't dry enough to play outside. (too wet)
The weather was ______ to play outside.
3 There's the right amount of space in the classroom for two more desks. (enough)
There's ______ .
4 The exam wasn't easy enough for me to complete in an hour. (too difficult)
The exam ______ .
5 Was there the right number of textbooks for the whole class? (enough)
Were there ______ ?

7 Complete the sentences with *so* or *such*.

1 That was *such* an interesting lesson.
That lesson was ______ interesting.
2 The test was ______ difficult.
It was ______ a difficult test.
3 The assignment was ______ long that I couldn't finish it.
It was ______ a long assignment that I couldn't finish it.
4 It was ______ a good outdoor-skills course that I wanted to do it again.
The outdoor-skills course was ______ good that I wanted to do it again.

PRESENT PERFECT AND SIMPLE PAST

Present perfect

The present perfect is used to talk about experiences or things that happened in the past without saying exactly when they happened.

The present perfect is used to talk about:

- actions in the past with a result in the present.
  *I've **lost** my keys and can't get into my house.*
- situations that started in the past and continue.
  *We**'ve** always **lived** in this house.*
- experiences that happened at an unspecified time.
  *She**'s traveled** to Canada several times.*

The present perfect is formed with *have* / *has* + the past participle of a verb.

*I**'ve traveled** to Asia.*

Add *never* to talk about experiences that haven't happened.

*I**'ve never traveled** to South America.*

Affirmative	Negative
I / You / We / They **have traveled** a long way.	I / You / We / They **haven't traveled** a long way.
He / She / It **has traveled** a long way.	He / She / It **hasn't traveled** a long way.

Question	Short answer
Have I / you / we / they **traveled** a long way?	Yes, I / you / we / they **have**. No, I / you / we / they **haven't**.
Has he / she / it **traveled** a long way?	Yes, he / she / it **has**. No, he / she / it **hasn't**.

ever, *never*, and *always*

Add *ever* before the participle to a question to mean *in your whole life*.

*Have you **ever** tried Indonesian food?*

Use *never* to say *not in my whole life*.

*I've **never** been to Peru.*

Never is not usually used in questions.

~~*Have you never been to China?*~~

A *Have you **ever** been to China?*

B *No, I've **never** been to China.*

Use *always* to say that a situation has continued your whole life.

*We've **always** lived in this house.*

Present perfect and simple past

When the present perfect is used, exactly when the action happened is not usually stated. When a speaker wants to say exactly when something happened, the simple past is used.

*You**'ve met** my cousin. You **met** her last year at my party.*

PRESENT PERFECT WITH *FOR*, *SINCE*, *ALREADY*, *JUST*, AND *YET*

Present perfect with *for* and *since*

Use *for* to talk about how long something has gone on.

*I**'ve known** Layla **for** four years.*

Use *since* to talk about when something began.

*He**'s lived** with his uncle **since** 2016.*

Present perfect with *just*, *already*, and *yet*

With the present perfect, use:

- *just* to talk about something very recent. *Just* always goes before the participle.
  *We**'ve just heard** a very funny joke.*
  ***Have** you **just arrived**?*
- *already* to talk about something that happened before now, without saying when. *Already* can come before or after the participle.
  *They're not here—they**'ve left already**.*
  *They**'ve already left**.*
  ***Has** he **gone** to bed **already**?*
  ***Has** he **already gone** to bed?*
- *yet* to talk about something that hasn't happened but is expected to happen.
  *I **haven't met** your parents **yet**.*
  ***Has** your cousin **arrived yet**?*

1 Complete the questions with the present perfect of the verbs.

go kiss meet play see take

1 ___Have___ you ever ________ to a big wedding?
2 ________ Michaela ________ the car?
3 ________ Erika ________ your new house?
4 ________ your brother ________ soccer with my friend Jakob?
5 ________ your grandparents ever ________ you?
6 ________ I ________ your uncle before?

2 Complete the answers below. Then match each answer to a question in Activity 1.

a _____
No, she ________ . Ricardo took it to go to work.

b ___2___
Yes, of course they ________ —every time I've visited them!

c _____
Yes, I ________ . I have a lot of older cousins, so I've been to five or six huge ones.

d _____
No, you ________ . That was my older brother.

e _____
Yes, he ________ . They've played together a few times.

f _____
No, she ________ . I haven't invited her over yet.

3 Underline the mistake in each sentence and write the correct sentence.

1 Have you seen your cousins when you were in Dubai last week?
____ .

2 I didn't ever go to a wedding.
____ .

3 They never met my best friend. This is the first time.
____ .

4 Has he enjoyed the celebration last night?
____ .

5 We've missed an exciting celebration yesterday.
____ .

6 My sister is only twelve, but she learned three foreign languages.
____ .

4 Choose the correct word to complete each sentence.

1 Have you been friends *for / since* a long time?
2 They've had the same teacher *for / since* three years.
3 So you've lived in Singapore *for / since* 2010?
4 Her grandmother has called every year on her birthday *for / since* Layla was born.
5 You've been my next-door neighbor *for / since* my whole life.
6 We've made each other laugh *for / since* the first time we met.

5 Complete the sentences with the present perfect of the verbs in parentheses and *for* or *since*.

1 My cousin ________ (live) in Madrid ________ fifteen years.
2 They ________ (know) Ed ________ he was a baby.
3 We ________ (be) friends ________ elementary school.
4 You ________ (have) the same friends ________ ten years.
5 I ________ (not see) you ________ last summer.
6 I ________ (meet) him every Friday ________ three months.

6 Complete the exchanges with the words given.

1 already / yet
A Have you ________ met your new neighbor?
B No, not ________ .

2 just / yet
A I've ________ seen Rory.
B Oh, really? I haven't seen him ________ .

3 already / just
A I've had lunch ________ . You?
B Yes, I've ________ eaten.

4 just / yet
A I haven't celebrated my fifteenth birthday ________ . Has your brother?
B Yes, he's ________ celebrated it. His birthday was last week.

IRREGULAR VERBS

BASE FORM	SIMPLE PAST	PAST PARTICIPLE
be	was/were	been
become	became	become
begin	began	begun
bring	brought	brought
build	built	built
buy	bought	bought
choose	chose	chosen
come	came	come
cost	cost	cost
do	did	done
drink	drank	drunk
eat	ate	eaten
fall	fell	fallen
feel	felt	felt
find	found	found
fly	flew	flown
forget	forgot	forgotten
get	got	gotten
give	gave	given
go	went	gone
grow	grew	grown
have	had	had
hear	heard	heard
hurt	hurt	hurt
keep	kept	kept
know	knew	known

BASE FORM	SIMPLE PAST	PAST PARTICIPLE
leave	left	left
learn	learned / learnt	learned / learnt
let	let	let
make	made	made
meet	met	met
pay	paid	paid
put	put	put
read	read	read
run	ran	run
say	said	said
see	saw	seen
sell	sold	sold
send	sent	sent
sit	sat	sat
sleep	slept	slept
speak	spoke	spoken
spend	spent	spent
swim	swam	swum
take	took	taken
teach	taught	taught
tell	told	told
think	thought	thought
understand	understood	understood
wake	woke	woken
wear	wore	worn
write	wrote	written

WRITING

UNIT 1 Introducing yourself

Use the person's name to greet them in the salutation (greeting).

Talk about your interests.

End by saying you look forward to hearing from the person and then end with a closing (Sincerely, Best regards, Yours truly, etc.) and your name.

Dear Thanh,

My name is Jayro. My friends call me Jay. I'm from Tabasco, Mexico. I'm a student in ninth grade.

My favorite subjects are art and music. I love drawing superhero comics, and I play the drums. I'm also really into soccer. I think I'm a great player, but my friends don't always agree! One thing that a lot of people don't know about me is that I speak three languages: Spanish, English, and Mayan, my family's language.

What about you? Are you into sports? What are your favorite subjects?

I look forward to hearing from you.

Best regards,

Jayro

Introduce yourself and say where you're from.

Ask the person you are writing to about his or her interests.

UNIT 2 Describing a visit to a house or place

What is the name of the place? What is it?

How old is it? When was it built?

What was the visit like?

Shuri Castle is a beautiful castle in the city I'm from—Naha, Japan. I went there last year when my cousin was visiting from Tokyo because the castle is famous in our area. The oldest part is about seven hundred years old. It has many beautiful buildings, gardens, and huge gates. That's the reason I like it. It's unlike any other place I've ever seen. A king used to live there, but now it is like a museum. When we were taking the tour, the tour guide showed us the inside of the castle and told us about its history. It's definitely the coolest house I've ever seen.
—Kana

Where is it?

Why is it special? Why do people like it?

UNIT 3 An opinion essay

Opinion essays will state the argument in the title or in the first paragraph.

Acknowledging other ideas can make your own argument stronger.

Use phrases like *in my opinion* and *for me* to show where you are stating your opinion.

Agree or disagree: Exercising every day is the best way to stay healthy

While it's true that doing a little exercise every day is good for you, I think eating well is more important than exercise.

One reason I think this is that exercise can make people eat too much. Everyone knows someone who exercises and then eats a lot of junk food as a reward. This doesn't improve their health. I believe that for the best health, everyone should first make sure they have a healthy diet.

Second, in my opinion no one should smoke, because cigarettes are bad for you. They're also bad for people around you.

For me, exercise is the third most important thing. It isn't necessary to go to the gym, but you should try to walk to school instead of going by car or bus.

Not smoking and getting exercise are important, but the best way to stay healthy is to have a good diet.

State your own opinion clearly at the beginning of the essay.

Clearly state your opinions and give reasons to support them.

Restate your opinion at the end of the essay.

UNIT 4 An inquiry email

Include the name of the school in the salutation. If you know the name of the person who will be reading the letter, include his or her name.

Ask questions about the company or program. Make sure that they show you've done some research.

Say *thank you.*

> Dear City Summer School,
>
> I saw your ad for the two-week course in videomaking on vacationcourses.com. I'm writing because I have a couple of questions.
>
> First, does each student make a video, or do students work in groups to produce projects? Second, do students have to choose to make a story or a documentary, or is it possible to do both?
>
> Thanks in advance for any information you can give me. I look forward to hearing from you.
>
> Yours sincerely,
>
> Alfonso Alongi

Say how you know about the company or program.

Say why you're writing.

End with a polite and professional closing, like *Sincerely*, *Cordially*, or *Best regards*.

UNIT 5 Invitations and responses

When you write an invitation, give the time, date, location, and type of event. Remember to ask the person to let you know if they can come.

> Hey Sylvia,
>
> I'm having a birthday party on Saturday the 25th from 5:00 to 10:00 at my house. We're going to have pizza and cake and watch a movie and play some games. Can you make it? R.S.V.P.
>
> Joanna

> Hi Davina,
>
> Thanks for inviting me to your graduation party. It sounds like a lot of fun. I'd love to come. What should I wear? Should I bring anything? Let me know A.S.A.P.!
>
> Lena

When you accept an invitation, begin by saying *thank you*. If you have any questions about the event, ask them. It can be polite to offer to bring something (food or drinks, for example).

> Anders,
>
> Thank you for the invitation to your New Year's party. I'm sorry, but I can't make it. I've already made other plans that night. I'm going to be with my family.
>
> Lucas
>
> P.S. I hope you have a great time! Let's catch up soon!

When you say no to an invitation, begin by saying *thank you*. Apologize that you can't make it and say why—without giving too many details if you don't want to. It can be polite to end by saying you hope they enjoy the event.

UNIT 1

active (adj) /ˈæktɪv/
afraid (adj) /əˈfreɪd/
angry (adj) /ˈæŋgri/
anonymously (adv) /əˈnɑnəməsli/
artful (adj) /ˈɑrtfəl/
be (v) /bi/
become (v) /biˈkʌm/
bored (adj) /bɔrd/
calm (adj) /kɑm/
cheerful (adj) /ˈtʃɪrfəl/
confident (adj) /ˈkɑnfədənt/
cool (adj) /kul/
easygoing (adj) /ˈizigoʊɪŋ/
excited (adj) /ɪkˈsaɪtɪd/
feel (v) /fil/
friendly (adj) /ˈfrendli/
frightened (adj) /ˈfraɪtənd/
funny (adj) /ˈfʌni/
get (v) /gɛt/
happy (adj) /ˈhæpi/
hard-working (adj) /ˌhɑrdˈwɜrkɪŋ/
helpful (adj) /ˈhɛlpfəl/
humanity (n) /hjuˈmænɪti/
image (n) /ˈɪmɪdʒ/
intelligent (adj) /ɪnˈtɛlədʒənt/
kind (adj) /kaɪnd/
language barriers (n) /ˈlæŋgwɪdʒ/ /ˈbæriərz/
lazy (adj) /ˈleɪzi/
look (v) /lʊk/
loud (adj) /laʊd/
mean (adj) /min/
nervous (adj) /ˈnɜrvəs/
nice (adj) /naɪs/
popular (adj) /ˈpɑpjələr/
proposal (n) /prəˈpoʊzəl/
relaxed (adj) /rəˈlækst/
seem (v) /sim/
serious (adj) /ˈsɪriəs/
shy (adj) /ʃaɪ/
smart (adj) /smɑrt/
sociable (adj) /ˈsoʊʃəbəl/
soulful (adj) /ˈsoʊlfəl/
struggling (v) /ˈstrʌgəlɪŋ/
talented (adj) /ˈtæləntɪd/
upset (adj) /ʌpsɛt/
virally (adv) /ˈvaɪrəli/
worried (adj) /ˈwʌrid/

UNIT 2

accommodation (n) /əˌkɑməˈdeɪʃən/
ad designer (n) /æd/ /dɪˈzaɪnər/
bamboo (n) /bæmˈbu/
building material (n) /ˈbɪldɪŋ/ /məˈtɪriəl/
business (n) /ˈbɪznəs/
construction (n) /kənˈstrʌkʃən/
crowded (adj) /ˈkraʊdɪd/
didn't feel right (phrase) /ˈdɪdənt/ /fil/ /raɪt/
direction (n) /dɪˈrɛkʃən/
earthquake-resistant (n) /ˈɜrθkweɪk/ /rɪˈzɪstənt/
education (n) /ˌɪdʒəˈkeɪʃən/
elegant (adj) /ˈələgənt/
exploration (n) /ˌɛkspləˈreɪʃən/
footprint (n) /ˈfʊtprɪnt/
historic (adj) /hɪˈstɔrɪk/
I've got to tell you (phrase) /aɪv/ /gɑt/ /tu/ /tɛl/ /ju/
lively (adj) /ˈlaɪvli/
location (n) /loʊˈkeɪʃən/
makes perfect sense (phrase) (v) /meɪks/ /ˈpɜrfekt/ /sens/
modern (adj) /ˈmɑdərn/
old-fashioned (adj) /ˌoʊldˈfæʃənd/
residential (adj) /ˌrɛzəˈdɛnʃəl/
rural (adj) /ˈrʊrəl/
shopping district (n) /ˈʃɑpɪŋ/ /dɪstrɪkt/
suburban (adj) /səˈbɜrbən/
sustainable material (n) /səˈsteɪnəbəl/ /məˈtɪriəl/
traditional (adj) /trəˈdɪʃənəl/
transport (v) /ˈtrænspɔrt/
treat you well (v) /trit/ /ju/ /wɛl/
urban (adj) /ˈɜrbən/
walkable (adj) /ˈwɔkəbl/

UNIT 3

block (v) /blɑk/
calm (adj) /kɑm/
dumb dodo (n) /dʌm/ /ˈdoʊdoʊ/
eyeglasses (n) /ˈaɪˌglæsɪz/
frightening (adj) /ˈfraɪtənɪŋ/
happiness (n) /ˈhæpinəs/
health (n) /hɛθ/
healthy (adj) /ˈhɛlθi/
hit the books (phrase) (v) /hɪt/ /ðə/ /bʊks/
hospital (n) /ˈhɑspɪtəl/
ignore (v) /ɪgˈnɔr/
illnesses (n) /ˈɪlnəs/
injuries (n) /ˈɪndʒəri/
institution (n) /ˌɪnstɪˈtuʃən/
medical (adj) /ˈmɛdɪkəl/
medicine (n) /ˈmɛdɪsən/
pain (n) /peɪn/
painful (adj) /ˈpeɪnfəl/
passed out (phrase) (v) /pæsd/ /aʊts/
patients (n) /ˈpeɪʃənts/
pseudonyms (n) /ˈsudənɪm/
quiet (adj) /ˈkwaɪət/
realize (v) /ˈriəlaɪz/
scary (adj) /ˈskeəri/
sick (adj) /sɪk/
sore (adj) /sɔr/
specialists (n) /ˈspɛʃəlɪsts/
stop (v) /stɑp/
take seriously (v) /teɪk/ /ˈsɪriəsli/
treatments (n) /ˈtritmənt/
understand (v) /ˌʌndərˈstænd/
unwell (adj) /ʌnˈwɛl/
wrestler (n) /ˈrɛslər/

UNIT 4

100 percent (n) /wʌn/ /ˈhʌndrɪd/ /pərsent/
applications (n) /ˌæpləˈkeɪʃənz/
art (n) /ɑrt/
attend (v) /əˈtɛnd/
blackboard (n) /blækbɔrd/
careful (adj) /ˈkɛrfəl/
careless (adj) /ˈkɛrləs/
creative (n) /kriˈeɪtɪv/
desk (n) /dɛsk/
develop (v) /dɪˈvɛləp/
drop out (v) /drɑp/ /aʊt/
education (n) /ˌɛdʒəˈkeɪʃən/
elementary school (n) /ˌɛləˈmɛntri/ /ˌskul/
exam (n) /ɪgˈzæm/
factor (n) /ˈfæktər/
geography (n) /dʒiˈɑgrəfi/
go into (phrase) (v) /goʊ/ /ˈɪntu/
grades (n) /greɪdz/
gratification (n) /ˌgrætəfɪˈkeɪʃən/
hard-working (adj) /ˌhɑrdˈwɜrkɪŋ/
high school (n) /ˈhaɪ/ /ˌskul/
hopeful (adj) /ˈhoʊpfəl/
hopeless (adj) /ˈhoʊpləs/
in other words (phrase) /ɪn/ /ˈʌðər/ /wɜrd/
in trouble (phrase) /ɪn/ /ˈtrʌbəl/
make it to (phrase) (v) /meɪk/ /ɪt/ /tu/
math (n) /mæθ/
notebook (n) /ˈnoʊtbʊk/
pen (n) /pɛn/
principles (n) /ˈprɪnsəpəlz/
private school (n) /ˌpraɪvət/ /ˈskul/
producing (v) /prəˈdusɪŋ/
public school (n) /ˌpʌblɪk/ /ˈskul/
science (n) /ˈsaɪəns/
self-discipline (n) /ˌsɛlfˈdɪsəplɪn/
skills (n) /skɪl/
stress-free (adj) /strɛs/ /fri/
stressful (adj) /ˈstrɛsfəl/
student (n) /ˈstudənt/
study (v) /ˈstʌdi/
take (v) /teɪk/
teacher (n) /ˈtitʃər/
test (n) /tɛst/
thankful (adj) /ˈθæŋkfəl/
useful (adj) /ˈjusfəl/
useless (adj) /ˈjusləs/

UNIT 5

aunt (n)	/ænt/
best friend (n)	/bɛst/
bonds (n)	/bɑndz/
bow (v)	/baʊ/
brother (n)	/ˈbrʌðər/
classmate (n)	/ˈklæsmeɪt/
contagious (adj)	/kənˈteɪdʒəs/
cousin (n)	/ˈkʌzɪn/
family (n)	/ˈfæmli/
friend of a friend (phrase) (n)	/frɛnd/ /əv/ /ə/ /frɛnd/
friends (n)	/frɛndz/
grandfather (n)	/ˈgrændfɑðər/
grandmother (n)	/ˈgrændmʌðər/
historical (adj)	/hɪstɔrɪkəl/
hug (v)	/hʌg/
international (adj)	/ˌɪntərˈnæʃənəl/
kiss (v)	/kɪs/
laughter (n)	/ˈlæftər/
neuroscientist (n)	/nʊroʊˈsaɪəntɪst/
odd (adj)	/ɑd/
origins (n)	/ˈɔrədʒɪnz/
partner (n)	/ˈpɑrtnər/
personal (adj)	/ˈpɜrsənəl/
primitive (adj)	/ˈprɪmətɪv/
roots (n)	/ruts/
say hello (phrase) (v)	/seɪ/ /hɛloʊ/
shake hands (phrase) (v)	/ʃeɪk/ /hændz/
silly (adj)	/ˈsɪli/
sister (n)	/ˈsɪstər/
social (adj)	/ˈsoʊʃəl/
stranger (n)	/ˈstreɪndʒər/
uncle (n)	/ˈʌŋkəl/
vocalize (v)	/ˈvoʊkəlaɪz/
wave (v)	/weɪv/
weird (adj)	/wɪrd/

4 (tl1) © Pascal Mannaerts, (tl2) © Tim Street-Porter/OTTO, (cl) Markus Kirchgessner/laif/Redux, (b11) The Washington Post/Getty Images, (bl2) © Alexandre Ayer/Barcroft USA, **5** (tl1) © James Duncan Davidson/TED, (tl2) © Bret Hartman/TED, (cl) © Ryan Lash/TED, (bl1) © Asa Mathat/TED, (bl2) © Bret Hartman/TED, **6** (tl1) Giordano Cipriani/Photolibrary/Getty Images, (tl2) Wok stir fry, as seen in The Photography of Modernist Cuisine, courtesy of The Cooking Lab, copyright 2013, (cl) Stringer/Reuters, (bl1) © Quang Tran, (bl2) © Thomas Jackson, **7** (tl1) © Bret Hartman/TED, (tl2) ©Dafjones.com/TED, (c) © James Duncan Davidson/TED, (bl1) © Bret Hartman/TED, (bl2) © Ryan Lash/TED, **8-9** © Pascal Mannaerts, **10-11** Richard Perry/The New York Times/Redux, **13** (t) Toru Hanai/Reuters, (bl) Kostenyukova Nataliya/Shutterstock.com, **14** XPACIFICA/National Geographic Creative, **15** Joel Sartore/National Geographic Creative, **16-17** © James Duncan Davidson/TED, **18-19** H. Mark Weidman Photography/Alamy Stock Photo, **20-21** © Tim Street-Porter/OTTO, **22** Gonzalo Azumendi/Getty Images, **24-25** (spread) (br) NASA, **26** Ekaterina Pokrovsky/Shutterstock.com, **27** © Andy Stagg, **28-29** © Bret Hartman/TED, **30-31** Sean Pavone/Alamy Stock Photo, **32-33** Markus Kirchgessner/laif/Redux, **34-35** Ken Gillham/robertharding/Getty Images, **37** Jeff Riedel/Getty Images, **38** (tl) Mark Hannaford/Getty Images, (cl) Kaz Chiba/Photodisc/Getty Images, (bl) Brian Gordon Green/National Geographic Creative, (bc) Monkey Business Images/Shutterstock.com, **39** (cl) Sabphoto/Shutterstock.com, (br) David Coleman/Alamy Stock Photo, **40-41** © Ryan Lash/TED, **42-43** Maremagnum/Photodisc/Getty Images, **44-45** The Washington Post/Getty Images, **46** © Cause Collective, **47** © 2014 UNRWA, Photo by Taghrid Mohammad, **48** Spencer Weiner/Los Angeles Times/Getty Images, **50** aldomurillo/E+/Getty Images, **51** Erik Lesser/EPA/Redux, **52-53** © Asa Mathat/TED, **54-55** Cem Ozdel/Anadolu Agency/Getty Images, **56-57** © Alexandre Ayer/Barcroft USA, **58-59** Pedro Mera Xinhua News Agency/Newscom, **61** The Washington Post/Getty Images, **62** The Asahi Shimbun/Getty Images, **63** David Alan Harvey/Magnum Photos, **64-65** © Bret Hartman/TED, **66-67** Rajesh Sachar/Pacific Press/LightRocket/Getty Images, **68-69** Giordano Cipriani/Photolibrary/Getty Images, **70** picturepartners/Shutterstock.com, **72-73** © Lewis Pugh, **74** PA Images/Alamy Stock Photo & © Mural by Lady AIKO, City Walk Dubai, **75** Frank Heuer/laif/Redux, **76-77** © Bret Hartman/TED, **78-79** Jianan Yu/Reuters, **80-81** © Wok stir fry, as seen in The Photography of Modernist Cuisine, courtesy of The Cooking Lab, copyright 2013, **82-83** Olivier Morin/AFP/Getty Images, **85** Antagain/E+/Getty Images, **86** Brimo/Alamy Stock Photo, **87** © Catherine Jaffee, **88-89** © Dafjones.com/TED, **90-91** Edwin Koo/New York Times/Redux, **92-93** Stringer/Reuters, **94** (tl) Debra Ferguson/Passage/Getty Images, (tr) Bloomberg/Getty Images, (c) Jostaphot/E+/Getty Images, (cl1) Christophe Lehenaff/Photononstop/Getty Images, (cl2) Bloomberg/Getty Images, (cl3) Hero Images/Getty Images, (cl4) Driendl Group/DigitalVision/Getty Images, **97** © Bureo Inc, **98** FL Wong/EPN/Newscom & © Paulo Grangeon, **99** ZCHE/Smithers of Stamford (Supplied by WENN)/Newscom, **100-101** © James Duncan Davidson/TED, **102-103** Rob Whitaker/EyeEm/Getty Images, **104-105** © Quang Tran, **106** Anand Varma/National Geographic Creative, **109** © Luca Locatelli/INSTITUTE, **110** Piotr Zajac/Alamy Stock Photo, **111** Gordon Chibroski/Portland Press Herald/Getty Images, **112-113** © Bret Hartman/TED, **114-115** Kelvin Murray/Taxi/Getty Images, **116-117** © Thomas Jackson, **118-119** (spread) William Albert Allard/National Geographic Creative, **118** (tl1) Adrio Communications Ltd/Shutterstock.com, (tl2) Roman Vukolov/Shutterstock.com, (tl3) best4u/Shutterstock.com, (tc) Zastolskiy Victor/Shutterstock.com, (tr1) Africa Studio/Shutterstock.com, (tr2) Scanrail1/Shutterstock.com, (tr3) blojfo/Shutterstock.com, **121** Handout/Getty Images News/Getty Images, **122** Lafforgue Eric/Hemis/Alamy Stock Photo, **123** AP Images/Martin Mejia, **124-125** © Ryan Lash/TED, **126** AP Images/Tony Avelar, **131** (tr1) Lorenzo Pesce/Contrasto/Redux, (tr2) David Burton/Photolibrary/Getty Images.

PERSPECTIVES 1

Workbook

Australia • Brazil • Mexico • Singapore • United Kingdom • United States

Perspectives 1

Publisher: Sherrise Roehr
Executive Editor: Sarah Kenney
Project Manager: Katherine Carroll
Media Researcher: Leila Hishmeh
Senior Technology Product Manager: Lauren Krolick
Director of Global Marketing: Ian Martin
Product Marketing Manager: Anders Bylund
Sr. Director, ELT & World Languages: Michael Burggren
Production Manager: Daisy Sosa
Senior Print Buyer: Mary Beth Hennebury
Composition: Lumina Datamatics, Inc.
Cover/Text Design: Brenda Carmichael
Art Director: Brenda Carmichael
Cover Image: Bernardo Galmarini/ Alamy Stock Photo

© 2018 National Geographic Learning, a part of Cengage Learning

ALL RIGHTS RESERVED. No part of this work covered by the copyright herein may be reproduced or distributed in any form or by any means, except as permitted by U.S. copyright law, without the prior written permission of the copyright owner.

"National Geographic", "National Geographic Society" and the Yellow Border Design are registered trademarks of the National Geographic Society
® Marcas Registradas

For product information and technology assistance, contact us at
Cengage Learning Customer & Sales Support, cengage.com/contact

For permission to use material from this text or product, submit all requests online at **cengage.com/permissions**
Further permissions questions can be emailed to
permissionrequest@cengage.com

Perspectives 1 Workbook

ISBN: 978-1-337-29731-8

National Geographic Learning
20 Channel Center Street
Boston, MA 02210
USA

National Geographic Learning, a Cengage Learning Company, has a mission to bring the world to the classroom and the classroom to life. With our English language programs, students learn about their world by experiencing it. Through our partnerships with National Geographic and TED Talks, they develop the language and skills they need to be successful global citizens and leaders.

Locate your local office at **international.cengage.com/region**

Visit National Geographic Learning online at **NGL.Cengage.com/ELT**
Visit our corporate website at **www.cengage.com**

Printed in China
Print Number: 02 Print Year: 2023

CONTENTS

1 Who are you?

1A Describe someone

VOCABULARY

1 Review Choose the best words to complete the sentences.

1 My father has no hair. He's *bald / beard / brown*.
2 My sister is *long / tall / curly*. She's a star on the basketball team.
3 **A:** Does your brother have *bald / a beard / glasses*?
B: No, he doesn't like hair on his face.
4 My hair isn't straight. It's *short / blond / curly*.
5 My mother, brother, and I all have dark hair, but my father's hair is different. It's *black / blond / long*.
6 I wear *a beard / glasses / short hair*, but only when I'm reading.

2 Review Look at the photos. Match each description to the correct person.

a

b

c

d

e

f

1 Carlos has long, curly brown hair and a beard. ____
2 Angela is tall and has long, curly blond hair. ____
3 Richard has very short dark hair. ____
4 Lily has short, straight, dark hair. ____
5 Nick is tall and bald, and he has a beard. ____
6 Emma has long, straight, brown hair and glasses. ____

3 Complete the adjectives to describe personality.

1 fr__ __ n __ __ __
2 s__ c __ ab__ __
3 con__ __ __ en__
4 t__ __en__ __ d
5 e__s__g__ __ __g
6 n __ __ v __ __s
7 p__ __ u__ __ r
8 in__ __ __ __ __ g __ __ t
9 ch__ __ __f__ __
10 r__ __ __ x __ __

4 Find the word that means the opposite of each description.

intelligent	lazy	loud	mean
nervous	serious	shy	weak

1 kind, helpful ____________
2 active, hard-working ____________
3 funny, cheerful ____________
4 sociable, confident ____________
5 calm, relaxed ____________
6 quiet ____________

5 Review the sentences and photos in Activity 2. Circle the correct word to describe each person.

1 Lily is *active / lazy*.
2 Emma is *smart / loud*.
3 Angela is *kind / nervous*.
4 Nick is *serious / cheerful*.
5 Richard is *calm / hard-working*.
6 Carlos is *funny / mean*.

6 Read the sentences. Are the adjectives logical (L) or not logical (N)?

1 I don't understand the math lesson, and I don't have time to study. I'm very confident about the test tomorrow! _____
2 A mean friend is usually fun to be with. _____
3 Good teachers are kind to their students. _____
4 A good worker is lazy. _____
5 It's always good to be honest when you answer a question. _____
6 A popular person is usually very sociable. _____
7 A shy person feels nervous talking to new people. _____
8 It's not easy for a smart person to understand new ideas. _____

7 Listen to the descriptions. Complete the sentence with the correct form of *be* and the adjective that best fits each description. 2

active	easygoing	funny	helpful
lazy	loud	mean	talented

1 Our teacher ____________________
2 We ____________________
3 The neighbors ____________________
4 My roommate ____________________
5 My aunt ____________________
6 You ____________________
7 My boss ____________________
8 I ____________________

8 **Extension** Put the adjectives into the correct categories.

affectionate	annoying	careless	generous
impatient	organized	patient	polite
rude	selfish		

Positive personality traits	Negative personality traits

9 **Extension** Listen to the descriptions. Circle all the adjectives that describe each person. 3

1 Homer intelligent / lazy / careless / organized / helpful / selfish / generous
2 Marge kind / helpful / active / affectionate / annoying / patient / selfish
3 Bart generous / rude / smart / funny / honest / annoying / hard-working
4 Lisa talented / intelligent / mean / hard-working / polite / impatient / neat

PRONUNCIATION -*s* verb endings

10 Listen. Choose the verb that has the same ending sound. 4

1 **a** goes **b** thinks **c** dances
2 **a** follows **b** acts **c** fixes
3 **a** enjoys **b** sits **c** touches
4 **a** plays **b** looks **c** watches
5 **a** feels **b** jumps **c** misses
6 **a** sees **b** puts **c** practices
7 **a** calls **b** stops **c** changes
8 **a** wears **b** laughs **c** wishes

LISTENING

11 Listen. Complete the sentence. 5

1 He's ________.
   a honest
   b friendly
   c hard-working

2 She's into ________.
   a music
   b art
   c sports

3 He's a little ________.
   a intelligent
   b loud
   c shy

4 He's into ________.
   a sports
   b books
   c photography

5 She's very ________.
   a popular
   b fit
   c kind

6 She enjoys ________.
   a writing
   b hiking
   c drawing

7 He's ________.
   a cool
   b serious
   c nervous

8 She really likes ________.
   a dancing
   b singing
   c reading

12 Listen. Complete each sentence with the name and the correct verb in the present tense. 6

be	like (x2)	paint
think	want (x2)	

1 ________ to see a movie.
2 ________ busy this afternoon.
3 ________ fruit and flowers.
4 ________ painting is difficult.
5 ________ action movies.
6 ________ DJ Spooky.
7 ________ to hang out tomorrow.

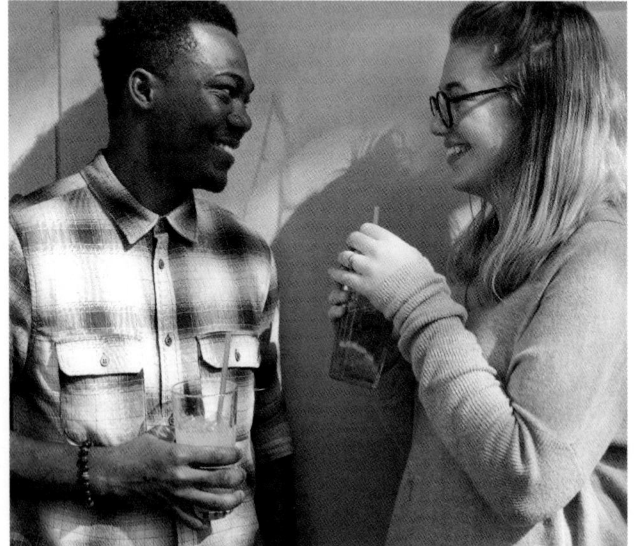

13 Listen. Are the sentences true (T) or false (F)? 7

1 The passage explains why we don't like some things. ____
2 People like something not only because it looks, smells, sounds, or tastes good. ____
3 What people think about something makes them like or dislike something. ____
4 People often believe that expensive things are good. ____
5 People like things that they connect with positive experiences. ____

14 Correct the false sentences in Activity 13. Listen again if necessary. 7

15 Listen to the lecture and answer the questions. 8

1 What is the lecture mainly about?
   a the United States of America in the 1930s
   b different characters from California
   c characters and personalities in a book
   d being a leader of a family

2 Why does the professor say this: "novel, or long story"?
   a The students had two assignments.
   b The novel is not true.
   c The book has many stories.
   d A novel is a long story.

3 Why did farmers leave their homes?
   a There was not enough rain.
   b Land was cheap in California.
   c They were angry with their neighbors.
   d A fire burned their crops and fields.

4 What does the professor probably think when he says this: "It's not easy to leave your home."?
   a People move around a lot.
   b Most of the professor's students live abroad.
   c Most people enjoy staying in the place they know.
   d Some people enjoy the weather at home.

5 What does the professor mean when he says this: "move their whole family across the country"?
   a The farmers had to move to a new country.
   b The farmers had to leave the United States of America.
   c The farmers had to move to a new place in the United States of America.
   d The farmers had to find a state with more rain.

6 There are two answers for the next question. Mark two answers.
   Which personality words does the professor say in the lecture?
   a fearful
   b calm
   c brave
   d helpful

GRAMMAR Simple present and present continuous

16 **Read the sentences and decide if the action is taking place right now (RT) or is a general truth (GT).**

1 Julia is working on an article for her school's website. _____
2 She is writing about the new students in her class this semester. _____
3 Julia's school welcomes new students at the beginning of each semester. _____
4 There are three new students in Julia's class this semester. _____
5 Alex is funny, laughs a lot, and tells jokes when he meets new people. _____
6 Min smiles a lot and seems really happy to be in the class. _____

17 **Complete the sentences with the simple present form of the correct verbs.**

be	create	go	hope
mind	practice	study	think
want			

1 Naomi ________________ to the best school in the city.
2 She ________________ a lot because she wants to go to college.
3 She ________________ to study computer science.
4 Sometimes she ________________ the only girl in her class.
5 But Naomi ________________ not ________________ because she ________________ computers are really interesting.
6 She ________________ that she can show other girls that computer science is cool.
7 Naomi ________________ coding at home.
8 She ________________ new apps for her friends to try.

18 **Choose the correct verb forms for each sentence.**

1 Bo has a new camera and _____ how to take better photos. He _____ to take photos of people.
a is learn; liking　**c** are learning; is like
b is learning; likes　**d** learning; like

2 His friends Mina and Jacob _____ him. They _____ to have their photo taken.
a help; liking　**c** help; are liking
b is helping; is liking　**d** are helping; like

3 Right now, Mina and Jacob _____ in front of a statue. They _____ taking selfies.
a standing; enjoying　**c** stand; enjoying
b are standing; enjoy　**d** stands; enjoys

4 For some reason, Mina and Jacob _____, and Bo _____ annoyed.
a not smiling; be　**c** are not smiling; is
b is not smiling; is being　**d** doesn't smile; being

5 Now he _____ them to smile because they _____ happy.
a ask; not looking　**c** is ask; look
b is asking; do not look　**d** is asking; no looking

6 They _____ to the park now because Bo _____ to take photos in front of the fountain.
a walks; want　**c** are walking; wants
b is walking; is wanting　**d** walking; wanting

19 **Complete the sentences with the correct form of the verbs in parentheses.**

1 My brother really ________________ (like) music and ________________ (listen) to it all the time.
2 He ________________ (play) the electric guitar and the drums. He's really talented!
3 He and his friends ________________ (be) in a band and ________________ (write) cool new songs.
4 My friend Mei plays keyboard and ________________ (sing) in the band with my brother and his friend Maia. The name of their band ________________ (be) Victory.
5 They ________________ (go) to have a concert in the park next month. All of us ________________ (go) to see them play.
6 That's why they ________________ (practice) every Saturday.
7 I ________________ (not, can) watch them every time they practice because I ________________ (study) for an important exam.
8 But I ________________ (go) to their big concert on the 25th!

20 **Choose the correct words to complete the questions.**

1 *Is / Does* he intelligent?
2 *Is / Are* your classmates kind?
3 *Do / Does* you like cool music?
4 *Does / Do* Simon play guitar?
5 *Am / Is* I late for class?
6 *Does / Is* it raining?
7 *Do / Does* the DJs play good music?
8 *Are / Do* you a good singer?

1B How are you feeling?

VOCABULARY BUILDING Collocations

1 Put the words in the correct order to make sentences and questions.

1 you / angry / are

____

______________________________?

2 the / she's / about / test / worried

____

______________________________.

3 get / easily / children / do / frightened

____

______________________________?

4 they're / about / presentation / nervous / the

____

______________________________.

5 excited / vacation / about / we're / our

____

______________________________.

6 by / students / the / the / seemed / lecture / bored

____

______________________________.

7 news / I / when / on TV / watch / upset / I / become / the

____

______________________________.

8 looks / about / he / angry / something

____

______________________________.

READING

2 Read the article. Answer the questions.

1 Why do Finnish researchers recommend that people spend about five hours a month outdoors?
  a in order to learn more about urban areas
  b so that they can stay healthy
  c because winters in Finland are very cold
  d because they work for the government

2 According to paragraph 4, which of the following is not true of the Saneum Healing Forest?
  a Visitors are offered a tea made from elm bark.
  b Visitors hike along creeks and through the forest.
  c Firefighters fought a fire there for three days.
  d Firefighters practice yoga in order to relax.

3 Which of the following best restates the saying "Body and soil are one" in paragraph 4?
  a Being aware of our natural surroundings can help us remain healthy.
  b It's important to wash your hands at least once every day.
  c People who are careful about what they eat sometimes grow their own food.
  d Being clean is the most important thing you can do in order to stay healthy.

4 What did a study in Japan show about the effects of being outdoors?
  a A walk in the woods takes at least 15 minutes.
  b Spending time outdoors can cause measurable changes in the body.
  c Forests and natural places are usually far from city centers.
  d People who live in city centers have high blood pressure.

3 Write the name of each country next to the correct statement.

Canada	Finland	Japan	South Korea

1 Researchers measured changes in the body caused by spending time outdoors. __________

2 The government wants to know more about its people's moods. __________

3 Researchers have found evidence that being outdoors contributes to the "happiness effect." __________

4 Local governments pay for healthy outdoor experiences for their people. __________

4 Read the phrases (a–e). Then scan the article to find which paragraph includes the information. Write the paragraph number next to the phrase.

a measurable effects of being outdoors _____
b a question we all want answered _____
c the "happiness effect" _____
d a weekly dose of nature _____
e a "Healing Forest" _____

This is Your Brain on Nature 9

1 What makes you happy? It's a question we all want an answer to. Does food make you happy? Do pictures of puppies make you feel calm? What about being outdoors, walking in the sun, or hiking in a forest?

2 "People underestimate the happiness effect" of being outdoors, says Lisa Nisbet, a psychology professor at Canada's Trent University. "We don't think of it as a way to increase happiness. We think other things will do this, like shopping or TV." But there's a lot of evidence* to show that being outdoors in nature makes people feel better. In fact, some countries are promoting nature experiences as one way to help people stay healthy.

3 In Finland, a large number of people become sad or depressed in winter. The Finnish government wants to know why. It pays researchers to ask people about their moods after visiting natural and urban areas. Do they feel more nervous or more relaxed? The researchers studied people's responses. They are recommending a minimum nature dose* of five hours a month, or several short visits a week, to a natural place.

4 In South Korea, many people deal with stress from work and school. But this very hard-working nation respects nature. A very old saying reminds South Koreans that "*Shin to bul ee*—Body and soil are one." At the Saneum Healing Forest, east of Seoul, "health rangers" offer visitors elm-bark tea, then take them on hikes along creeks, and through forests of red maple, oak, and pine-nut trees. During one visit, forty firefighters take part in a free, three-day program sponsored by the local government. After a morning of hiking, they enjoy practicing yoga and arranging delicate dried flowers. Among them is Kang Byoung-wook, a 46-year-old firefighter from Seoul. "It's a stressed life," he says. "I want to live here for a month."

5 Researchers can measure how a 15-minute walk in the woods causes changes in the body. A study in Japan compares people who spend time in forests and in city centers. The people who spend time in nature show a lower level of stress, and lower blood pressure and heart rate. Yoshifumi Miyazaki, one of the researchers, believes our bodies relax in pleasant, natural surroundings because they are originally from natural places. When we slow down, stop working, and take in beautiful natural surroundings, we often feel more cheerful, and our mental* performance improves. Our senses are better at interpreting information about plants and streams, Miyazaki says, than traffic and high-rises!

evidence *a sign that shows something is true or correct*
dose *an amount of something, usually medicine*
mental *related to the mind*

1C Needs, wants, likes

GRAMMAR Verb patterns: Verb + *-ing* or infinitive with *to*

1 Listen and complete the sentences. 10

1 When the musicians begin ________________, you must stop talking.
2 Do you plan ________________ after you graduate?
3 I always enjoy ________________ with my friends after class.
4 He prefers ________________ before dinner.
5 Oscar can't help ________________ when he hears sad music.
6 Mei tries ________________ her grandfather every week.
7 I hope ________________ ten countries before my 21st birthday.
8 Young children learn ________________ by listening to other people.

2 Choose the correct words to complete the sentences.

1 She usually manages *studying / to study* during the week so that she can relax on the weekends.
2 I don't want *arguing / to argue* with you.
3 She enjoys *helping / to help* her younger sister.
4 He enjoys *going / to go* for a long run on the weekend.
5 Taavi wants *writing / to write* an email to his friend in Canada.
6 Can you learn *speaking / to speak* English on your own?
7 I don't mind *seeing / to see* that movie again with you.
8 Lana avoids *going / to go* to the gym on the weekends. It's so busy!

3 Complete the sentences with the verb + *-ing* or the infinitive with *to* form of the verbs in parentheses.

1 My dad plans ________________ (read) five books while he's on vacation.
2 Does he enjoy ________________ (study) history?
3 I think it's possible to avoid ________________ (tell) her about the surprise party.
4 Frank wants to start ________________ (exercise) more starting on January 1.
5 Ted can't help ________________ (laugh) every time Seth tells a joke.
6 Do you think you can manage ________________ (get) your work done before Friday?
7 I promise ________________ (come) to your party early. Then I can help you get ready.
8 Devan is beginning ________________ (look) for a job.

4 Are the verbs in bold correct? Correct the incorrect verbs.

1 He enjoys **to go** on vacation with his family.
________________.
2 I want **to see** that new movie next weekend.
____
3 Do you enjoy **trying** new restaurants?
____
4 She needs to learn **eating** with chopsticks.
____
5 Jim hates **going** to the movies alone.
____
6 I need **talking** with you about our homework for tomorrow.
____
7 Does she want **to call** him or **to speak** to him in person?
____
8 I'm trying to avoid **to spend** too much money on vacation.
____

5 Put the words in the correct order to make sentences and questions.

1 hates / class / Jean / being / late / for
________________.
2 job / he / have / before / he / hopes / a / graduates / to
________________.
3 the / at / I / stop / need / store / to
________________.
4 us / with / come / he / does / to / want
________________?
5 loves / she / history / about / reading
________________.
6 checking / after / dinner / avoids / Emily / email / her
________________.
7 salad / he / a / eating / prefers / lunch / for
________________.

6 Complete the conversations with the verb + *-ing* or the infinitive with *to* form of the verbs in parentheses. Some sentences have two correct answers.

1 **A:** What can I do when I feel sad?
B: I suggest __________ (go) on a long walk.

2 **A:** Are you going to the beach this weekend? I really want to go!
B: I don't know. I promise __________ (call) you if I go.

3 **A:** How's your homework going?
B: Well, I hate __________ (ask) for help, but it's really hard.

4 **A:** Can you drive a car?
B: No, I have __________ (take) the bus or walk.

5 **A:** Do you read books by the author Isabelle Youngman?
B: I do. I often begin __________ (laugh) when I'm reading because her books are so funny.

6 **A:** Do you want to get some sushi with me?
B: Yes! I love __________ (eat) sushi!

7 Read the questions. Choose the correct answer.

1 What are you doing?
a I'm starting to make dinner.
b I'm starting making dinner.

2 What are you doing this weekend?
a I hope to see a movie with my sister.
b I hope seeing a movie with my sister.

3 Do you want to study together for the test?
a Sure! I don't mind to study with other people.
b Sure! I don't mind studying with other people.

4 Do you have enough money to pay for school?
a I think I can manage to save enough by next year.
b I think I can manage saving enough by next year.

5 What should we do for dinner?
a I want to go to the new Thai restaurant downtown.
b I want going to the new Thai restaurant downtown.

6 Can you play the piano?
a A little. I'm learning to play now.
b A little. I'm learning playing now.

7 Do you want cake for dessert?
a It looks so good! I want to trying a piece.
b It looks so good! I want to try a piece.

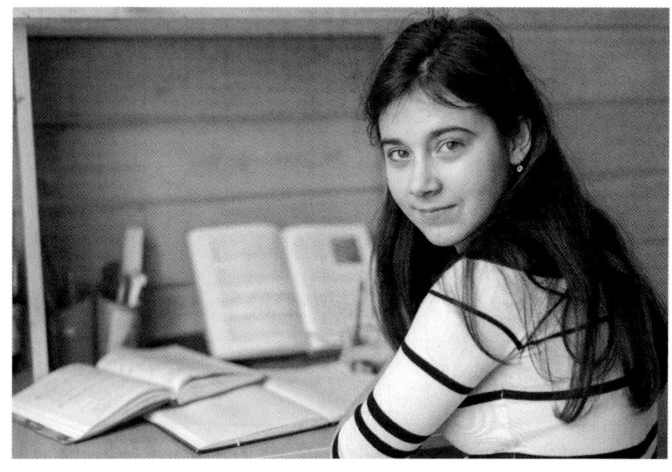

8 Choose the correct words to complete the sentences. In some sentences both answers are correct. Are any of the sentences true for you?

1 My friends and I like *helping / to help* each other.
2 I want *visiting / to visit* my grandparents in Poland this summer.
3 My parents want me *spending / to spend* more time studying.
4 They're right. I need *studying / to study* more.
5 It's easy *wasting / to waste* time on social media.
6 I avoid *using / to use* social media.
7 I don't enjoy *watching / to watch* movies on my laptop.
8 I prefer *watching / to watch* them on TV or at the movie theater.
9 In fact, the best place *watching / to watch* movies is the new 20-screen theater in my city.
10 I usually have a chance *going / to go* to that theater every month.

9 Complete the sentences with a verb + *-ing* or an infinitive with *to* so they are true for you.

1 My family needs __________.
2 I need __________.
3 I want __________.
4 My friend wants __________.
5 I like __________.
6 I don't like __________.
7 I enjoy __________.
8 My friends and I enjoy __________.

1D Half a million secrets

TEDTALKS

AUTHENTIC LISTENING SKILLS

1 Listen to the TED Talk. Complete the sentences. 11

2004	3,000	half-million
two	three	four

1. It all started with a crazy idea in November of ________.
2. I printed up ________ self-addressed postcards.
3. You can see my wife struggling to stack a brick of postcards on a pyramid of over a ________ secrets.
4. I had this postcard posted on the PostSecret blog ________ years ago on Valentine's Day.
5. For ________ years, my girlfriend and I, we've made it this Sunday morning ritual to visit the PostSecret blog together.
6. My son's birth is on this camera. He turns ________ tomorrow.

WATCH

2 Choose the correct words to complete the sentences.

1. People *make / are making* their own postcards.
2. Frank *shares / is sharing* people's secrets on PostSecret.
3. Frank *collects / is collecting* secrets on PostSecret right now.
4. People *send / are sending* him emails with secrets.
5. Matty *takes / is taking* the pictures off the cameras.
6. The man says his hands *shake / are shaking*.

3 Match the adjectives from the talk with the situations.

1 exuberant ____
2 crazy ____
3 special ____
4 ingenious ____
5 desperate ____
6 emotional ____

a people who lose their cameras and pictures
b Matty's idea
c Frank's idea in November of 2004
d email of a family that Matty shows Frank
e man asks girlfriend to marry him
f the secrets in Frank's collection

4 Are the sentences true (T) or false (F)?

1. People buy postcards from Frank. ____
2. PostSecret is hard to use. ____
3. Only people with special secrets can use PostSecret. ____
4. People can send lost cameras to Matty. ____
5. The pictures go back to the people who lost their cameras. ____
6. Matty and Frank work together. ____

5 Choose the correct answers.

1 What is the speaker mainly discussing?
  a how many people visit his blog a day
  b the secrets from his collection
  c why secrets are important

2 What is PostSecret?
  a a website
  b a place where people mail their secrets
  c a place in Washington, D.C.

3 Why does the speaker mention Matty?
  a to talk about how students use PostSecret
  b to show that people in Canada use PostSecret
  c to explain how people's lives have changed through PostSecret

4 What is the speaker's opinion of IFoundYourCamera?
  a He doesn't think it is helpful.
  b He thinks it is important.
  c He thinks only people who like pictures will use it.

5 What can be inferred about the speaker and PostSecret?
  a The speaker will continue to work on PostSecret.
  b The speaker will stop doing PostSecret to start another idea.
  c The speaker will sell the secrets on PostSecret.

6 Why does the speaker say this: "Secrets can take many forms. They can be shocking or silly or soulful."?
  a to explain that everyone has secrets
  b to explain a good secret
  c to explain that secrets are different

VOCABULARY IN CONTEXT

6 Match the words to the correct definitions.

1 struggling ____
2 calm ____
3 proposal ____
4 image ____
5 language barriers ____

a a picture
b relaxed
c when a person asks another person to marry him or her
d the difficulties people have because they don't speak the same language
e to have a hard time with something

1E What are you into?

SPEAKING

Useful language

Talking about likes and dislikes	
Are you into…	*sports / music / gaming / cycling?*
I play… *I love to watch…* *I'm not that interested in…* *I don't mind…* *I can't stand…*	*baseball / basketball / soccer.*
Do you have a favorite…	*team / kind of music / place to go hiking?*
I'm really into…	*Real Madrid / hip-hop / going to the mountains.*
That's cool. / Really? / Wow!	

1 Put the words in the correct order to make sentences.

1 into / are / music / you

____________________?

2 interested / I'm / in / not / gaming / that

____________________.

3 basketball / to / I / watch / love

____________________.

4 do / a favorite / have / team / you

____________________?

5 really / skating / into / I'm

____________________.

6 cool / wow / that's

____________________!

7 mind / don't / hip-hop / I

____________________.

8 pop / I / stand / music / can't

____________________.

2 Complete the sentences. Then listen and check your answers. 12

Are you into (x3)	Do you have a favorite (x2)
I can't stand	I don't mind
I love to (x3)	I'm not that interested in
I'm really into (x3)	I play

1 **A:** __________ sports?
B: __________ watch soccer.
__________ Real Madrid.

2 **A:** __________ kind of music?
B: __________ the saxophone so
__________ listen to jazz music.

3 **A:** __________ gaming?
B: A little. __________ playing games,
but __________ pro-gaming!
Watching other people play is so boring.

4 **A:** __________ place to hang out?
B: __________ shopping so
__________ go to the mall.

5 **A:** __________ cycling?
B: __________ road cycling, but
__________ mountain biking.

3 You are on vacation in another country and meeting new people.

Look at the questions from the dialogs in Activity 2. For each question, use the useful language and make some notes for how you would answer it.

4 Write responses that are true for you. Use the useful language.

1 Are you into sports?

____

2 Are you into clothes?

____

3 What are you into?

____

4 What kind of music do you like?

____

5 What kind of movies do you like?

____

6 What TV shows are you into?

____

5 Listen, and follow the instructions. 13

Now listen to a sample response. 14

WRITING

1 Match the sentence halves.

1 My name is ____
2 I'm from ____
3 I'm in grade 9 ____
4 My favorite subjects are ____
5 I love watching ____
6 I'm also ____
7 What ____
8 What's your ____

a science and math.
b about you?
c Osaka City in Japan.
d favorite type of music?
e at high school.
f really into hip-hop.
g Ken Sato.
h action movies.

2 Choose the correct word or phrase to complete each sentence.

1 When you introduce yourself in writing, the first thing you tell the other person is ____.
a your school b your name c your city

2 The second thing you write is ____.
a what you enjoy b how you feel c where you're from

3 ____ usually tell each other what grade they are in at school.
a Students b Teachers c Classmates

4 In a new paragraph, you should write about ____.
a your classmates b the weather c your hobbies

5 It's polite to ask the other person some questions about ____.
a their interests b their grades c their problems

6 ____ by telling the other person that you look forward to hearing from him or her.
a Start b Finish c Learn

3 Read the postcard to a student in California. Then read the questions and circle the answers.

Dear Julie,

My name is Ana Cristina. I'm from Mexico City. It's a big and busy place! I'm in grade 10 at high school.

At school, my favorite subjects are history and English. In my free time, I play the piano, and I love singing songs in English. I'm also really into music festivals.

What about you? Do you play any instruments? Who is your favorite singer?

I look forward to hearing from you, Julie.

Best wishes,
Ana Cristina

1 What is the name of the person introducing herself?
2 Where is she from?
3 What grade is she in at school?
4 What are her favorite subjects?
5 What instrument does she play?
6 What language does she like to sing in?
7 What else is she into?
8 She asks Julie about playing an instrument and what else?

4 Complete the postcard from Charlie to Amir. Write one word in each space.

Dear Amir,

My ____________ is Charlie Ford. I'm ____________ Vancouver in Canada. I'm a ____________ in grade 8.

My favorite ____________ are geography and physics. I ____________ the guitar, but I'm not very good! I ____________ traveling to new places, and I'm also ____________ into video games.

What ____________ you, Amir? Are you ____________ video games, too? What are your favorite subjects at school?

I look forward to ____________ from you.

Best regards,
Charlie

5 Read the profile. Imagine you are Alex Green, and write a postcard introducing yourself.

PROFILE

Who:	*Alex Green*
What:	*High school student, grade 10*
Where:	*New York City, USA*
Favorite subjects:	*chemistry and economics*
Musical instruments:	*none*
Hobbies:	*web design and basketball*

	Dear ________,
1 Include your name and other information.	*[Paragraph 1]*
2 Write about your favorite subjects and your hobbies.	*[Paragraph 2]*
3 Ask the other person some questions.	*[Paragraph 3]*
4 Write six sentences. 5 Use some of the phrases you learned in this unit.	*I look forward to hearing from you.* *Best wishes,* *Alex*

Review

1 **Circle eight adjectives that describe the singer's personality.**

Angélique Kidjo is a popular African singer and songwriter. She is from Benin, a small country in West Africa. She wears her hair very short and blond. She's small, not tall, but she has a lot of personality! She's very cool and confident. She's very active. She travels a lot to perform her shows around the world. Angélique is talented, but she is also intelligent, kind, and helpful. She started an organization, the Batonga Foundation, to help African women and girls get an education.

Angélique Kidjo

2 **Match the related sentences.**

1 Angélique Kidjo is talented. _____
2 She is popular. _____
3 She's very active. _____
4 She's kind. _____
5 She's intelligent. _____
6 She's confident. _____

a Education is important to her.
b She helps women and girls in Africa.
c She's calm, not nervous, in front of people.
d She's a great singer and songwriter.
e Many people like her.
f She travels and performs a lot.

3 **Correct the errors with the verb forms.**

1 Sofia and her friends are liking ________________ hanging out at the mall on the weekend.
2 They going ________________ there almost every Saturday afternoon.
3 They are often seeing ________________ their friends from school there.
4 Filipe always buying ________________ clothing or books.
5 Sofia is always looks ________________ at the latest mobile phones.
6 Right now, Nele and Sofia drink ________________ coffee and chatting.
7 They do not wanting ________________ to see a movie with Filipe.
8 Sometimes they are forgetting ________________ where the car is.

4 **Choose the correct words to complete the sentences.**

1 I _____ the instructions for the exam.
a am reading **b** is reading **c** doesn't read **d** don't reading

2 She _____ a newspaper every morning.
a buy **b** doesn't buying **c** is buying **d** buys

3 They _____ computer class today.
a has **b** don't have **c** doesn't have **d** having

4 Are you _____ the piano?
a practice **b** is practicing **c** doesn't practice **d** practicing

5 My aunt is a pilot. She _____ a plane.
a don't fly **b** flies **c** fly **d** flying

6 _____ they rent an apartment in the city?
a Doing **b** Does **c** Do **d** Doesn't

7 We never _____ in the ocean.
a swim **b** are swimming **c** do swim **d** swims

5 **Use the prompts to write sentences with the verb + *-ing* or the infinitive with *to*. Some sentences have more than one correct answer.**

1 I / would like / buy / a new jacket
____

2 They / usually / like / talk online
____

3 She / hate / shop for clothes
____

4 Do / you / like / help / your sister / learn English?
____

5 What / he / want / read / before bed?
____

6 I / want / tell you / about the end of movie
____

2 Where the Heart Is

2A Different places

VOCABULARY Describing where you live

1 Review Complete the sentences with the correct words.

apartment	bedroom	city
kitchen	quiet	wall

1 There's a clock on the ________ in our classroom.
2 I don't live in a house. I live in a(n) ________.
3 My roommate is sleeping in his ________.
4 The food is in the ________.
5 I don't live in a small town. I live in the ________.
6 My street is busy. It's not ________.

2 Review Complete the text with the correct words.

bathrooms	bed	bedroom	dining room
kitchen	living room	walls	yard

My family moved into a new house two months ago. So far, I love it. The only problem is that the (1) ________ are all white. It's a bit boring. We want to paint them different colors!

My favorite room is the (2) ________ because I love to cook! We usually eat there, too. There's also a big (3) ________ in the house, but we only eat there when we invite friends to dinner.

I spend a lot of time in the (4) ________, where I read or watch TV.

I sleep well at night because my (5) ________ is in the back of the house, away from the street, so it's very quiet. Also, my (6) ________ is soft and comfortable!

There are two (7) ________, which is great. One is upstairs and one is downstairs. When someone is taking a shower upstairs, I don't have to wait for them to finish. I can just use the one downstairs!

Finally, there's also a big (8) ________ outside in the back of the house. It's beautiful. There are lots of trees and flowers.

3 Label the photos with the correct words.

chairs	a couch	decorations	a door	light
a refrigerator	stairs	a table	a window	

1 ________

2 ________

3 ________

4 ________

5 ________

6 ________

7 ________

8 ________

9 ________

4 Complete the sentences with the correct words.

1 Please open the w________________. It's hot in here.
2 You have to put the milk in the r________________.
3 The whole family is sitting on the c________________ and watching a movie.
4 You can put the flowers in a vase on the dining room t________________.
5 The young girl has large photos of cute animals as d________________ in her bedroom.
6 There are 12 s________________ between the first and second floors.
7 The d________________ to the bathroom is closed. Is someone in there?
8 The l________________ are off and the house is dark. Everyone is sleeping.

5 Match the words to the definitions.

1 urban ____
2 walkable ____
3 business district ____
4 traditional ____
5 modern ____
6 historic ____
7 suburban ____
8 shopping district ____
9 crowded ____
10 residential area ____
11 lively ____

a a place where there are a lot of office buildings
b not quiet or boring
c not old-fashioned
d a place where there are a lot of houses or apartments
e an area that people visit when they want to buy things
f not too far; safe for people traveling on foot
g full of people
h from an important time in the past
i not rural
j in an area outside of a city
k an old way of doing things

6 Choose the correct words to complete the sentences.

1 Madrid is very *residential / lively* at night. Many people go out, and they stay out very late.
2 Tokyo is a *crowded / rural* city, with a population of almost 38 million.
3 In Oaxaca, Mexico, you can eat many *traditional / walkable* foods such as *tlayudas* and *tamales*.
4 Lined with expensive stores and restaurants, the Champs-Élysées in Paris is one of the most famous *shopping / residential* districts in the world.
5 Ho-Ho-Kus, New Jersey is a quiet *urban / suburban* town near New York City.
6 If you like *modern / historic* buildings, then you should visit the 306-meter-tall Cayan Tower in Dubai, opened in 2013.

7 Listen. Choose the correct description for each place. 15

1 **a** It's modern.
b It's walkable.
c It's crowded.
2 **a** It's the shopping district.
b It's a residential area.
c It's very lively.
3 **a** The area is very walkable.
b It's a rural area.
c It's the historic part of town.
4 **a** There's no furniture.
b It's a very small apartment.
c It's a traditional house.
5 **a** It's a historic area.
b It's very modern.
c It's a lively shopping district.
6 **a** It's a business.
b It's a modern house.
c It's old-fashioned.

8 Extension Fill in the missing vowels to form more words for things in a house or building.

1 st__v__
2 cl__s__t
3 c__b__n__t
4 c__rp__t
5 fl__ __r
6 c__ __l__ng
7 s__nk
8 c__rt__ __ns
9 t__ __l__t
10 __l__v__t__r

9 Extension Complete the text with the correct words.

cabinets	carpets	ceiling	curtains
driveway	floor	sinks	toilet
traditional			

There is an upside-down house in Moscow that is not a (1) ________________ house! There, the lights are on the (2) ________________ and all the furniture and the (3) ________________ are on the (4) ________________. The (5) ________________ hang from the "bottom" of the windows instead of the "top." Cups and plates are upside-down inside the kitchen (6) ________________. Even the car in the (7) ________________ is upside-down! The (8) ________________ in the kitchen and the bathroom can't work because the water would go in the wrong direction. And there isn't any water in the (9) ________________—it would fall out!

PRONUNCIATION

10 Read the sentences aloud. Circle your pronunciation. Listen to confirm your answers. 16

1 Finding an apartment used to be a lot easier.
/jus/ /juzd/ /just/

2 Didn't you use to live in London?
/jus/ /juzd/ /just/

3 They used all recycled materials to build the house.
/jus/ /juzd/ /just/

4 Did you use to live in an apartment?
/jus/ /juzd/ /just/

5 He used a lot of bamboo to build the house.
/jus/ /juzd/ /just/

6 The city used to be a lot less crowded.
/jus/ /juzd/ /just/

LISTENING

11 Listen and decide if each sentence is fact (F) or opinion (O). 17

1 _____ 5 _____
2 _____ 6 _____
3 _____ 7 _____
4 _____ 8 _____

12 Listen and check the topics the speaker talks about. 18

1 construction materials _____
2 the Amazon _____
3 pollution _____
4 saving forests _____
5 cutting down and planting _____
6 hunting animals _____
7 recycling _____
8 the future of our planet _____

13 Listen again and answer the questions. 18

1 What is the gist, or central idea, of what she is talking about?
a the need to replace all forests with bamboo
b reducing construction to protect the trees
c only building with bamboo in the future
d important ways to protect our forests

2 What adjective does she use meaning *to not think about the future*?
a thoughtless **c** old-fashioned
b short-sighted **d** traditional

3 What word does she use to describe a new tree?
a seedling **c** replacement
b baby **d** harvesting

4 What does she say about bamboo?
a It's very inexpensive.
b It doesn't grow in a forest.
c It grows very quickly.
d It can't be recycled.

5 What else does she talk about protecting?
a seeds **c** rivers
b air **d** animals

6 What do you think the speaker is trying to do?
a persuade people not to use wood or paper products
b convince people to be careful about what they use and buy
c get people to stop using bamboo construction materials
d encourage people to only cut down new seedlings to protect the forests

14 Listen and answer the questions. 19

1 How would you describe this young woman?
a crazy
b thoughtful
c selfish

2 Who would you expect to care more about pollution?
a the young woman
b her colleague
c both of them

3 What do you imagine is more important to the young woman?
a a new car
b good public transportation
c inexpensive taxis

4 What negative things does she mention about getting a car?
a traffic, pollution, and safety
b cost, parking, and pollution
c parking, traffic, and insurance

5 Which statement describes her attitude?
a She doesn't care about her quality of life.
b She only cares about others quality of life.
c She cares about everyone's quality of life.

6 What saying do you think she would agree with more?
a We're all in this together.
b You worry about your life and let me worry about mine.
c You can never have enough.

GRAMMAR Simple past

15 Write the missing simple present or simple past form for each verb.

Simple present	Simple past
are	
	became
change	
fly	
	went
grow	
	had
	lived

Simple present	Simple past
	looked
make	
	moved
see	
	spoke
take	
think	
	worked

16 Choose the correct verb forms to complete the text.

My mother and I *need / am needing / needs* to find a new place to live. We *work / worked / are working* with a real estate agent to find a new apartment. We *see / are seeing / saw* three different apartments yesterday. The first one *not is / was / weren't* in a quiet neighborhood and *had / have / is having* a big kitchen and bedroom. But it *costed / cost / costing* too much for us. The second one *be / was / are* really cheap, but it *was / are / being* ugly and too far from my school. The third apartment *is having / had / have* lots of windows and *is getting / get / got* lots of light. We *go / are going / going* to move in next month!

17 Complete the sentences with the simple past form of the verbs in parentheses.

1 Before we ____________ (move) here, we ____________ (live) in a suburb far from the city.
2 Back then, my brother and I ____________ (go) to school in the city. We ____________ (take) a bus from our town into the city.
3 Our parents ____________ (work) in the city and ____________ (drive) to work every day.
4 Eventually, all of us ____________ (become) tired of it because we ____________ (spend) so much time commuting.
5 My parents ____________ (decide) it would be better if we ____________ (move) to the city.
6 At first, I ____________ (think) this was a bad idea because I ____________ (not, want) to leave my friends.
7 I ____________ (be) afraid of not having friends and being lonely in the big city.
8 But I ____________ (change) my mind when I ____________ (realize) that my friends want to visit me here in the city!

18 Write a question for each answer.

1 ____
I walked to the movie theater and met my friends there.
2 ____
He didn't go to the concert yesterday. It was on Friday.
3 ____
Yes, I think cities need green spaces and public parks.
4 ____
We lived in a city and walked everywhere.
5 ____
We didn't want to live in an historic house because it cost too much to maintain.
6 ____
My friend's house had a large swimming pool and a big yard.

19 Complete the sentences with the correct form of ***use to***.

1 I ____________ watch a lot of TV when I was younger, but now I don't.
2 I never ____________ watch movies on my computer, but now I do.
3 Like lots of kids, I ____________ want to be an astronaut. Now I want to be a lawyer.
4 My sister didn't ____________ like vegetables, but now she's a vegetarian!
5 Our cat ____________ stay inside, but now he goes outside every day.
6 I ____________ play games on my computer like my friends, but now I do.
7 What kind of games ____________ you ____________ play as a child?
8 I did not ____________ study every day, but now I do, and my grades are much better!

2B Floating cities

VOCABULARY BUILDING

1 Complete each sentence with the noun form of the verb in parentheses.

1 Did you send Max an __________ (invite) to the party?
2 The __________ (explore) of North America didn't begin with Columbus.
3 The detectives did a thorough __________ (investigate) of the crime scene.
4 What's the __________ (locate) of that restaurant?
5 I like to use public __________ (transport) whenever I can.

READING

2 Match the words from the article to their definitions. Two words are extra.

1 business ____
2 construction ____
3 district ____
4 imagination ____
5 walkable ____
6 residential ____
7 suburban ____
8 traditional ____
9 urban ____

a an area marked for a specific purpose
b the customary way of doing things
c easy to get around on foot
d the ability to form new ideas and see things that aren't real yet
e suitable for living in
f referring to the city instead of the country
g where people work, buy and sell goods and services

3 Read the statements. Do the statements match the information in the article? Is the information true (T), false (F), or not given (NG)?

1 Floating cities are home to 7 billion people. ____
2 Over 100,000 people could live in a Green Float city. ____
3 A floating Lilypad city would be completely self-sufficient. ____
4 Each Lilypad would contain around 50,000 homes. ____
5 Floating cities like Lilypad only exist on paper. ____
6 Coastal cities may someday be threatened by flooding. ____

4 Choose the correct heading for each paragraph.

Paragraph 1:
a Where will we live in the future?
b Would you like to live in a city?

Paragraph 2:
a Designing a new type of city
b People all over the world are building new ships and cities

Paragraph 3:
a An underwater farm!
b Another type of floating city

Paragraph 4:
a Inventors and their imaginations
b Why floating cities matter

5 Read each question. Choose the correct answer.

1 According to the information in paragraph 2, it is NOT true that
a people are thinking about developing cities on the ocean.
b the first floating cities will be near Brazil.
c a Japanese company is working on a floating city idea.
d the plans for Green Float include walkable neighborhoods.

2 Why does the author mention Lilypad's sources of energy?
a to show that it is self-sufficient.
b to explain why there are no cars.
c to contrast it with the energy sources of Green Float.
d to give an example of farming below the water.

3 Why does the author say floating cities "only exist on paper"?
a Because floating cities appear on maps of the Pacific Ocean.
b Because only 100,000 people can live in a floating city.
c Because floating cities don't exist yet.
d Because they are in science fiction stories.

4 In the article, the word *inventors* in paragraph 4 is closest in meaning to
a residents.
b builders.
c creators.
d instructors.

Floating Cities of the Future 20

1 We all know that the ocean covers a large part of the Earth's surface. We also know that with 7 billion people on this planet, space for housing is running out! Where do you want to live in the future? In a city? Near the ocean? How about a city in the ocean?

2 In the past, people thought that floating cities were only in science fiction stories. Today, people are developing plans for new types of buildings and cities, including some that float on the surface* of the ocean. Japan's Shimizu Corporation is working on a "Green Float" idea. The company wants to build a floating city in the Pacific Ocean. And just like the cities we know today, the plan for Green Float's city on the ocean includes residential areas, shopping districts, walkable neighborhoods, and business districts.

3 Another plan for a floating city takes its name and inspiration from a plant. An architect designed Lilypad to be an ecologically friendly, ultra-modern city that's completely self-sufficient*. A Lilypad city gets energy from the sun, wind, and the ocean's tide. Boats and other floating vehicles are the only transportation for the 50,000 future residents of a Lilypad.

4 Today, cities like the Lilypads only exist on paper, and in the imaginations of their inventors. But these new ideas for housing are important for the future. Traditional ways of living need to change. Major urban centers are becoming more and more crowded every day. Floating cities are one possible answer to the need for more housing.

Lilypad

surface *the top of something*
self-sufficient *able to provide for its needs*

2C What were you doing?

GRAMMAR Past continuous

1 Read the paragraph. Circle the past continuous verbs.

When I went to Prague last year I was planning to visit historic buildings, and I did. But I was not expecting to see a historic elevator. This unusual elevator was running nonstop! It also didn't have doors! People stepped into the elevator as it was moving up or down. I was thinking how unsafe it was when the tour guide told us the name. It's called a *paternoster* after a prayer that people said as they rode it. People prayed because the elevator was dangerous. The guide explained that the elevator was working like a Ferris wheel, moving people up and down in a circle. The important thing about riding the *paternoster* was making sure that you got off before it reached the top, turned over, and went down.

Ferris wheel

2 Read about Raul's day. Complete the sentences using the past continuous.

7:00–8:30 exercised at the gym
8:45–9:15 had breakfast with his uncle
9:15–9:45 took the bus to school
10:00–10:30 met with his study group
10:30–12:15 studied in the library
12:15–12:45 ate lunch with his friend David
1:00–2:15 attended his English class

1 At 8:15, Raul *was exercising at the gym*.
2 At 9:00, Raul ______.
3 At 9:30, Raul ______.
4 At 10:15, Raul ______.
5 At 11:00, Raul ______.
6 At 12:30, Raul ______.
7 At 1:45, Raul ______.

3 Choose the correct words to complete the sentences.

1 Hana *arrived / was arriving* an hour early for her flight to Seoul.
2 I *relaxed / was relaxing* at home when I got a call from my boss.
3 I saw Raj at the Student Union and *asked / was asking* him if he had time to help me prepare for my math exam.
4 Pedro *listened / was listening* to music when suddenly the power went out.
5 Last night, my sister *cleaned / was cleaning* up the kitchen after dinner.
6 Congratulations on your new job! I *heard / was hearing* the good news last week.
7 I *saw / was seeing* him walk past my office on his way to the meeting.

4 Complete the sentences using past continuous or simple past.

1 The bus drove by while we ______ (walk) to school.
2 I looked out the window and ______ (notice) it was snowing.
3 After Kira ______ (make) breakfast, she washed the dishes.
4 She ______ (ask) me to help her move into her new house.
5 She ______ (play) soccer with her friends but had to stop to take her little brother to his piano lesson.
6 I ______ (meet) Antonio at the party last night.
7 Elena wrote a letter to her grandmother last week but ______ (forget) to send it.
8 I ______ (watch) TV when I heard the news.

5 Use the prompts to write sentences with the past continuous and simple past. Add any necessary words.

1 I / do the laundry / while / my mother / make dinner
2 I / make lunch / when / my phone / ring
3 she / fall down / while / ride bike
4 we / run / down the street / when / bus / leave the station
5 Claire / shop / new couch / when / find / great sale
6 while / they / save money / a new house / win the lottery
7 Jaime / read book / when / mom / call
8 I / break / laptop / while / board / boat

6 Complete the conversation with the past continuous of the verbs in parentheses.

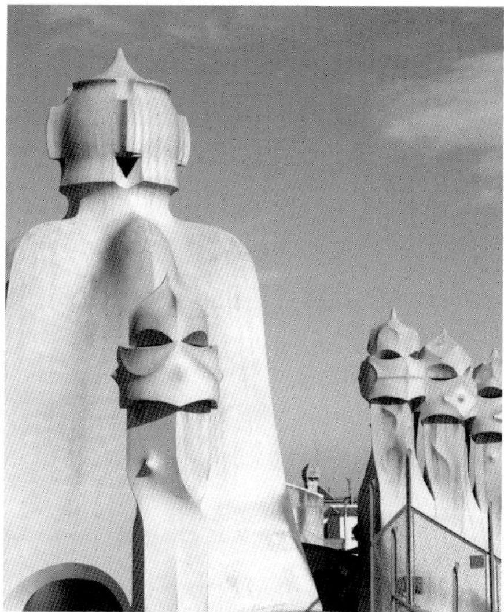
Chimneys on the roof of Casa Mila

A: Hey, Julia! Welcome back! (1) *Were you traveling* (travel) last semester?

B: Yes, I was. I (2) ______________ (study) in Barcelona.

A: That is so cool! Where (3) ______________ (live)?

B: I (4) ______________ (live) in this really cool neighborhood called the Eixample. It's pretty famous for its architecture. It's a nice area—residential, but there is still a lot of shopping and restaurants. Do you know it?

A: Yeah, I do. Is that where Antoni Gaudi (5) ______________ (work) in the late 1800s?

B: Yes! His buildings are so amazing! I (6) ______________ (stay) in a house just two blocks away from Casa Mila, a famous apartment building he designed.

A: You're so lucky! I (7) ______________ (hope) to visit Barcelona when I went to Spain last year, but I ran out of time.

B: Well, I'm sure you (8) ______________ other places.

A: Yeah, but I (9) ______________ (hear) so many great things about the parks and monuments in Barcelona from everyone! Now, (10) ______________ Gaudi (11) ______________ (build) something when he died? A church?

B: Yes, he (12) ______________ (work) on a large cathedral, the *Sagrada Familia*. It still isn't finished, but the city (13) ______________ (work) on it when I left!

7 Which choice is closest in meaning to the original sentence?

1 I was listening to my brother tell me about his day when someone rang the doorbell.
- **a** I started listening to my brother. Then someone rang the doorbell.
- **b** The doorbell rang. Then I started listening to my brother.

2 He was eating lunch outside because it stopped raining.
- **a** It stopped raining. Then he ate lunch outside.
- **b** He ate lunch outside. Then it stopped raining.

3 Sam was practicing the trumpet when he suddenly heard his roommate asking him for help.
- **a** Sam's roommate asked for help before Sam practiced the trumpet.
- **b** Sam's roommate asked for help while Sam was practicing the trumpet.

4 She hurt her leg while she was playing basketball.
- **a** Because she hurt her leg, she played basketball.
- **b** Because she was playing basketball, she hurt her leg.

5 Before I moved to Tokyo, I was living in Amsterdam.
- **a** I lived in Amsterdam. Then I lived in Tokyo.
- **b** I moved to Tokyo. Then I lived in Amsterdam.

6 Yesterday Beatrix was listening to music while she cleaned her apartment.
- **a** Beatrix started listening to music. Then she cleaned her apartment.
- **b** Beatrix listened to music and cleaned her apartment at the same time.

7 I was thinking about going back to school but decided to take a new job instead.
- **a** I went back to school and also took a new job.
- **b** I thought about going back to school. But I didn't.

8 Choose the correct response for each question.

1 Did you read *Animal Farm* when you were in high school?
- **a** Yes, we read it in ninth grade.
- **b** Yes, we were reading it in ninth grade.

2 Where were you when I tried to call you?
- **a** I talked to my mother.
- **b** I was talking to my mother.

3 Why did you call me?
- **a** I wanted to ask you to go on a hike next weekend.
- **b** I was wanting to ask you to go on a hike next weekend.

4 Did you hear what I said?
- **a** No, sorry. I was concentrating on my work.
- **b** No, sorry. I concentrated on my work.

5 Where did you meet your friend Amy?
- **a** We were meeting in college.
- **b** We met in college.

6 Did they graduate in 2017?
- **a** No, they were graduating in 2016.
- **b** No, they graduated in 2016.

7 Where did you buy this comfortable chair?
- **a** I found it at a furniture store near school.
- **b** I was finding it at a furniture store near school.

8 What were you doing at 8:15 this morning?
- **a** I was exercising before I caught the bus for work at 9:30.
- **b** I caught the bus while I was exercising at 9:30.

2D Magical houses, made of bamboo

TEDTALKS

AUTHENTIC LISTENING SKILLS

1 Listen to the TED Talk extracts. Choose the correct answers. 21

1 What is the gist of this extract?
   a the different homes in Bali
   b the homes Elora designed
   c different parts of any home
2 What is the gist of this extract?
   a a special kind of bamboo
   b how her father builds with bamboo
   c how tall bamboo plants grow
3 What is the gist of this extract?
   a trucks that go through mountains
   b the plants the family grows
   c a really strong bamboo
4 What is the gist of this extract?
   a why bamboo is a good material
   b how the children study in Bali
   c how to stay safe in an earthquake
5 What is the gist of this extract?
   a how to be an extraordinary person
   b how to be an architect
   c how to build something great with bamboo

WATCH

2 Are the statements true (T) or false (F)?

1 Bamboo is a wild grass ___.
2 There are seven species of bamboo around the world ___.
3 Betung is as strong as steel ___.
4 Betung is so heavy that many people need to carry it ___.
5 Bamboo can be easily broken by earthquakes ___.
6 Bamboo is a material that is good for the environment ___.

3 Put the events in order.

___ Her father plants a bamboo called *Dendrocalamus asper niger*.
___ Elora draws a picture of her dream home.
___ Elora realizes how bamboo is important and thinks about what else she can do with it.
___ Elora sees one of the buildings from the Green School in Bali.
___ Her mother builds a home that looks like a fairy mushroom.

4 Choose the correct answers.

1 What is the speaker mainly discussing?
   a how she is a good home designer
   b why bamboo is a great material
   c the way everyone should build their homes
2 What does the speaker mean when she says this: "Bamboo will treat you well if you use it right."?
   a Bamboo has to be carefully used.
   b Bamboo can be used the same way by everyone.
   c Bamboo can take care of people.
3 What can be inferred about the speaker's father?
   a His main job is a farmer.
   b He builds homes and buildings like Elora.
   c He works for Elora.
4 Why does the speaker say: "protect it (bamboo) from water"?
   a Water can make the bamboo grow bigger.
   b Water is not a good building material.
   c Water can be bad for bamboo when building.
5 Why does the speaker mention designing in 3D?
   a to explain how easy it is to design in 3D
   b to show how much planning she does before building
   c to give an example of the best way to design
6 What is a *blueprint*?
   a a piece of bamboo
   b a part of a home
   c a plan for a home

VOCABULARY IN CONTEXT

5 Match the expressions to the situations.

1 It didn't feel right. ___
2 I've got to tell you something. ___
3 It looks elegant. ___
4 It will treat you well. ___
5 It makes perfect sense. ___

a You see a stylish jacket and you really like it.
b When you take care of something and you expect it will be good to you.
c Someone tells you a good idea that solves your problems.
d Someone tells you to do something you aren't comfortable doing.
e When you learn exciting and new information you want to share.

6 Elora Hardy talks about designing houses for the tropics, where it can get very hot. Think about your home. Can you give an example of how it was designed for the place you live?

2E Inside and outside

SPEAKING

Useful language

Giving reasons

Use *The reason…*, *because*, *so*, and *since* to give reasons.

***The reason** he went there was to get away from his money problems.*

*He went **because** his business failed.*

*She thought life was too hard, **so** she left.*

***Since** he loved living a simple life in a tiny house, he didn't want to leave.*

1 Complete the sentences with words from the Useful language box. Listen to check your answers. 22

1 I used to spend a lot of time outside ____________ I lived in a small apartment.
2 ____________ I went to Barcelona was to see the amazing architecture.
3 My house is in a rural area, ____________ I spend a lot of time by myself.
4 ____________ I have four brothers and sisters, our place was very noisy.

2 Listen again to the sentences from Activity 1. Are the reason words stressed or weak? 22

1 stressed / weak
2 stressed / weak
3 stressed / weak
4 stressed / weak

3 Think about some things you don't do, and the reasons why. Complete the sentences about yourself.

Example: *Since I don't like shopping, I don't go to the mall a lot.*

1 The reason I don't ____________ is to ____________.
2 Since I don't ____________, I ____________.
3 I don't ____________, so ____________.
4 I don't ____________ because ____________.

4 You are designing a dream house. Look at the options in the box and choose four to include in your design. Use the prompts to explain reasons for your choices. Use the useful language.

bamboo	solar panels
big windows	swimming pool
energy-saving lights	wall insulation
rainwater tank	water recycling system

1 The first thing a dream house needs is ____________.
____
2 It's also important that the house have ____________.
____
3 Another thing it should have is ____________.
____
4 Finally, I think ____________ is very important.
____

When you complete the sentences, listen to the sample answers and compare them with your answers. 23

5 Answer the questions and give reasons for your ideas, using the useful language. Then listen to the sample answers and compare them with your ideas. 24

1 Do you prefer spending your free time at home or going out?
2 Tell me a little about your hometown.
3 What did you like about where you lived as a child?
4 What do you do in your free time in your hometown?

WRITING

1 **Match each question with a logical answer.**

1 Where is it? ____
2 When did you go there? ____
3 How old is it? ____
4 What does it look like? ____
5 Who lives there? ____
6 What did you see or do there? ____

a It's a huge house with beautiful gardens and views of New York City.
b I really enjoyed visiting the art gallery on the first floor of the house.
c My favorite house is in Westchester County, New York.
d The house is more than 100 years old. It was built in 1913.
e A few weeks ago, my aunt and uncle took me to visit this house.
f It's the home of a very rich American family called the Rockefellers.

2 **Read the paragraph. Put the information in order, 1–6.**

I stayed in the most amazing apartment in Dubai. I went there a few months ago with my best friend, Amira, when we were on our way to Australia. It's only a few years old, and it's definitely the most modern apartment I've ever seen. It has white walls and a huge balcony, and a swimming pool! It belongs to Amira's uncle, but he only lives there sometimes, because he travels a lot for business. When we were there, we swam in the pool every morning and drank tea on the balcony every evening. It was such a wonderful home to visit. –Laura

When Laura went there: ____
What she did there: ____
What it looks like: ____
Where it is: ____
How old it is: ____
Who lives there: ____

3 **Complete the paragraph with the correct words.**

designed	family	garden	gates
saw	special	tower	years

I love the Gaudi House in Barcelona, which is in Spain. I went there on a trip with my (1) ____________ last month. It's in Park Guell and it's now a museum. The house is about 100 (2) ____________ old, and it's amazing. One part has a tall (3) ____________, which looks like a castle! It's pretty big, with four floors, many windows, and huge (4) ____________. It's (5) ____________ because a famous architect, called Antoni Gaudi, lived there for almost 20 years. He (6) ____________ many incredible buildings in Barcelona, but not this house! When I went there, I (7) ____________ lots of beautiful art and some strange furniture. After our visit, we had a picnic in the (8) ____________. It was really nice. –Ken

4 **Read the paragraph in Activity 3 again. Choose the correct options to complete the sentences.**

1 The Gaudi House is in a city called *Barcelona / Spain*.
2 Ken went there last *year / month*.
3 The house is *100 / 20* years old.
4 Part of the house looks like a *museum / castle*.
5 The house is quite *small / large*.
6 A famous man called *Gaudi / Guell* used to live there.
7 The furniture that Ken saw there was *unusual / beautiful*.

5 **Read the notes and imagine you visited the house in the picture. A friend has asked you about it. Write a paragraph (80–100 words) describing your visit. In your paragraph you should say:**

- Where it is and when you went there
- How old it is; its location; and what's special about it
- Who used to live in it, and what you did or saw there

Notes about the house:
- in Ireland
- visited cousin there last summer
- house was built in 1757
- pretty cottage in the countryside
- very old furniture
- great grandparents used to live there
- baked bread in the old stove

6 **A teacher gave you an assignment to write a story. The first sentence of the story is: *The lighthouse where I stayed at in Canada was the best house I ever visited.* Write the story (100 words) in your notebook.**

Review

1 Unscramble the letters to form furniture or items in a house.

1. arsist ____________
2. scriha ____________
3. fergritroare ____________
4. orcastedino ____________
5. blate ____________
6. gilth ____________

2 Read the sentences about houses. Choose the best word to complete each sentence.

1. The elevator doesn't work, so we have to take the ____________ up to our hotel room.
   a door **b** stairs **c** window
2. My aunt lives in a ____________ house from the 1700s.
   a modern **b** walkable **c** historic
3. There are six ____________ in the dining room—one for each dinner guest.
   a chairs **b** tables **c** couches
4. His apartment is very plain and boring. He has basic furniture but no ____________ at all.
   a lights **b** refrigerators **c** decorations
5. If a restaurant is always ____________, that usually means the food is pretty good.
   a old-fashioned **b** crowded **c** traditional
6. Adrian and Martin ____________ school last week.
   a studied **b** went **c** finished

3 Correct the errors in the exchanges.

1. **A:** When do you moved to your new apartment? ____________
   B: I was move in last week. ____________
2. **A:** Do you saw anything interesting at the store? ____________
   B: No, I didn't saw anything new. ____________
3. **A:** Did you took the subway to the train station? ____________
   B: No. I taked the bus. It's faster. ____________
4. **A:** Did you drew this picture of your grandparents? ____________
   B: Yes, I did. I drawed it last night. ____________
5. **A:** I readed a good article in the sports magazine last night. ____________
   B: Really? Did you enjoyed it? ____________
6. **A:** I didn't used to like to dance, but now I love it! ____________
   B: Really? What change your mind? ____________

4 Complete the chart.

Infinitive	Simple past	Past continuous
grow	*grew*	*was growing*
watch		
dance		
love		
buy		
fly		
leave		
ride		

5 Complete the sentences based on information provided.

1. I ate lunch before you called.
   I ____________ lunch when you called.
2. He took English classes. During one of those classes, he decided to study in Australia.
   While he ____________ English classes, he ____________ to study in Australia.
3. They fell asleep before the train stopped.
   They ____________ when the train ____________.
4. I think I remember you went shopping for a new wallet.
   ____________ you ____________ to find a new wallet?
5. I looked for a new wallet at the mall. While I was at the mall, I found a wallet I wanted to buy.
   I ____________ for a new wallet and finally ____________ one at the mall.
6. We talked about our friend Ana at the same time we rode our bikes to the pool.
   We ____________ our bikes to the pool while we ____________ about our friend Ana.
7. You studied for the exam. I want to know if your sisters bothered you then.
   ____________ your sisters ____________ you while you ____________ for the exam?

3 Health and Happiness

3A Treating the Whole Person

VOCABULARY Being well

1 Review Choose the correct words to complete the sentences.

1 You see with your ______.
 a eyes **b** teeth

2 Your back is part of your ______.
 a body **b** face

3 When your tooth hurts, you go to the ______.
 a doctor **b** dentist

4 When you catch a cold, you feel ______.
 a fine **b** sick

5 When you don't feel well, you go to the ______.
 a doctor **b** dentist

6 You usually know someone by looking at their ______.
 a back **b** face

7 Smoking isn't good ______.
 a to you **b** for you

2 Review Listen. Match the descriptions to the images.

 25

a
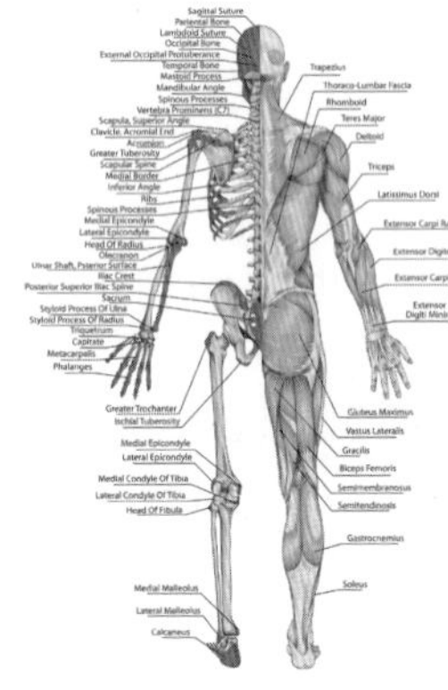

b

c
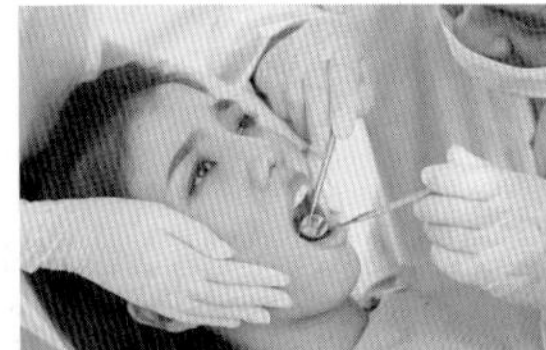

d

e

f

g

h

1 ____ 2 ____ 3 ____ 4 ____ 5 ____ 6 ____ 7 ____ 8 ____

3 Put the words into the correct categories.

backache chest flu foot mouth
pain seasickness shoulder stomach virus

Body part	Illness

4 Write the correct words.

1 ______________
2 ______________
3 ______________
4 ______________
5 ______________
6 ______________
7 ______________
8 ______________

5 Complete the paragraph. Two words are extra.

broken	happiness	healthy	hospital
illnesses	injuries	medicine	pain
patient	unwell	viruses	

We all know that laughing makes us feel good—in fact, there is a saying that "laughter is the best (1) ________________." Positive thoughts and happy feelings can certainly take some of our (2) ________________ away. But many scientists and doctors believe there is an even stronger connection between (3) ________________ and health. Some studies show that happier people heal faster after (4) ________________ such as a (5) ________________ leg. They also show that positive feelings can help prepare your body to fight (6) ________________ better. On the other hand, negative feelings like stress can lead to (7) ________________ such as heart disease and diabetes over time. In short, happier people are more likely to be (8) ________________ and make fewer visits to the (9) ________________.

6 Listen. Match each talk (a–f) to the correct topic (1–6). 26

1 a common virus ____
2 seasickness ____
3 a problem with a pain medicine ____
4 patients who get sicker instead of better ____
5 reading people's faces and body language ____
6 sports injuries ____

7 **Extension** Where is it? Choose the correct answer for each body part.

1 brain
a inside the head
b inside the chest

2 finger
a part of the foot
b part of the hand

3 toe
a part of the foot
b part of the face

4 cheek
a below the neck
b part of the face

5 wrist
a part of your arm
b part of your leg

6 chin
a inside the body
b you can see it

7 bones
a inside the body
b you can see them

8 lungs
a inside the body
b you can see them

9 ankles
a inside the body
b you can see them

10 blood
a on your face
b in your whole body

8 **Extension** Complete the sentences with the correct words.

accident	ankles	blood	bone	brain	chin
heart	lungs	recover	toe	wrists	

1 Your ________________ thinks and controls everything in your body.
2 Your ________________ is inside your chest, and it pumps ________________ around your body.
3 Your ________________ are also inside your chest. They take air in and push it out.
4 If you have an ________________, you could break a ________________ in your leg or your arm.
5 It's very painful to hit your big ________________ on a table when you walk by it.
6 Your forehead and your ________________ are both parts of your face.
7 Your ________________ help you move your hands. Your ________________ help you move your feet.
8 When you ________________ from an illness or injury, you get better.

9 **Extension** Choose the correct words to complete the text.

In 2013, motorcyclist Nick Matthews had a terrible *blood / accident*. His neck was broken and his *back / heart* was broken in three places. He also had a broken *wrist / cheek*, two broken *fingers / brains*, and several broken *bones / ankles* in his chest area. To make matters worse, he had a serious *lung / chin* injury, which caused him to stop breathing. In the hospital, the doctors thought he might not walk again. But three weeks later, Matthews walked out of the hospital. He *recovered / injured* completely and ran in the Berlin Marathon, just one year later!

PRONUNCIATION Nuclear stress

10 Listen and choose the stressed word or phrase. One sentence has two stressed phrases. 27

1 **a** you said
b a few
c problems

2 **a** no
b knee
c neck

3 **a** How much
b you
c it costs

4 **a** kind
b mind
c matter

5 **a** biggest
b problem
c world

6 **a** kidding me
b call
c a little

LISTENING

11 Listen. Choose the illness or injury in the description. 28

1 **a** the flu
b a broken hand
c an earache

2 **a** a broken nose
b bad cold
c backache

3 **a** shoulder injury
b knee injury
c headache

4 **a** broken temperature
b high temperature
c sore injury

5 **a** neck injury
b nose injury
c knee injury

6 **a** the flu
b seasickness
c a broken stomach

7 **a** seasickness
b a headache
c the flu

12 Listen. What is the speaker mainly talking about? 29

a People who go to the doctor and take medicine are sensitive.
b Medical professionals don't believe in mind over matter.
c The mind-body connection is important in understanding health.
d Meditation is better than visiting a doctor or taking medicine.

13 Listen again and answer the questions. 29

1 What phrasal verb does the speaker use meaning to *handle* or *manage*?
a take control
b deal with
c depend on
d look after

2 What adjective does the speaker use for people who don't handle pain well?
a anxious
b serious
c stressful
d sensitive

3 What phrasal verb does the speaker use meaning to *stop* or *end*?
a cut off
b take out
c turn off
d able to

4 What adjective does the speaker use to describe doctors?
a prescription
b professional
c patient
d serious

5 What two things are connected in the idea of mind over matter?
a symptoms and pain
b body and mind
c patient and doctor
d prescription medicine and meditation

6 According to the speaker, what can some people do that others cannot?
a tolerate pain
b describe their symptoms
c deal with their doctor
d meditate

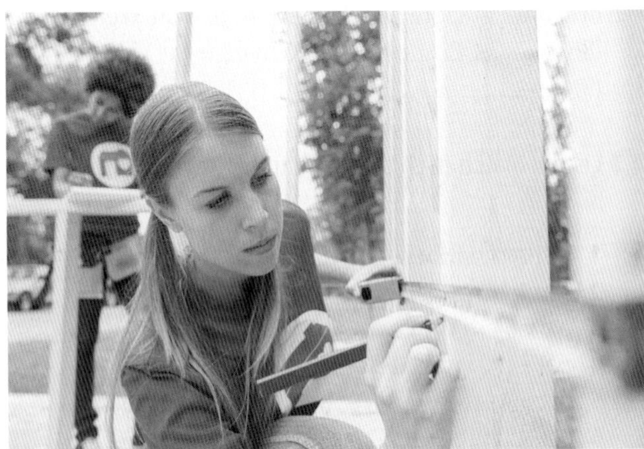

A volunteer works on a house.

14 Listen. Are the sentences true (T) or false (F)? 30

1 She used to enjoy showing off her money and success. _____
2 She was very unhappy earlier in her life. _____
3 She was missing the company of close friends. _____
4 She wasn't sure what was missing in her life. _____
5 She learned about Habitat for Humanity from a friend. _____
6 Habitat for Humanity charges a lot of money for their homes. _____
7 Her boss allowed her to take time off from work. _____

GRAMMAR Quantifiers

15 Put the words into the correct categories.

air	arm	ear	exercise
eye	the flu	hand	health
hospital	injury	leg	medicine
patient	skin	water	

Countable	Uncountable

16 Choose the correct option to complete each sentence.

1 My doctor gave me _____ really good suggestions for things I can do to get back into shape.
a some
b any

2 She told me that I should do _____ exercise every couple of hours—just a few minutes is enough.
a a few
b a little

3 She said that _____ people think they have to go to the gym to exercise, but you can do some exercises at home without expensive equipment.
a a lot of
b a little

4 For _____ of the exercises, you can use the weight of your body.
a much
b many

5 The intensity of the exercise depends on how _____ you weigh.
a many
b much

6 Another tip from my doctor was to drink _____ water throughout the day.
a a lot of
b a few

7 And to eat _____ grapes as a snack rather than chips or cookies.
a a little
b a few

17 Complete the questions and statements with *how much* or *how many*.

1 _______________ time do you spend at the gym?
2 _______________ times do you meditate each week?
3 _______________ medicine do you take every day?
4 _______________ pills do you take at breakfast?
5 _______________ did you weigh the last time you went to the doctor?
6 I don't know _______________ times I was sick last year.
7 My doctor told me _______________ sleep I should get every night.
8 No one knows _______________ people got sick from the flu.

18 Complete the sentences with the correct words. Some items have more than one correct answer.

a little	any	many	much
not any	not much	some	

1 I still have _______________ pain in my shoulder after working on the house.
2 The doctor told me I still have _______________ more weight to lose.
3 My grandparents take _______________ pills every day because they are sick.
4 We didn't have _______________ junk food in our house, so we had to eat fruit.
5 The coach showed us _______________ really fun exercises you can do with a chair.
6 Do you have _______________ bandages? I cut my finger, and it's bleeding.
7 The doctors do _______________ have _______________ idea how long the illness will last.
8 We do _______________ have _______________ food in the house, so we should go to the supermarket.

19 Correct the quantifier in each sentence.

1 Last night, I went to the hospital because I had much pain in my stomach. _______________
2 I don't know how much hours I waited there, but I finally saw the doctor around midnight. _______________
3 She asked me how many pain I had. _______________
4 I told her there was a few pain in my stomach and that I could barely walk. _______________
5 She asked me if I ate too many food at dinner. _______________
6 I told her that I ate too many pizza, and then I ate a lot of ice cream. _______________
7 She asked me a lot of slices of pizza, and I told her, "Six." _______________
8 She said I was in pain because I ate too many food! _______________

3B Health at Every Size

VOCABULARY BUILDING

1 Match the words or phrases to their synonyms.

1	happy	well
	healthy	sickness
	unwell	content
	illness	sick
2	discover	combine
	mix	find
	entire	whole
	think	believe
3	angry	try
	attempt	upset
	several	normal
	typical	some

READING

2 Read the article. Choose the correct answer for each question.

1 What do some people mean when they say that they want to "go on a diet"?
   a They want to eat more grains and beans.
   b They mean more than one thing.
   c They want to eat every day.
   d They want to lose weight.

2 What can happen when you lose weight suddenly?
   a You skip a few meals every week.
   b Your body thinks there's a problem.
   c You eat more meat and fish.
   d Your body type varies.

3 What does Linda Bacon recommend that you do in order to stay healthy?
   a Eat less food and miss several meals a week.
   b Worry about whether you're too big or too small.
   c Move your body and try to find foods that you enjoy.
   d Keep eating even after you're full.

4 What is a "diet"?
   a the food you normally eat
   b a fun physical activity
   c a type of exercise
   d a way to stay alert

5 According to HAES, what are two ways to avoid feeling unwell?
   a Go on a diet and lose weight suddenly.
   b Eat less and miss a few meals.
   c Eat good food and get physical activity.
   d Sleep a lot and worry about your weight.

3 Choose the correct words to complete the sentences.

1 It's important to be aware of what you ________ in order to stay healthy.
   a wear
   b eat
   c say
   d hear

2 Many people think that going on a diet is a good way to ________ weight.
   a avoid
   b recognize
   c lose
   d feel

3 Being aware of what you eat can help you avoid certain ________.
   a illnesses
   b diets
   c weight
   d hungry

4 HAES doesn't believe that everyone should be the same ________.
   a height
   b age
   c weight
   d way

5 In order to stay healthy, your body needs many different ________.
   a nutrients
   b experiments
   c mix
   d weights

4 Read the statements. Write the number of the paragraph in the article that includes the information in each statement. Numbers may be used more than once.

a recommendations for healthy eating and activities ____
b two easy ways to avoid feeling unwell ____
c a description of how bodies react to sudden weight loss ____
d two definitions for the word "diet" ____
e a description of how people vary physically ____
f how listening to your body can help you feel well ____

Health at Every Size 31

1 The word "diet" can mean a couple of things. What you normally eat every day is your regular diet. If you eat meat or fish, grains or beans, fruits or vegetables, then those foods are part of your diet. But "diet" also has another meaning, one that you may be more familiar with. When people say that they want to "go on a diet," they usually mean that they want to lose some weight. They may think that by eating less, missing a few meals, or eating only certain foods, they'll lose weight and become healthier.

2 Of course, everyone wants to stay healthy, avoid illnesses, and live longer, but dieting isn't always the best way to do it! Like height or skin color, weight and body type are different from person to person. A person's ideal weight range* is called their "set-point" weight. When you go on a diet and lose weight quickly, your body thinks the sudden weight loss is a problem or challenge. It will do whatever it can to get you back to your set-point, or average weight.

3 Health at Every Size (HAES) is a group that encourages healthy eating and fun physical activity as two easy ways to avoid feeling unwell and live longer. HAES doesn't believe weight loss through dieting is the way to become healthy. As Linda Bacon, a researcher and the author of *Health at Every Size: The Surprising Truth About Your Weight*, says, "Health at Every Size is about taking care of your body without worrying about whether you're "too" big or small. Saying everybody needs to be the same weight is like saying all people should be the same height."

4 "What's good for thin kids, fat kids, and everyone in between, it turns out, is moving their bodies, and a healthy mix of foods that taste good and nourish their bodies. Finding the activities you enjoy might mean sports or workouts, but it could also be walking, jumping rope with friends, or dancing," Bacon says. She recommends trying out a variety of foods to find those that you enjoy most or make you happy. (Within reason—of course that doesn't mean you should eat a lot of junk food!) "This means learning to listen to your body so you can recognize when you're hungry and when you're full, and what foods satisfy you. So mix it up and get a range of nutrients in you to keep you alert* and in a good mood. Experiment with food to see which ones make you feel best!"

range *the highest and lowest numbers in a series*
alert *paying attention; wide awake*

3C What Makes Us Happy?

GRAMMAR Phrasal verbs

1 Put the verbs into the correct categories.

belong to	bring back	carry out (do)
deal with	eat out	go in
keep up	look around	pick up
put on (music)	sit down	take off (clothing)
wake up	write down	

Separable	Inseparable

2 Complete the second sentence so that it means the same as the first. Use three words or fewer in each blank.

1 He brought the book back to the library.
He ________________ the book to the library.

2 She wrote her information on the application.
She ________________ her information on the application.

3 He filled out the form and gave it to the teacher.
He filled out the form and ________________.

4 She took off her hat.
She ________________ off.

5 Please pass on the book after you read it.
Please ________________ the book ________________ after you read it.

6 Did you pick the coffee up on your way to work?
Did you ________________ the coffee on your way to work?

7 I turned down the TV after my neighbor said it was too loud.
I ________________ the TV ________________ after my neighbor said it was too loud.

3 Choose the correct words to complete the sentences.

1 I handed it _____ already.
a in
b on
c with

2 How many times did you work _____ at the gym last week?
a with
b up
c out

3 I wrote his name and phone number _____.
a into
b about
c down

4 Please bring it _____ by Friday.
a back
b out
c down

5 He looked _____ moving to Brazil.
a back
b into
c off

6 I give _____! I just can't do it.
a up
b on
c with

7 I was turning _____ the lights when my friend Luiz walked into the room.
a back
b on
c out

8 Let's put the movie _____ after we eat dinner.
a on
b out
c into

4 Match the first and second part of each sentence.

1 You can't give ____
2 Did you hand ____
3 They're looking ____
4 Did he put ____
5 He's dealing ____
6 Please take ____
7 Were you hanging ____
8 Remember to turn ____

a out at the movies last weekend?
b on the oven 30 minutes before you put in the pizza.
c in your assignment on time?
d up—just keep trying!
e into getting someone to help around the house.
f with a lot of problems at work.
g on his new suit before the interview?
h out the trash before you leave.

5 Complete the sentences with the correct words.

deal with	get along with	get on
give up	hang out	look after
put on	work out	

1 Hurry! ____________ the train before it leaves.
2 Dina ____________ her roommate.
3 Francis likes to ____________ at the beach every Saturday.
4 She ____________ her sister before their mom gets home from work.
5 How do you ____________ the stress of working and going to school?
6 I told him he needs to ____________ smoking.
7 Let's go to the gym and ____________ today.
8 I was ____________ my jacket when the phone rang.

6 Read the incorrect sentences. Then write the correct sentences.

1 I picked my friend from the train station up.
____
2 Let's hang into Gina and Ruby on Friday.
____
3 Rae deals her pain with by doing yoga.
____
4 Suneeta is looking in her neighbor's cat while he's on vacation.
____
5 Please down sit.
____
6 My mom left a voicemail message for me, so back her I called.
____
7 He spoke with the need to eat well and exercise.
____

7 Re-order the words to make sentences.

1 on / she / earrings / put / favorite / her
____
2 TV / turned /on / I / the
____
3 along / roommate / get / new / I / my / with
____
4 too / he / easily / up / gave
____
5 while / I / out / with / my / brother / was / he / studied / hanging
____
6 looking / car / she / was / new / buying / into / a
____
7 I / out / yesterday / worked
____
8 to / remember / trash / the / out / take
____

8 Listen and choose the correct response. 32

1 **a** Yes, I wrote down his number.
b Yes, I wrote his down number.

2 **a** We looked around the Opera House.
b We looked the Opera House around.

3 **a** He grew with in New York.
b He grew up in New York.

4 **a** Yes, I need to lie down and rest.
b Yes, I need to lie off and rest.

5 **a** She woke at 7:30 up.
b She woke up at 7:30.

6 **a** Let's eat out at the new Italian restaurant.
b Let's eat about at the new Italian restaurant.

7 **a** Yes, I filled in all the information.
b Yes, I filled all in the information.

8 **a** Sure. I'll turn it down now.
b Sure. I'll turn down it now.

3D The Amazing Story of the Man Who Gave Us Modern Pain Relief

TEDTALKS

AUTHENTIC LISTENING SKILLS

1 Complete the sentences.

1 The *lion tamer / wire-walker* had an emergency during an act.
2 John J. Bonica didn't tell anyone that he *was a medical student / worked for the army.*
3 John spoke to *patients / doctors* to do research on pain.
4 John read *7,700 / 14,000* pages of medical textbooks. He found that the word "pain" appeared on *17.5 / 27* pages.
5 John wanted doctors to *understand pain / be more careful with surgeries.*
6 Hundreds of *pain clinics / hospitals* opened because of John's work.

WATCH

2 Put the events in order.

_____ John writes the "Bible of Pain."
_____ The circus arrives to Brookfield, New York.
_____ John goes to Madigan Army Medical Center.
_____ There is an announcement that a doctor is needed.
_____ John gives the lion tamer mouth-to-mouth.
_____ John speaks to specialists and reads every medical textbook he can.

3 Underline the things that are true about John J. Bonica.

He used other names like Masked Marvel and Bull Walker.
He was a lion tamer.
He worked at a circus.
He had two jobs while he was in the circus.
He wrote a book about the circus.
He wanted to help patients feel better.

4 Complete each sentence about the talk with the correct word or short phrase. 33

1 The strongman _______________ the lion tamer's life.
2 The strongman kept _______________ from the other people to protect himself.
3 The same year, he was crowned the Light Heavyweight Champion _______________.
4 Over the years, John had two jobs. He was a wrestler and _______________.
5 John was _______________ of all pain control in one of the largest army hospitals in America.
6 _______________ had ever focused on pain like John had.
7 For the next _______________ John would talk about pain.
8 The _______________ wasn't to make patients better; it was to make patients to feel better.

VOCABULARY IN CONTEXT

5 Choose the correct meaning for the words in bold.

1 Alison **passed out** and fell to the ground after running ten miles.
   a stopped being awake
   b kept going
   c felt well
2 Mr. Chen is **a specialist** who takes care of people with cancer.
   a a teacher
   b an expert
   c a writer
3 Louisa has three tests tomorrow, so she has to **hit the books** tonight.
   a borrow books from the library
   b study
   c hit books so they get softer
4 Edwin wants to create **an institution** that helps people with their pain.
   a an organization
   b a company
   c a website
5 My mom and dad **take** lies **seriously**. They don't get as mad about other things, but lying is not OK.
   a see as important
   b understand
   c don't know how to joke
6 Jisuk could not **ignore** the pain of others. She decided to become a doctor.
   a not see
   b not think about
   c look at carefully

6 Bonica's contributions to science have helped millions of people live more comfortable lives. Can you give an example of someone in your life who has benefited from his work?

3E Opinions About Health and Happiness

SPEAKING

1 Put the phrases in the correct categories. Then listen and check your answers. 34

Are you kidding?
I believe...
I think...
In my opinion...
Sorry, but I don't think so.
Why do you say that?
Could you explain that a bit more?
I don't agree.
I'm not sure about that.
Really?
Well, that's true...
You're right that...

Saying what you think	Disagreeing
Asking follow-up questions	**Conceding a point**

2 Use the phrases from Activity 1 to complete this conversation between two friends.

A: It's so depressing, there are so many people getting sick these days because they don't do enough exercise.
B: I know. And they say that getting more exercise actually makes you happier.
A: (1) ________________ everyone should have to do two hours of exercise every week. It should be the law.
B: (2) ________________. I think that's a bit extreme.
A: (3) ________________. The health system spends lots of money treating illnesses, when people could stop some problems by doing regular exercise.
B: (4) ________________ my grandad's 85 and since he swims every day, he's a lot healthier than my other grandparents. But (5) ________________, you can't make people do exercise.
A: (6) ________________.
B: Well, (7) ________________ exercise is good for us, but it's not that simple. The reason some people may not enjoy exercise is that it actually causes them pain, and anyway, not everyone has enough time to exercise. Some people have really busy lives and have family to take care of.
A: (8) ________________. Exercise reduces the risk of lots of diseases and lowers stress so (9) ________________ people should make time to do this. It's their responsibility to stay healthy.
B: (10) ________________. I think it's each person's choice if they want to do exercise. There are other ways to stay healthy.
A: (11) ________________.
B: Well, people can eat healthy food, and not smoke or drink alcohol. Some people also take vitamins and do meditation, things like that.
A: (12) ________________. These things may help a little, but it's not the same as doing exercise to keep your body fit and working.
B: Maybe, but I don't think you can make a law telling people they have to exercise.

3 Match the statements with their replies.

1 Teenagers are under more and more pressure from their friends these days. ___
2 Students have too much stress from school. ___
3 If you get sick in the jungle you're going to die. ___
4 It would be great not to feel any pain. ___
5 Teenagers don't have very healthy diets. ___
6 The way to stay thin is to eat less. ___
7 Smartphones are really bad for your health. ___
8 I believe the best way to stay healthy is to exercise every day. ___

a **Are you kidding?** That's what stops us from getting more serious injuries.
b **I don't agree.** Your body needs a good supply of healthy food and some regular exercise.
c **I'm not sure about that.** Emergency health services can help you in most places.
d **In my opinion,** junk food should be banned from school cafeterias.
e **Really?** I think being happy is just as important for your health as exercise.
f **Sorry, but I don't think so.** People just worry about the effects of new technology.
g **Well, that's true.** Students don't have enough time to relax these days.
h Yes, **I think** social media makes the problem worse.

4 You will hear three questions. Listen to each question and make notes about how you would answer it. Speak for at least one minute and record yourself. Then listen to the sample answer. 35

Now listen to a sample response. 36

WRITING An opinion essay

1 Re-order the words to make sentences.

1 fast food / I think / convenient / While it's / that / is unhealthy, / true / very / it's

____

____

2 easier / believe that / understand / should / to / I / food labels / be

____

____

3 health care / opinion, / smokers / my / In / should / get / any / not

____

____

4 acceptable / sometimes / food / For / is / junk / me,

____

____

5 think this / us / I / reason / jealous / is / makes / that / One / social media

____

____

6 because / don't / too / exercise / expensive / We / gym membership / is

____

____

2 Choose the correct options to complete the opinion essay.

Agree or disagree: Everyone should be forced to do one gym class every day

One reason I think this is / While it's true that joining gym classes is a good way to get exercise and stay healthy, *I think / because* forcing people to do it is a bad idea.

For me, / One reason I think this is that we are less likely to do things we don't enjoy. So it's a bad idea *because / in my opinion* people stop enjoying anything they are forced to do. *I believe / For me,* that everyone should be encouraged to go to the gym, but not forced. Whatever people do to stay healthy should be their own choice.

Second, *because / in my opinion*, many of us already exercise and stay healthy without going to the gym. For example, some people walk or cycle to school or work.

While it's true that / For me, hiking in the countryside or swimming is how I get exercise. It's healthy… and it's fun!

It doesn't matter how people exercise as long as they try to do some physical activity most days. Forcing everyone to go to daily gym classes will not work.

3 Read the opinion essay in Activity 2 again. Do the statements match the information in the text? Are they true (T), false (F), or not given (NG)?

1 The writer mainly disagrees with the statement. _____
2 The writer doesn't feel that getting exercise is important. _____
3 The writer thinks people should enjoy getting exercise. _____
4 The writer believes the gym is the best place to get exercise. _____
5 The writer exercises and is overweight. _____
6 Overall, the writer feels it's best if people have a choice. _____

4 In this writing activity you will read a statement and write a response to it. In your written response, give your opinion and reasons and examples to support it.

We would be healthier if we stopped eating meat.

To support your answer, use specific reasons and the expressions you learned in this unit.

Acknowledging other ideas:
While it's true that…, I think…

Giving your opinion:
I believe…
In my opinion, …
For me, …

Giving reasons for your opinion:
One reason I think this is…
… because…

Review

1 Choose the word that doesn't belong with the others.

1 mouth	ear	nose	knee
2 throat	elbow	hand	finger
3 stomachache	seasickness	happiness	high temperature
4 well	unwell	healthy	fine
5 doctor	virus	dentist	patient
6 feet	chest	arm	eyeglasses

2 Read the descriptions of some parts of the body. What is the word for each one? The first letter is already provided.

1 It's the part of your leg that bends. k ___ ___ ___

2 It's the part of your arm that bends. e ___ ___ ___ ___

3 Dogs and cats have four of these, but birds and people have only two. l ___ ___ ___

4 Your toes are part of these. f ___ ___ ___

5 You have ten of these on your hands. f ___ ___ ___ ___ ___ ___

6 You can hurt this if you fall or if you lift something very heavy. b ___ ___ ___

7 These are at the top of your arms, on either side of your neck. s ___ ___ ___ ___ ___ ___ ___ ___

8 It's where your food goes. s ___ ___ ___ ___ ___ ___

3 Complete the text with the correct quantifiers. There may be more than one correct answer for some items.

Infected mosquitos make (1) ________________ people sick with malaria. (2) ________________ people get sick from malaria? In 2015, about 210 million people in 91 countries were sick with malaria, and 400,000 people with malaria died. (3) ________________ of the symptoms of malaria are fever, joint pain, and headaches.

To protect against malaria, (4) ________________ people hang mosquito nets over their beds. This keeps (5) ________________ of the mosquitos away. Since 2000, UNICEF (United Nations International Children's Emergency Fund) has given out almost 1 billion nets in (6) ________________ countries.

With medicine, (7) ________________ people with malaria can get better. Organizations like Medecins Sans Frontieres (Doctors Without Borders) provide treatment to (8) ________________ people with malaria. In 2015, Medecins Sans Frontieres treated 2.2 million cases of malaria.

4 Complete the sentences with the correct quantifier and words. Some sentences have two correct answers.

bring back	pick up	put on	sit down
spoke about	turn in	wrote down	

1 I ________________ ________________ notes during class.

2 ________________ assignments did you ________________ last week?

3 Do you want to ________________ ________________ music ________________?

4 Did you ________________ ________________ dinner ________________ with you?

5 ________________ food did you ________________ on your way home?

6 ________________ people at the meeting ________________ the need for a new gym.

7 ________________ times a day do you ________________ to check your email?

5 Circle the verb phrase which <u>cannot</u> be separated.

1 look around / call back / keep up

2 write down / speak about / take off

3 turn down / look after / take up

4 deal with / fill in / pass on

5 put on / bring back / complain of

6 grow up / write down / hand in

4 Learning

4A How We Learn

VOCABULARY Education

1 Review Label the photos with the correct words.

classroom dictionary homework library map teacher university

1 ______________

2 ______________

3 ______________

4 ______________

5 ______________

6 ______________

7 ______________

2 Review Choose the correct words to complete the sentences.

1 My favorite *class / classroom* is Spanish. Today's *lesson / teach* was about the past tense.
2 When I don't understand a word, I look it up in my English-Spanish *map / dictionary*.
3 I always *teach / pass* all of my courses. I work hard because I don't want to *fail / take*.
4 My classes start at 7:30am. I have to take the *books / school bus* at 7:00. Sometimes it's late, but usually I am the one who is late!
5 My classes end at 2:15pm, but in the evening I have a lot of *maps / homework* to do.
6 There are a lot of books at our school *library / university*.
7 My mother *fails / teaches* Chinese classes at the *dictionary / university*.

3 Add vowels to complete the words related to school.

1 b__ cr__ __t__v__
2 h__rd-w__rk__ng
3 __l__m__nt__ry sch__ __l
4 n__t__b__ __k
5 d__v__l__p sk__lls
6 __n __d__c__t__ __n
7 __nl__n__ l__ __rn__ng

4 Match the words or phrases to their definitions.

1 what students write in ____
2 to go to classes ____
3 to become good at something ____
4 to have new, interesting ideas ____
5 to do and study a lot ____
6 piece of furniture students sit at ____
7 learning ____
8 internet-based classes ____
9 what you get in a class to show how you did ____

a desk
b be creative
c notebook
d online learning
e attend school
f be hard-working
g develop a skill
h grade
i education

5 Read the sentences. Complete the words.

1 It's important to get an e______________. At school, children learn and develop s______________ they will need in life, like reading and math.
2 In developed countries, most children a______________ school during the day. Younger kids go to e______________ school, and older kids go to h______________ school.
3 In a typical classroom, students sit at d______________ and the teacher stands in front and writes on a b______________.
4 The government pays for p______________ schools, so all children can go there. Some parents choose to pay to send their children to p______________ schools. These can be very expensive.

5 Class s__________ can vary a lot. There may be only three or four students in a class, or there may be 30–40! It depends on the area and the school.
6 School is usually fun for younger students, but as they get older, it gets more difficult. They start to worry about taking t__________ and getting good g__________.

6 Complete the text with the correct words.

attend	classes	creative	desks
develop	education (x2)	elementary	online learning
public	students	study	teacher

In rural Bangladesh, heavy rains make it hard for many children to (1) __________ school. An organization called Shidhulai Swanirvar Sangstha found a (2) __________ solution to this problem: Floating (3) __________ schools! Twenty boats pick up children near their homes, then they stop and (4) __________ begin. So the boats are both school buses *and* classrooms! Inside, there are (5) __________ and chairs for the (6) __________, and a board for the (7) __________ to write on. There are also computers with internet for (8) __________. The children (9) __________ for three hours on the boats, then they go home and work on their homework.

Some of their parents go to the floating schools, too. There are seven boats for adult (10) __________. In the classrooms, the men and women (11) __________ skills for farming and good health. The schools for both the children and the adults are (12) __________ they don't have to pay for their (13) __________.

7 **Extension** Write the subjects in the correct categories.

algebra	biology	chemistry	drama club
geography	geometry	history	orchestra
physics	sports		

Science: __________

Math: __________

Social studies: __________

After-school activities: __________

8 **Extension** Write the class or club that each person belongs in.

algebra	ancient history	band	biology
chemistry	drama club	orchestra	social studies
sports team			

1 I'm interested in plants and animals. __________
2 I like reading about people who lived a very long time ago. __________
3 I play soccer and tennis. __________
4 I want to be a theater actor, or maybe be in movies. __________
5 I'm learning to play the guitar. I love pop and rock music. __________
6 I want to learn about other cultures and the world we live in. __________
7 I enjoy finding out what things are made of. I also like doing interesting experiments! __________
8 I'm good with numbers, but I'd like to develop my skills more. __________
9 I play the violin. I love Mozart and Beethoven. __________

PRONUNCIATION

9 Listen and underline the stressed word. 37

1. Saruka is hopeful about attending college in Kyoto next year.
2. The test was stressful because I didn't study for it.
3. Alex was thankful his teacher allowed extra time to complete the assignment.
4. Haru didn't get a good grade on the math test because he made careless mistakes.
5. Maria thinks computers are a useful way to learn.

LISTENING

10 Listen and choose the subject that each speaker talks about. 38

1 **a** history
b geography
c art

2 **a** computer science
b art history
c foreign language

3 **a** science
b geography
c history

4 **a** math
b gym
c science

5 **a** math
b computer science
c foreign language

6 **a** music
b gym
c math

11 Listen and choose the best title for the talk. 29

1 **a** Remote education
b Online classes
c Distance learning
d Modern technology

12 Listen to the speaker again and answer the questions. 39

1 How many other names does the speaker use for distance learning?
a 1 **b** 2 **c** 3

2 What does the speaker say makes online learning possible?
a the internet and computers
b colleges and universities
c teachers and students

3 What adjective does the speaker use for areas that are distant and isolated?
a faraway **b** remote **c** secluded

4 What does the *e* in *e-learning* stand for?
a everybody **b** electronic **c** everything

5 What is one reason the speaker gives for people not choosing e-learning?
a wanting to be with other students
b fear of being with others
c frustration with technology

6 What is another word for *choices* that the author uses?
a opinions **b** opportunities **c** options

13 Listen and complete the sentences. 40

1. Online learning is a lot ____________ for me than attending a college.
2. Technology is ____________ for me. I prefer to be in a classroom.
3. My online classes are ____________ expensive than attending a university.
4. Learning with others is ____________ interesting than studying alone.
5. I think distance education is clearly the ____________ way to learn.
6. I'm happy that people have lots of ____________ these days.

GRAMMAR Comparatives and superlatives

14 **Complete the sentences with the correct form of the adjective in parentheses.**

1 If I had a ________________ (big) desk, I could see my notes and my books at the same time.
2 If my chair were ________________ (comfortable), I wouldn't need to stand up so often.
3 My eyes wouldn't hurt when I read if my lamp were ________________ (bright).
4 I can use several programs at the same time with a ________________ (good) computer.
5 If our teacher chose ________________ (interesting) books, reading would be more fun.
6 I need a ________________ (new) notebook because this one is almost full!
7 I'm going to ask my friends to recommend some ________________ (cool) music to listen to when I study.
8 I asked for a ________________ (expensive) laptop because I need more storage space.

15 **Complete the sentences with the correct comparative form of the adverbs.**

attentively	clearly	early	hard
often	regularly	well	

1 How should I change my study habits to do ________________ in school?
2 I need to study ________________ so I can get better grades.
3 If I do my homework ________________, I wouldn't have to study so much before tests.
4 I could ask the teacher to explain things I don't understand if I read the textbook ________________.
5 I know I need to listen to my teachers ________________.
6 I should write ________________ so I can read my notes and study from them later.
7 I would do better on tests if I started studying for them ________________.

16 **Put the words in the correct order to make correct sentences.**

1 the best / in the whole city / is / school / our school
____
2 nicer / and bigger / than / the other schools / near here / is / the building
____
3 than / are / better / teachers in / other schools / our teachers
____
4 place / in the school / the library / the quietest / is
____
5 has / computers / our / computer lab / the fastest
____
6 the other / than / classes / is / my class / smarter
____
7 because we / learning / we study / than / harder / like / other classes
____
8 also have / soccer team / we / best / the
____

17 **Write questions using the correct superlative forms of the words in bold.**

1 **A:** what / **old** / university in the world?
____
B: The University of Karueein (also known as Al Quaraouiyine University) in Morocco started in 859.

2 **A:** what country / **large** / number of students?
____
B: According to the 2011 census, there are 315 million students in India, which has a population of 1.3 billion people.

3 **A:** where / **big** / school in the world?
____
B: In India. The Lucknow City Montessori School in Uttar Pradesh has 2,500 teachers who teach more than 52,000 students in 1,000 classrooms.

4 **A:** how large / **small** / school in the world?
____
B: A school in Turin, Italy, has just one student.

5 **A:** who / **old** / high school graduate in the US?
____
B: Fred Butler was 106 years old when he graduated from high school.

6 **A:** who / **young** / high school graduate in the US?
____
B: Michael Kearney graduated from high school when he was six years old! He graduated from college when he was eight!

7 **A:** where / students / **long** and **short** / summer vacation?
____
B: In Ethiopia, some schools have 12–15 weeks of summer vacation. In Germany, most students have only six weeks of summer vacation.

8 **A:** where / students / receive / **more** / homework?
____
B: In China, where students have to do more than 14 hours of homework a week!

4B What do you want to know?

VOCABULARY BUILDING

1 Complete the sentences using the word in parentheses in the correct form. Add the suffix *-ful* or *-less*, and make changes to spelling where necessary.

1. Finnish schools believe that studying subjects together is more ____________ (use) than studying them separately.
2. When students work together, they may be more ____________ (care) about what they do than when they work alone.
3. Learning about ____________ (beauty) works of art is part of a complete education.
4. Working together in groups can help students become more ____________ (skill) learners.
5. Working with a group is a good way to avoid making ____________ (care) mistakes.

READING

2 Choose the correct answers.

1 According to paragraph 1, which of the following is true of Finnish schools?
   a Students only learn about their favorite subjects.
   b Finnish schools don't teach history and geography.
   c Students learn about different subjects at the same time.
   d Students work in cafes.

2 Which TWO of these points about Finnish schools does the writer make?
   a Working in groups is a good way to be exposed to many different points of view.
   b Some students prefer to study science rather than geography or history.
   c Studying topics, as opposed to subjects, is a useful way to learn.
   d Finnish students study math, art, and history.

3 According to paragraph 3, how is Finland making changes to learning environments?
   a by creating courses about World War II
   b by encouraging students to work in groups
   c by building new school buildings without separate classrooms or hallways
   d by preparing students for jobs in the future

4 According to the article, what do students learn by studying topics instead of subjects?
   a They learn how to look for a job.
   b They study the history of wars, including World Wars I and II.
   c They develop the skills needed to work in a restaurant.
   d They learn to share information and apply skills to a variety of tasks.

5 In the article as a whole, the writer appears to feel that
   a schools should have separate classrooms and hallways.
   b recent changes in Finnish education are good for students.
   c some students prefer to work alone and not in groups.
   d most Finnish teachers usually work very long days.

3 Which phrase completes each sentence? Write the letter.

a working together is the best
b isn't as useful as studying
c students in Finland study some
d students need to be able to

1. According to the article, _____ subjects together.
2. Rather than study subjects on their own, _____ way to learn.
3. Working in groups, _____ work together successfully.
4. Studying one subject at a time _____ them together.

4 The article has four paragraphs. Match the headings to the paragraphs.

a The advantages of working together
b Schools that make a difference
c Finland's new approach to education
d Giving students the skills to succeed

Paragraph 1 _____
Paragraph 2 _____
Paragraph 3 _____
Paragraph 4 _____

What do you want to know? 41

1 What's your favorite school subject? Do you love math? Does English interest you? Are you not as excited about art as you are about music? Or are you more of a science buff*? We all have favorite subjects, but what if, instead of learning about each subject separately, you studied two or more together? That's exactly how some students in Finland are learning.

2 When students learn about topics such as world events, they study several subjects together. For example, in a course about World War II, the students study history, geography, and math. Learning about topics, not just one subject, helps students see several points of view. In another course,* called "Working in a Cafe," students study English language, communication skills, and economics. In courses like this, students use many skills as they are learning.

3 Finnish educators* believe that students learn better when they work in small groups to solve problems. Working together is a very useful skill that helps students develop their ability to communicate. At this point, students in Finland don't spend their whole school day working in groups. They still attend "regular" classes and study some subjects separately. But Finland is serious about making changes to the school day and to how students learn. The country has already built several new school buildings that don't have separate classrooms or hallways.

4 Finnish schools are making this change because many educators there believe that working together to study topics is the best way to learn. They believe that working alone and studying only one subject at a time is not the best way to learn. They feel that students who work together with teachers and other students to choose and study topics they care about are better learners. They also feel that students who learn in this way are better prepared for jobs, once they've completed their education.

buff *a fan; someone who likes something a lot*
course *class*
educators *teachers and school directors*

4C How much fun is it?

GRAMMAR Comparative forms

1 Complete the sentences below with *so* or *such*.

1 Computer skills are ____________ important for students.
2 There is ____________ a need for computers in every classroom.
3 The book was ____________ interesting Airi read it in one day!
4 Tomas is ____________ a talented writer. Do you read his blog?
5 That test was ____________ easy!
6 The English exam was ____________ challenging.
7 We saw ____________ a fun play on Friday night.

2 Listen and complete the sentences. 42

1 Victor hopes the essay he wrote is ____________. It's 200 words.
2 Grammar is ____________ vocabulary for me.
3 Studying for your exams is ____________ doing your homework.
4 I thought our assignment was ____________.
5 The classroom wasn't ____________ for 14 students.
6 My classmate decided the study group wasn't ____________ for her to attend.
7 Watching movies in English is ____________!
8 I watched ____________ film last weekend.

3 Choose the correct options to complete the sentences.

1 Playing soccer **isn't as fun as** swimming.
The phrase *isn't as... as* ____.
a shows that the quality described by an adjective is more than wanted or needed
b compares things and says how they are similar or different
c makes the adjective stronger

2 My soup was **not hot enough,** so I sent it back.
The phrase *not... enough* ____.
a shows that the quality described by an adjective is more than wanted or needed
b says that the quality described by the adjective is the right amount
c says that the quality described by the adjective is less than the right amount

3 Tom has **such a great** car.
The word *such* ____.
a shows that the quality described by an adjective is more than wanted or needed
b compares things and says how they are similar or different
c makes the adjective stronger

4 His score was **high enough** to earn him an award.
The word *enough* ____.
a shows that the quality described by an adjective is more than wanted or needed
b says that the quality described by the adjective is the right amount
c says that the quality described by the adjective is less than the right amount

5 I love that book! It's **so interesting**.
The word *so* ____.
a shows that the quality described by an adjective is more than wanted or needed
b compares things and says how they are similar or different
c makes the adjective stronger

6 This shirt is **too big** for me.
The word *too* ____.
a shows that the quality described by an adjective is more than wanted or needed
b compares things and says how they are similar or different
c makes the adjective stronger

4 Are the words in bold correct or incorrect? Write the correct words if they're incorrect.

1 It is **such cold** today. ____________
2 Chen isn't **as old enough** his brother. ____________
3 The wifi in this cafe is **so bad**. ____________
4 The train is **enough fast** to get us to Granada by 4:00. ____________
5 This is **such a slow bus**. I don't think we'll get to class on time. ____________
6 The bus was **enough slow**—we didn't get to class on time. ____________
7 Is it **hot such** to go swimming today? ____________
8 My math class has three students in it. It **isn't as big as** my English class. ____________

5 Which choice is closest in meaning to the original sentence?

1 Math is as easy as history.
 a Math is easy and history is easy.
 b History is not as challenging as math.

2 My new neighborhood is a lot safer than where I lived last year.
 a My old neighborhood isn't as safe as my new neighborhood.
 b My new neighborhood isn't as safe as my old neighborhood.

3 Lara's car wasn't big enough for us all to ride in.
 a Lara's car was small enough.
 b Lara's car was too small.

4 Antoni's car is noisy. Lila's car is quiet.
 a Antoni's car isn't as quiet as Lila's car.
 b Lila's car isn't as quiet as Antoni's car.

5 I went to Athens, but I was only there for two days. It was a very quick trip!
 a My trip to Athens was quick enough.
 b My trip to Athens was so quick.

6 Katya thinks studying is as important as working to make money.
 a Katya thinks studying is important enough.
 b Katya thinks studying is important. She also thinks making money is important.

7 I wasn't old enough to go see that movie.
 a I was too young to see that movie.
 b I was so young to see that movie.

8 It is very challenging to climb Mt. Everest.
 a Mt. Everest is such a challenging mountain to climb.
 b Mt. Everest is challenging enough to climb.

6 Complete the second sentence so that it means the same as the first. Use no more than three words in each space.

1 I thought the exam was very stressful.
 I thought the exam was ________________ stressful.

2 That coffee was awful!
 That was ________________ bad coffee.

3 I am 17 years old, and my friend Zach is 17 years old.
 I am ________________ Zach.

4 Wei is very popular, but his friend Kwan is not.
 Kwan ________________ as Wei.

5 I really loved that book!
 That book was ________________ good!

6 I needed to get to the theater by 8:00 to get a good seat; I got there at 7:50.
 I got to the theater early ________________.

7 I gave up because I was afraid.
 I gave up because I wasn't ________________.

7 Put the words in the correct order to make sentences.

1 was / cool / the / to / drink / enough / tea

____

2 the / too / were / hot / peppers

____

3 we / enough / to / have / a / salad / vegetables / make

____

4 there / people / were / to / class / play / the / game / in / enough

____

5 my / tomorrow / is / at / the / important / school / interview / so

____

6 teacher / us / our / easy / gave / an / such / assignment

____

7 as / Josh / father / is / as / his / tall

____

8 can / as / I / run / as / can / fast / Leo

____

8 Choose the correct words to complete the sentences.

1 My tea was too hot, so
 a I didn't drink it.
 b I heated it up.

2 The birthday cake was so good, so
 a I didn't have any.
 b I ate two pieces.

3 He wasn't serious enough when he practiced for the competition, so
 a he came in last place.
 b he came in first place.

4 The chemistry course wasn't challenging enough for me, so
 a I took a different class.
 b I got a bad grade.

5 She doesn't think watching TV is as interesting as seeing films, so
 a she went to see a film.
 b she stayed home and watched TV.

6 I had enough money to buy my mom a really nice birthday present, so
 a my mom was sad and didn't like her present.
 b my mom loved her present and was really happy.

7 The trip took such a long time, so
 a we got there late at night and were really tired.
 b we got there really quickly and had a lot of time to hang out before bed.

4D Don't Eat the Marshmallow!

TEDTALKS

AUTHENTIC LISTENING SKILLS

1 **Listen to the TED Talk. Choose the correct words to complete the sentences.** 43

1 In the US research, *one out of three / two out of three* children ate the marshmallow.
2 *One out of three / Two out of three* children did other things, like walking around.
3 *A great percentage / A few* of the children who ate the marshmallows were in trouble years later.
4 In Colombia, *one out of three / two out of three* ate the marshmallow.
5 Joachim made *one / two* marshmallow book(s) for children in Korea.

WATCH

2 **Choose the correct answers.**

1 Who started the first research?
  a Joachim de Posada
  b a group of children
  c a professor at Stanford
2 How long did the children have to wait in the room?
  a four minutes
  b fifteen minutes
  c two hours
3 What did the children get if they waited?
  a one more marshmallow
  b two more marshmallows
  c coffee
4 What does Joachim de Posada say is the most important factor for success?
  a being able to control yourself
  b knowing how to get more of what you want
  c asking for a better opportunity or deal
5 What did Joachim want to find out in Colombia?
  a if Hispanic children liked marshmallows
  b if Hispanic children acted differently than American children
  c if the first research was correct
6 Why does Joachim think the research is so important?
  a People are eating too many sweets like marshmallows.
  b People should teach their children to stop eating sweets.
  c People are using more than they are giving back.

3 **Match the words to the correct paraphrased line.**

1 principle
2 question
3 experiment
4 message
5 factor

a I'm here because I have **something very important to say**.
b I think we have found the most important **reason** for success.
c The children already, at four, understood the most important **rule** for success.
d I have **something I want to ask**...
e I did the same **test** in Colombia.

4 **Underline the things that are true about the children who did not eat the marshmallows.**

They knew how to wait.
They grew up to be successful.
They did not like marshmallows.
They did not make it to university.
They had good grades.
They were in trouble.
They had good eating habits.

VOCABULARY IN CONTEXT

5 **Listen and complete each sentence with the correct word or short phrase.** 44

1 What did they find? They went to look for these kids who were now 18 and 19. And they found that ________________ of the children that had not eaten the marshmallow were successful.
2 A great percentage of the kids that ate the marshmallow, they ________________.
3 They did not ________________ university. They had bad grades. Some of them dropped out.
4 This little girl was interesting; she ate the inside of the marshmallow. ________________, she wanted us to think that she had not eaten it, so she would get two. But she ate it.
5 She should not ________________ banking, for example, or work at a cash register. But she will be successful.
6 We are eating more marshmallows than we are ________________. Thank you so much.

4E It's Such a Cool Subject

SPEAKING

1 Read the conversation and complete the sentences with the correct phrases. Then listen to the conversation and check your answers. 45

is the best choice	isn't as useful as this
isn't it expensive	look the most useful
looks more exciting	more interesting
think it's useful enough (x2)	too boring

A: Hey, I'm looking for an app to practice my English with, do you know any?
B: That's a good idea. I've never thought of that. Which ones (1) ______________________?
A: Well, there's this one here, which has flash cards and some grammar exercises, and it's free.
B: Is it (2) ______________________, maybe?
A: I don't know, it's for school anyway, but do you (3) ______________________?
B: Well, you get what you pay for. What about that one, with the star logo?
A: That looks (4) ______________________. There are things to read and listen to.
B: And there are some collocation activities for vocabulary too.
A: Excellent! Teachers always tell us to practice them. We'll be awesome.
B: Yeah, that first one (5) ______________________.
A: Are there any more?
B: I had a look and there's this one. It (6) ______________________, with lots of games to play with words and grammar.
A: Let's see. Oh yeah, but (7) ______________________?
B: Well, it is a little. Do you (8) ______________________ to pay for?
A: I'm not sure. I guess you have to pay to find out.
B: Yeah. I think the star one (9) ______________________.

2 You are writing an article for the school website about things students like and dislike about the school.

Think about the three different people described below and make notes about their answers to the questions. Then listen to the sample answers to compare your ideas. 46

1 What's the most fun thing about being at this school?
2 Which subjects are the most interesting?
3 Do you think that school is useful enough for your future?

- A student in the first year at the school, who is quite lazy.
- A student in their last year at school, who is captain of the soccer team.
- A student in the middle year at school, who plans to go to college.

3 Listen and follow the instructions. 47

Listen to the sample answer. 48

WRITING

1 Choose the correct answers to the questions.

1 What greeting would you use in an email to someone you don't know?
   a Dear Evening Class Coordinator,
   b Hi Evening Class Coordinator,

2 How would you say how you know about the course?
   a I'm really interested in this course.
   b I saw an ad for this course online.

3 How would you introduce your reason for emailing?
   a I wanted to do a course in printmaking last year.
   b I'm writing because I have a couple of questions.

4 What kind of information would you ask?
   a Are all the materials for the course provided?
   b Do you prefer printmaking or photography?

5 How would you thank the person you are emailing?
   a Thank you in advance for any information.
   b Thanks a lot. I really appreciate your help!

6 What closing expression would you use?
   a See you soon,
   b Yours sincerely,

2 Put the six sections of the email of inquiry in the correct order.

_____ First, is the course suitable for complete beginners? Second, is there a focus on sound editing, or do you mainly cover mixing techniques?
_____ Dario Cafolla
_____ Thanks for any information you can provide. I look forward to hearing from you.
_____ Yours sincerely,
_____ I saw your poster for the five-day music production course when I was at the train station this morning. I'm writing because I'd like some more information.
_____ Dear Sound Studios,

3 Read the email of inquiry. Then choose the correct information for the categories. Two items are not used.

> Dear Sound Studios,
>
> I saw your poster for the five-day music production course when I was at the train station this morning. I'm writing because I'd like some more information.
>
> First, is the course suitable for complete beginners? Second, is there a focus on sound editing, or do you mainly cover mixing techniques?
>
> Thanks for any information you can provide. I look forward to hearing from you.
>
> Yours sincerely,
> Dario Cafolla

Dario Cafolla	five days	formal
informal	music production	sound editing
Sound Studios	train station	

1 Course venue: __________
2 Course title: __________
3 Length of course: __________
4 Question: __________
5 Sender: __________
6 Tone of email: __________

4 Read the email of inquiry. Find and correct six errors in it.

> Dear Happy Language School,
>
> I saw you're ad for the four-week course in Business English on your website. I'd like to ask about a couple of things.
>
> First, what is the language level of most students who take this course? First, is your Certificate of Achievement recognized by industry professionals!
>
> Thanks for any informations you can give me. I look forward to hearing for you.
>
> Your sincerely,
> Joan Cho

5 This is part of an ad for a course you have seen online.

> **Introduction to Lead Guitar**
> Experienced instructor gives group lessons every Monday, 6pm to 8pm. Efficient teaching method. Useful exercises, techniques, and tips. Contact *Guitar Experts Inc.* at info@GEI.com.

Now, write an email of inquiry to the course directors. Say:

- where you saw the course advertised, and why you are emailing
- ask about the style of music taught, and the cost of a lesson
- use polite language for your greeting, closing statement, and closing expressions

Review

1 A word or phrase is missing in each of the following sentences. Four answer choices are given below each sentence. Choose the correct words to complete the sentences.

1 Teachers give _____ to students to see what they have learned.
a skills
b tests
c grades
d notebooks

2 Teachers give _____ to show students how well they did in the class.
a pens
b education
c grades
d skills

3 For _____, you need a computer, tablet, or smartphone.
a classrooms
b online learning
c public school
d studying math

4 A hard-working student _____.
a sometimes attends school
b never does homework
c gets bad grades
d always studies for tests

2 Look at the scrambled words. Unscramble them and match them to the correct descriptions.

enolni rangilen | melterayne closoh | ontobesko | sksde | upbicl loshosc

1 Students sit here when they study. ____________
2 Students write with pens in these. ____________
3 You need the internet for this. ____________
4 They are free for all students. ____________
5 Classes here are for very young students. ____________

3 Complete the charts with the correct forms of the comparative and superlative adjectives and adverbs.

Adjective	Comparative	Superlative
bad	worse	
old	older	
useful	more useful	
hard-working		the most hard-working
interesting		the most interesting

Adverb	Comparative	Superlative
fast		the fastest
late	later	
hard		the hardest
well	better	
recently	more recently	
slowly		the most slowly

4 Complete the conversation with the correct words.

best | better | important enough | is as important as | isn't as fun as | more useful | so fun | too hard

A: I think swimming is (1) ____________.

B: I think swimming (2) ____________ playing soccer. Soccer is the (3) ____________!

A: I am (4) ____________ at swimming than I am at playing soccer.

B: I think sports are a fun way to stay healthy! But what do you think—is it (5) ____________ to eat well or exercise a lot?

A: Experts say eating well (6) ____________ exercising.

B: Yes, but sometimes it is (7) ____________ to find enough time to exercise.

A: I agree, but exercising is (8) ____________ to make sure you do it every day.

5 Family and Friends

5A The people in my life

VOCABULARY How's it going?

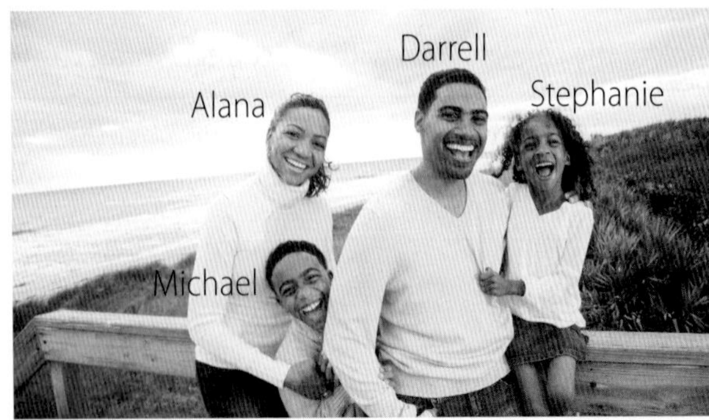

1 Review Look at the picture. Circle the correct words to complete the sentences.

1 They are *friends / a family*.
2 Michael is a *boy / man*.
3 Alana is a *girl / woman*.
4 Alana and Darrell are *married / divorced*.
5 Stephanie is Darrell's *son / daughter*.
6 Darrell is Michael's *father / mother*.
7 Alana and Darrell are Stephanie and Michael's *children / parents*.
8 Darrell is Alana's *wife / husband*.

2 Review Complete the sentences with the correct words.

1 Before people get married, they are s_ _ _ _ _ _.
2 If someone was married but now he's not, he's d_ v _ _ _ _ _ _.
3 Your mother and father are your p_ _ _ _ _ _ _.
4 Boys and girls are c_ _ l _ _ _ _.
5 Fathers are m_ _.
6 Mothers are w_ _ _ _.

3 Put the people into the correct categories.

aunt brother classmate cousin daughter
father friend husband mother sister
son stranger uncle

man / boy	woman / girl	either

4 Match the words to the definitions.

1 aunt
2 uncle
3 partner
4 teammate
5 stranger
6 kiss
7 hug
8 wave

a a person you don't know
b a person you play soccer or baseball with
c touch someone's cheek with your lips
d the brother of your mother or father
e move your hand in the air
f put your arms around someone
g a person you work together with on a project
h the sister of your mother or father

5 Listen. Match to the photos. 49

a

b

c

d

e

f

1 ________
2 ________
3 ________
4 ________
5 ________
6 ________

6 Choose the correct words from the multiple choice items to complete the text. Write the letter of the correct word on the line.

A Big Family

Having a big family can be fun. I have one older (1) _____, and he's not always nice to me, but I also have three younger (2) _____, and we are very close. We live with our parents and my (3) _____, who is my father's mother. Her husband, my (4) _____, died two years ago.

My father was an only child, but my grandparents on my mother's side had two sons and four daughters, which means I have two (5) _____ and three (6) _____.They all had children, too, so I have a lot of (7) _____ on that side of the family.

There are also some other people I think of as part of my family, for example my (8) _____. She comes to my house every weekend and celebrates holidays with us, too. There are also my volleyball (9) _____. We are like a family at school; we're always together and helping each other.

1	**a** sister	**b** father	**c** brother	**d** stranger
2	**a** sisters	**b** parents	**c** aunts	**d** classmates
3	**a** aunt	**b** grandmother	**c** uncle	**d** grandfather
4	**a** aunt	**b** grandmother	**c** uncle	**d** grandfather
5	**a** mothers	**b** cousins	**c** aunts	**d** uncles
6	**a** brothers	**b** grandfathers	**c** aunts	**d** uncles
7	**a** partners	**b** cousins	**c** brothers and sisters	**d** strangers
8	**a** stranger	**b** friend of a friend	**c** best friend	**d** cousin
9	**a** classmates	**b** teammates	**c** strangers	**d** partners

7 Complete the sentences with the correct words.

best friend	partner	say hello	shake
strangers	teammates	wave	

1 When I meet someone for the first time, I smile and ________________ their hand.

2 When I see my friends across the street, I ________________ my hand and ________________.

3 In class, we often have to work with a ________________ on an activity.

4 A lot of people don't enjoy talking to ________________ on the bus or the train, but there are some people who are friendly with everyone!

5 In a basketball game, all of the ________________ must work together to win.

6 Some people don't have just one ________________ but many people who they spend a lot of time with.

8 **Extension** Listen. What is each person's relationship to Rachel, the second speaker? Listen again and circle the answers. 50

1	Dan	brother	stepbrother
2	Steve	stepfather	father-in-law
3	Max	half-brother	stepbrother
4	April	sister-in-law	stepsister
5	Olivia	niece	half-sister
6	Amanda	sister-in-law	half-sister
7	Jared	half-brother	nephew

9 **Extension** Complete the text with the correct words.

brother-in-law	ex-wife	father-in-law
half-brother	half-sister	mother-in-law
nephews	nieces	stepbrothers
stepfather	stepmother	stepsisters

Our families often grow as we do. If you have a sister and she gets married, then you will have a new (1) ________________. If they have children, you will have (2) ________________ and (3) ________________. Then, if you get married, you will have a husband or wife, and his or her mother and father will become your (4) ________________ and (5) ________________.

Or, you might become part of a blended family. When a married couple gets divorced, or someone loses a wife or husband, sometimes they get married again. The man marries a new woman, and his children get a (6) ________________. If his new wife has children, too, then his children will also have new (7) ________________ and (8) ________________. If the father and his new wife have a baby together, this child will be the (9) ________________ or (10) ________________ of the children from the first marriages. If the man's (11) ________________ also marries someone new, then the kids will also have a (12) ________________ and another new family!

PRONUNCIATION

10 Read the sentences aloud and write the pronunciation of the *-ed* verb you hear. Write /d/, /t/, or /ɪd/. Then listen and check your answers. 51

1 I've already selected my outfit for the party. _____
2 I learned how to dance from my father. _____
3 Have you tasted the cake yet? _____
4 My uncle photographed the football team. _____
5 I tried to invite her, but she said no. _____
6 Everyone at the celebration looked great! _____
7 We haven't celebrated yet. _____
8 My aunt was sick so she stayed home. _____

LISTENING

11 Listen to the conversations. Are the statements correct (YES) or incorrect (NO)? Check the boxes. 52

		YES	NO
1	He invited her to the party.	☐	☐
2	She invited him to the celebration.	☐	☐
3	She accepted his invitation.	☐	☐
4	He didn't accept the invitation.	☐	☐
5	She accepted his invitation.	☐	☐
6	She invited everyone to the celebration.	☐	☐

12 Listen to the speaker and complete the text with the correct words. 53

I recently graduated from high school. We had a fantastic (1) __________________ with family and friends. And to be honest, it was both sad and happy for me. Sad because I'm leaving a lot of people that I have (2) __________________ for years. Happy because a whole new period in my life is beginning.

I've been (3) __________________ to three different universities. I haven't decided on one (4) __________________, but they're all good. I feel really lucky. And my parents are really supportive. They want me to follow my dreams. My mother told me that she'll be (5) __________________ of me no matter what I decide to do.

It's impossible to predict the future, but I feel really good about things. I'm (6) __________________, I have a wonderful family, and I feel like almost anything is possible. I'd better stop talking before I get too (7) __________________.

13 Listen to the sentences about each photo. Write the letter (a, b, c, d) of the sentence that best describes the photo. 54

1 _____

2 _____

3 _____

4 _____

GRAMMAR Present perfect and simple past

14 Choose the correct verb forms to complete the exchanges.

1 A: How long *have / had / has* you had your computer?

B: I haven't *has / had / having* it very long—only a year.

2 A: How many books has Ms. Brenner *ask / asks / asked* you to read this semester?

B: She *has / have / had* assigned two books so far.

3 A: *Had / Has / Have* you found your smartphone yet? I know you had it yesterday.

B: No, I *don't have / haven't / haven't had*. I don't know where it is.

4 A: Have you *knows / known / know* your best friend for a long time?

B: Yes, I have. We *had / having / have* been friends since we were ten!

5 A: How many years has our class *studies / study / studied* English? Three? Four?

B: I think we have *has / have / had* English for four years now. We're getting pretty good!

6 A: I have *work / worked / works* at the bookstore since the summer. I really like it.

B: That's awesome! *Has / Had /Have* you thought about working there after you graduate?

15 Rewrite the negative sentences to be affirmative, and the affirmative sentences to be negative.

Example: Marco hasn't finished his homework.
Marco has finished his homework.

1 Celia has seen her parents all day.

____

2 Yuri and Natasha have seen a lot of really good movies.

____

3 Our teacher has given us a lot of homework this weekend.

____

4 My friends have not called yet.

____

16 Complete the text with the present perfect form of the verbs in parentheses.

My family and I like to travel. We (1) ________________ (take) advantage of every chance to travel. Together and separately, we (2) ________________ (visit) some really exciting places. My parents (3) ________________ (be) to Peru many times. They (4) ________________ (see) Machu Picchu and (5) ________________ (hike) the Inca Trail. My brother and I (6) ________________ (go) to Europe a couple of times. We (7) ________________ (kayak) on fjords and (8) ________________ (ski) on glaciers in Scandinavia. And my sister and I (9) ________________ (take) the train from London to Paris.

We (10) ________________ (never, travel) to Japan, so I (11) ________________ (not, eat) "real" sushi, and I (12) ________________ (not, be) able to see the cherry trees in bloom. I (13) ________________ (not, go) to Africa yet either. I (14) ________________ (always, look) forward to going on safari and seeing lions and giraffes.

17 Complete the questions with the correct form of the verbs in parentheses.

1 ________________ you ________________ (ever, read) about people in Lhasa sticking out their tongues? It's a polite greeting there.

2 ________________ they ________________ (not, tell) you about the *mano*? That's where young Filipinos sometimes press the hand of an older person to their own forehead. It's very polite.

3 ________________ you ________________ (not, see) people touching each other's feet in India? It's a greeting called the *pranāma*.

4 ________________ anyone ________________ (do) the *kunik* with you in Greenland? People put their nose and top lip on your cheek and breathe in. It's a special way of greeting someone there.

5 ________________ you ________________ (rub) noses with anyone? For traditional Bedouins, it is a respectful greeting.

6 ________________ you ________________ (hear) people clap to greet each other? That's what the Shona people in southern Africa do.

7 ________________ you ________________ (not, ever, notice) people raising their eyebrows as a greeting? They do that in the Marshall Islands.

8 ________________ you ________________ (not, say) that you went to Niger? Then you probably saw people shaking their fists near their heads and saying "Wooshay!" to greet each other.

5B Going Walkabout

VOCABULARY BUILDING

1 **Complete the sentences. Change the nouns in parentheses to adjectives ending in *-al*.**

1 Going walkabout is an important ________________ tradition among the Yolngu people. (culture)
2 A ________________ walkabout can last for up to six months. (tradition)
3 Going walkabout can be a very ________________ experience for a boy. (emotion)
4 Songs and singing are part of the ________________ aspect of going walkabout. (music)
5 Boys going walkabout are surrounded by ________________ sights and sounds. (nature)

READING

2 **Read the article. Complete the summary with the correct words.**

aboriginal	ancestral	desert
grandfather	skills	tradition

It is a (1) ________________ for some young Australian (2) ________________ boys to go walkabout for up to six months, completely on their own and without supplies. A walkabout is a journey that reminds the boys of similar journeys that they believe their (3) ________________ spirits made thousands of years ago. The boys follow songlines that help them find their way through the Australian (4) ________________. Sometimes, the boys travel part of the walkabout with a male relative, for example, their father or (5) ________________. They need to develop many important (6) ________________ in order to survive the walkabout.

3 **Read each question. Choose the correct answer.**

1 How long have the Yolngu people lived in Australia?
a ten thousand years
b hundreds of years
c over 50,000 years

2 What is the aboriginal term for an invisible pathway that crosses the land?
a song
b songline
c ritual

3 According to the Yolngu, who created the songlines they follow?
a ancestral spirits
b Australians
c outsiders

4 How long does a walkabout last?
a six months
b 12–13 years
c 1,000 days

5 What is the main reason for going walkabout?
a to make maps
b to look for footprints
c to survive alone in the desert

6 Who might teach a Yolngu boy about his ancestral songlines?
a his grandfather
b his sister
c his aunt

4 **Do the statements match the information in the article? Write true (T), false (F), or not given (NG).**

1 The Yolngu are an aboriginal group that has lived in Australia for tens of thousands of years. ___
2 Songlines are pathways that are visible to anyone in the desert. ___
3 The Yolngu believe that ancestral spirits look after the boys while they go walkabout. ___
4 A Yolngu boy usually learns his clan's songlines from his father, grandfather, and other male relatives. ___
5 Yolngu girls learn about their ancestral songlines from their mothers and grandmothers. ___
6 Going walkabout is one way that Yolngu boys demonstrate that they're ready to take on new responsibilities. ___

Going Walkabout 55

1 Imagine waking up in the morning alone, hundreds of miles away from anyone you know, with no supplies, in the middle of a desert. This is what one day of "going walkabout" is like for a young Yolngu, or Australian aboriginal*, boy. The Yolngu have lived in Australia for approximately 60,000 years. In fact, they and other aboriginal people lived on the continent of Australia for tens of thousands of years without seeing people from any other places. The land was theirs. As a result, they respect tradition and have a strong connection to the land.

2 One of their oldest traditions is called "going walkabout" in English. The Yolngu and other aboriginal clans, or family groups, believe that invisible trails, called songlines, cover the land. According to their beliefs, songlines are secret pathways that follow the journeys made by ancestral* spirits as they created the earth. These ancestors sang names for everything that crossed their paths, and, in the process, created and named everything in the world. Aboriginal people consider songlines to be the footprints of their ancestors.

3 Going walkabout is a coming of age event for 12–13-year-old aboriginal boys. When young males go walkabout, they follow the songlines of their ancestors. They sing traditional songs in order to navigate, or find their way, as they walk. And they often walk very far. Some boys travel up to 1,000 miles, without any supplies, in the six months of a typical walkabout! They need to develop important skills in order to make the journey. The goal of going walkabout is to be able to survive alone in the wild just as their ancestors did.

4 Before they go walkabout, boys learn about songlines from the older people in the clan. Some walk parts of their ancestral songlines with their father, grandfather, or another male relative or friend. They learn to use songlines as a kind of map. They use the songs to identify parts of the landscape, such as caves or hills, and to connect to the stories that their ancestors have told for thousands of years.

5 When the boys return from going walkabout, they celebrate with their families and friends. They have made the passage from childhood into the adult world. They have already proven that they can take care of themselves during the six months of going walkabout, and that they're ready for new responsibilities.

aboriginal *the first people in a place*
ancestral *related to people in your family who lived long before you*

5C How long have you been. . .?

GRAMMAR Present perfect with *for, since, already, just,* and *yet*

1 Complete the sentences with the correct words. Some have more than one correct answer.

already | for | since | yet

1 **A:** Do you want to go to the gym with me this afternoon?
B: No, I ________ worked out this morning.
2 He hasn't called his brother ________ last month.
3 Natalie has studied ________ three hours.
4 **A:** Did you hear Aunt Sofia is coming to visit next week?
B: Yes! I ________ heard the news.
5 **A:** Have you started your English homework ________?
B: Actually, I have ________ finished it.
6 **A:** Have you asked your teacher for help ________?
B: No, I haven't asked him ________. I think I'll talk to him tomorrow.
7 Arata has been living with his cousins ________ two years.
8 Yasmin has ________ celebrated her *fiesta de quince años.*

2 Circle the present perfect verbs.

Do you know that humans aren't the only species that has rich social lives and family ties? For example, chimpanzees do as well. How do we know this? Well, have you ever heard of Jane Goodall? She is a scientist who has studied chimpanzees since 1960. She has learned a lot about chimpanzees since then. And she has shared this knowledge with both the scientific community and the rest of the world. For example, Goodall has taught us that not only do chimpanzees have rich social lives and family ties, they also make and use tools. She has set a very high standard for studying apes in the wild and has focused on individual characteristics as well as group patterns.

3 Match each question and answer.

1 Is the plane here yet? ____
2 How long have you taken English classes? ____
3 Do you know my friend Tammy? ____
4 Have you tried some of this pizza yet? ____
5 How long has your brother worked at that company? ____
6 How long have Shen and Jun been friends? ____
7 Have you finished your assignment? ____

a He has been there since 2015.
b Yes, I've eaten some already.
c They met in 2011 and have been friends ever since.
d No, I have not met her yet.
e Yes, I've just turned it in to our teacher!
f Yes, it's already arrived.
g I've studied English for two years.

4 Put the words in the correct order to make sentences.

1 called / three times / has / already / she / .
____
2 the test / have / yet / for / studied / you / ?
____
3 got / I / from school / just / home / .
____
4 been / never / the students / to another country / have / .
____
5 we haven't / we have / met / cousins / that / even / !
____
6 since / has studied / 2017 / Jana / English / .
____
7 for / my best friend / Renato / five years / has been / .
____

5 Answer the questions so they are true for you. Write complete sentences.

1 Have you learned to drive yet?
____
2 Have you already done your homework for this week?
____
3 What is something you just finished doing?
____
4 How long have you been a student at this school?
____
5 Have you ever visited an English-speaking country?
____
6 What is one food you never want to eat?
____
7 How long have you known your best friend?
____

6 Use the prompts to write sentences with the present perfect. You may need to add words.

1 I / live Bangalore / for / three years
____

2 I / listen that song / two times / already
____

3 She / not / go rock climbing / since / last year
____

4 Alex / be / my friend / since / four years old
____

5 We / just / go / beach
____

6 Nate / eat breakfast / already
____

7 They / just / finish / take test
____

8 I / not talk / new neighbor / yet
____

7 Which choice is closest in meaning to the original sentence?

1 I've just taken a walk.
   a I took a walk not long ago.
   b I have been taking walks for a long time.

2 Niko's teacher was surprised to find out she had already learned about ancient Roman history.
   a Niko's teacher was surprised she had studied history.
   b Niko's teacher didn't expect her to know about ancient Roman history.

3 He's lost his book.
   a He doesn't have his book now.
   b He lost his book but has it now.

4 I haven't learned all of the new vocabulary yet.
   a I did not learn all of the new vocabulary, but I plan to soon.
   b I did not learn all of the new vocabulary, and I am not planning to.

5 He has just come from Dubai.
   a He recently arrived from Dubai.
   b He arrived from Dubai more than a month ago.

6 It's 2017 now, and Kim has known Eliza for three years.
   a Kim met Eliza in 2014.
   b Kim knows Eliza now but didn't know her in 2014.

7 She hasn't made plans for after graduation yet.
   a She knows what she's doing after she graduates.
   b She doesn't know what she's doing after she graduates.

8 My cousins have already seen the film.
   a My cousins saw the film.
   b My cousins did not see the film.

8 Read each question. Choose the correct response.

1 How long have you had that phone?
   a I've had it for last week.
   b I've had it since last week.

2 Do you know how to get to the art museum?
   a No, I don't. I haven't gone there for I was a child.
   b Yes, I've been going there since I was a child.

3 Have you seen the new painting at the museum?
   a No, I've seen it already.
   b Yes, I've already seen it.

4 Did you talk to Tavish yesterday?
   a No, I haven't talked to him since last week.
   b Yes, I have talked with him yesterday.

5 Have you started your piano lessons yet?
   a Yes, I've started my lessons already.
   b Yes, I've just been started my lessons.

6 How long have you been playing the piano?
   a I was playing the piano for 2009.
   b I've played the piano since I was six years old.

7 Have you invited your teammates to the party yet?
   a No, I haven't invited them yet.
   b Yes, I have invited them yet.

5D Why we laugh

TEDTALKS

AUTHENTIC LISTENING SKILLS

1 Listen and complete each sentence about the excerpt with the correct word or short phrase. 56

1 Sophie noticed laughter when she was a ________________.
2 She saw her parents doing something ________________, where they were laughing.
3 They were ________________ with laughter. She didn't know what they were laughing at, but she wanted to join.
4 Her parents were laughing at a ________________ that people used to sing.
5 The song ________________ around signs in toilets in trains.
6 She says that the English have a sophisticated ________________.

WATCH

2 Choose the correct answers.

1 What does Sophie say about laughing with other people?
   a People aren't really laughing at jokes.
   b People laugh less when they are with other people.
   c People make other people laugh with jokes.
2 What do people try to show when they are laughing in a group?
   a that they think things are funny
   b that they are part of the group
   c that they have feelings
3 Who thought that humans were the only animals that laugh?
   a Sophie Scott
   b Robert Levenson
   c Nietzsche
4 What is *posed laughter*?
   a when someone laughs because something is funny
   b when someone laughs at a silly song
   c when someone makes a fake laugh
5 How does laughter affect relationships?
   a It helps people become less stressed.
   b It makes people annoyed.
   c It makes people speak better.
6 What does Sophie say about laughter?
   a It is a new behavior.
   b It is an old behavior.
   c It is something humans do to be different from other animals.

3 Circle the things that are true about laughter.

1 Laughter is most similar to human speech.
2 Laughter sounds like animals calling each other.
3 Humans are the only animals that laugh.
4 People are more likely to laugh if they are with other people.
5 Laughter is a social interaction or activity.

4 Match the words to the correct definitions.

1 social ____
2 laughter ____
3 voluntary ____
4 involuntary ____
5 emotional ____
6 funny ____
7 joke ____
8 mammals ____

a a group of animals that includes humans
b something that involves other people
c connected with feelings
d making a person laugh
e an act or something people say that makes people laugh
f the sound of a laugh
g when someone does something without being asked
h when someone does something because he can't control himself

VOCABULARY IN CONTEXT

5 Choose the correct word to complete each sentence.

1 My parents thought the song was really ____. They laughed really hard.
   a silly **b** weird **c** strange
2 When people laugh, they make ____ and strange sound. It isn't a usual sound.
   a a silly **b** an odd **c** a stupid
3 I cared about laughter and when I became a neuroscientist I cared about it again. It's a ____ thing to care about. Not many people care about it.
   a scary **b** dangerous **c** weird
4 I wanted to find out the beginnings of laughter. The ____ of it.
   a origins **b** ending **c** sounds
5 Laughter has two different ____. There are two causes for it.
   a problems **b** meanings **c** roots

5E Invitations

SPEAKING

1 Listen and complete the conversations with the correct words. 57

1 **A:** Hey, Marta,
_______________________________________?
B: _______________________________________. Why?
A: Well, I'm having a party at my house. Can you come?
B: Oh _______________________________________.
What time should I come over?
A: Any time after 8.

2 **A:** _______________________________________?
B: _______________________________________. I usually hang out with my family in the afternoon.
A: Well, a few of us are going hiking. Want to come?
B: Um, _______________________________________.
Can I let you know later?
A: Yeah, just text me, OK?

3 **A:** Jane, have fun playing at the concert tonight!
B: Thanks! Would you like to come and hear the band?
A: _______________________________________.
B: No problem.

4 **A:** Hey, listen.
_______________________________________?
B: _______________________________________. Why?
A: There's this new skate meet at the youth club.
B: Oh yeah, _______________________________________.
A: It starts at 7.
B: Cool! I'll be there!

5 **A:** Hey, Lucy! I just wondered. You haven't replied to see the play my brother's starring in.
B: Oh yeah, _______________________________________.
One sec.
A: Sure.
B: Yeah, I thought so.
_______________________________________.
B: Oh, that's too bad.

2 Find and correct the errors in the sentences. Then decide the function of the sentence or question. Write the letter on the line.

(A) asking if someone is available
(S) saying if you are available or not
(Y) accepting an invitation
(N) saying no to a an invitation

1 Are you near next Saturday? ___
2 I need to make my schedule. ___
3 Sure, I love to. ___
4 She depends. ___
5 This sounds great! ___
6 Thanks for inviting me, but I'm worried I've got something else on. ___
7 I'll go to ask my parents. ___
8 Are you making anything on Tuesday night? ___
9 Sorry, I can't take it. But thank you for inviting me. ___
10 Are you above on Sunday? ___
11 I (don't) think that. ___
12 I'm not definitely. ___

3 Describe an invitation you got recently.

You should say:

- who gave you the invitation
- how you know them
- what the invitation was for
- how you responded to the invitation
- why you gave this response

You will talk about the subject for one to two minutes. Record yourself. Take one minute to think about what you're going to say. You may make notes to help you. Then compare your recording with the sample answers. 58

WRITING Informal invitations and replies

1 **Write the missing letters of the following abbreviations.**

1 A.__.A.__. as soon as possible
2 __.S.__.P. reply and say if you can make it
3 __.S. let me also add this

2 **Complete the text with the correct words about writing, accepting, and saying *no* to invitations.**

apologize	begin	date	enjoy
know	make it	offer	say

When you write an invitation, you should include the time, (1) __________, location, and type of event. Remember to ask the person to let you know if they can come.

When you accept an invitation, (2) __________ by thanking the person who invited you. Ask any questions you might have about the event. You could also (3) __________ to bring something (food or drinks, for example).

If you can't go to the event, you should still (4) __________ *thank you* for the invitation. Then (5) __________, and if you want to, you can give a short explanation about why you can't (6) __________. It's polite to end by saying you hope they (7) __________ the event.

3 **Read the invitation. Then circle the answers to the questions below.**

Jason,

I'm having a surprise party for Pablo on Sunday the 18th from 7pm to 10pm at the tennis club. We're celebrating his success at the tennis finals last weekend. Can you make it? R.S.V.P.

Mike

1 Who is the invitation to?
2 What kind of party is it?
3 Who is the party for?
4 What day and date is the party at?
5 What time does the party end?
6 Where is the party being held?
7 What is the reason for the party?
8 Who is sending the invitation?

4 **Read the note. Then put the points in the correct order, 1–6.**

Hi Boris,

Thanks for inviting me to the block party on Friday. It sounds like fun, but I'm really sorry, I can't make it. I've already made plans with my cousin. (We're going to a concert in town.)

Hugo
P.S. I hope everyone has a fantastic time at the block party!

____ hopes people enjoy the block party
____ explains why he can't go
____ gives a greeting
____ says *no* to the invitation
____ apologizes
____ says *thank you* for the invitation

5 **Pretend you are Pat. This is an invitation you have received from your friend, Erika.**

Hey Pat,

I'm having a dinner party on Thursday the 9th at 7:30 at my house. I'm going to cook curry and rice. Can you make it?

R.S.V.P.
Erika

Write a note to Erika accepting or saying no to the invitation. Include the following information:

If you can make it
- thank the sender for the invitation
- say you can make it
- offer to bring something
- ask a question

If you can't make it
- thank the sender for the invitation
- say you can't make it
- explain why
- say you hope the party goes well

Review

1 Unscramble the words for family members and other people.

1 onrmadhretg ______
2 rgantres ______
3 scamletsa ______
4 tessir ______
5 nuta ______
6 nulce ______
7 robhert ______
8 scunoi ______

2 Complete the sentences with the correct words.

1 Your mother's sister and brother are your ______ and ______.
2 Your mother's brother's kids are your ______.
3 If your parents have other kids besides you, they are your ______ and ______.
4 Your father's mother and father are your ______ and ______.
5 People that you don't know are ______.
6 People you go to school with are your ______.
7 People you play sports like football or hockey with are your ______.
8 Waving, shaking hands, kissing, hugging, and bowing are all ways to ______.

3 Correct the present perfect errors in the sentences.

1 Scientists have document multi-generational family groups of elephants which have up to 12 members and are led by the oldest female. ______
2 Researchers has observed wolves giving up their own lives to protect other wolves in their pack. ______
3 Young orcas that scientists have studying spend their entire lives with their parents in the wild. ______
4 People has spot dolphins that tried to save people from shark attacks. ______
5 Scientists have notice that female lions lick other lions, both male and female, to strengthen the social bonds in their group. ______
6 Researchers have make videos of chimps grooming each other, which is important for maintaining chimp "friendships." ______
7 Zookeepers has noticed that Asian small-clawed otters spend nearly all their time together—even when they sleep! ______

4 Put the words in the correct order to make sentences.

1 I / minutes / ridden / bike / just / for / my / have / fifteen
______.
______.
2 she / party / already / has / planned / the
______.
______.
3 new / a / he's / built / just / house
______.
______.
4 school / already / from / she's / high / graduated
______.
______.
5 in / long / how / you / lived / Denmark / have
______.
______?
6 long / London / how / has / to / school / in / she / gone
______.
______?

5 Choose the correct option to complete the sentences.

1 He hasn't written his paper *yet / just*.
2 She has lived with her sister *for / since* seven months.
3 Connie has practiced the piano *yet / already*.
4 He has *since / just* read the letter from his grandfather.
5 She's watched that TV show *for / since* it began.
6 They *had traveling / have traveled* to Mexico every summer since they were eight years old.
7 Marty *is feeling / has felt* sick for three days.

VOCABULARY LIST

UNIT 1

Review

bald (adj)	/bɔld/
beard (n)	/bɪrd/
black (adj)	/blæk/
blond (adj)	/blɑnd/
brown (adj)	/braʊn/
dark (adj)	/dɑrk/
curly (adj)	/ˈkɜrli/
glasses (n)	/ˈglæsəz/
hair (n)	/hɛr/
long (adj)	/lɔŋ/
short (adj)	/ʃɔrt/
straight (adj)	/streɪt/
tall (adj)	/tɔl/

Unit Vocabulary

active (adj)	/ˈæktɪv/
calm (adj)	/kɑm/
cheerful (adj)	/ˈtʃɪrfəl/
cool (adj)	/kul/
confident (adj)	/ˈkɑnfədənt/
easygoing (adj)	/ˈizigoʊɪŋ/
friendly (adj)	/ˈfrendli/
funny (adj)	/ˈfʌni/
happy (adj)	/ˈhæpi/
hard-working (adj)	/ˌhɑrdˈwɜrkɪŋ/
helpful (adj)	/ˈhɛlpfəl/
honest (adj)	/ˈɑnəst/
intelligent (adj)	/ɪnˈtɛlədʒənt/
kind (adj)	/kaɪnd/
lazy (adj)	/ˈleɪzi/
loud (adj)	/laʊd/
mean (adj)	/min/
nervous (adj)	/ˈnɜrvəs/
nice (adj)	/naɪs/
personality (n)	/ˌpɜrsəˈnælɪti/
popular (adj)	/ˈpɑpjələr/
relaxed (adj)	/rəˈlækst/
serious (adj)	/ˈsɪriəs/
shy (adj)	/ʃaɪ/
smart (adj)	/smɑrt/
sociable (adj)	/ˈsoʊʃəbəl/
talented (adj)	/ˈtæləntɪd/
weak (adj)	/wik/

Extension

affectionate (adj)	/əˈfɛkʃənət/
annoying (adj)	/əˈnɔɪɪŋ/
careless (adj)	/ˈkɛrləs/
generous (adj)	/ˈdʒɛnərəs/
impatient (adj)	/ɪmˈpeɪʃənt/
neat (adj)	/nit/
organized (adj)	/ˈɔrgəˌnaɪzd/
patient (adj)	/ˈpeɪʃənt/
polite (adj)	/pəˈlaɪt/
rude (adj)	/rud/
selfish (adj)	/ˈsɛlfɪʃ/

Vocabulary Building

be (v)	/bi/
become (v)	/bɪˈkʌm/
afraid (adj)	/əˈfreɪd/
angry (adj)	/ˈæŋgri/
bored (adj)	/bɔrd/
excited (adj)	/ɪkˈsaɪtɪd/
feel (v)	/fil/
frightened (adj)	/ˈfraɪtənd/
get (v)	/gɛt/
look (v)	/lʊk/
seem (v)	/sim/
upset (adj)	/ʌpsɛt/
worried (adj)	/ˈwʌrid/

Vocabulary in Context

feel calm (phrase)	/fil kɑm/
image (n)	/ˈɪmɪdʒ/
language barrier (n)	/ˈlæŋgwɪdʒ/ /ˈbæriərz/
proposal (n)	/prəˈpoʊzəl/
struggle (n)	/ˈstrʌgəl/

UNIT 2

Review

apartment (n)	/əˈpɑrtmənt/
bathroom (n)	/ˈbæˌθrum/
bed (n)	/bɛd/
bedroom (n)	/ˈbɛˌdrum/
city (n)	/ˈsɪti/
dining room (n)	/ˈdaɪnɪŋ rum/
kitchen (n)	/ˈkɪtʃən/
living room (n)	/ˈlɪvɪŋ rum/
quiet (adj)	/ˈkwaɪət/
wall (n)	/wɔl/
yard (n)	/jɑrd/

Unit Vocabulary

business district (n)	/ˈbɪznəs ˈdɪstrɪkt/
chair (n)	/tʃɛr/
couch (n)	/kaʊtʃ/
crowded (adj)	/ˈkraʊdɪd/
decoration (n)	/ˌdɛkəˈreɪʃən/
door (n)	/dɔr/
historic (adj)	/hɪˈstɔrɪk/
light (adj)	/laɪt/
modern (adj)	/ˈmɑdərn/
refrigerator (n)	/rəˈfrɪdʒəˌreɪtər/
residential area (n)	/ˌrɛzɪˈdɛntʃəl ˈɛriə/
rural (adj)	/ˈrʊrəl/
shopping district (n)	/ˈʃɑpɪŋ/ /dɪstrɪkt/
stairs (n)	/stɛrz/
suburban (adj)	/səˈbɜrbən/
table (n)	/ˈteɪbəl/
traditional (adj)	/trəˈdɪʃənəl/
urban (adj)	/ˈɜrbən/
walkable (adj)	/ˈwɔkəbl/
window (n)	/ˈwɪndoʊ/

Extension

cabinet (n)	/ˈkæbənət/
carpet (n)	/ˈkɑrpət/
ceiling (n)	/ˈsilɪŋ/
closet (n)	/ˈklɑzət/
curtains (n)	/ˈkɜrtənz/
driveway (n)	/ˈdraɪˌvweɪ/
elevator (n)	/ˈɛləˌveɪtər/
floor (n)	/flɔr/
sink (n)	/sɪŋk/
stove (n)	/stoʊv/
toilet (n)	/ˈtɔɪlət/

Vocabulary Building

accommodation (n)	/əˌkɑməˈdeɪʃən/
communication (n)	/kəmˌjunəˈkeɪʃən/
imagination (n)	/ɪˌmædʒəˈneɪʃən/
construction (n)	/kənˈstrʌkʃən/
direction (n)	/dəˈrɛkʃən/
education (n)	/ˌɛdʒəˈkeɪʃən/
exploration (n)	/ˌɛkspləˈreɪʃən/
location (n)	/loʊˈkeɪʃən/
transportation (n)	/ˌtrænspərˈteɪʃən/

Vocabulary in Context

I've got to tell you (phrase)	/aɪv gɑt tu tɛl ju/
didn't feel right (phrase)	/ˈdɪdənt/ /fil/ /raɪt/
elegant (adj)	/ˈələgənt/
make perfect sense (phrase)	/meɪk ˈpɜrˌfɪkt sɛns/
treat you well (phrase)	/trit ju wɛl/

UNIT 3

Review

back (n)	/bæk/
body (n)	/ˈbɑdi/
dentist (n)	/ˈdɛntəst/
doctor (n)	/ˈdɑktər/
eyes (n)	/aɪz/
face (n)	/feɪs/
fine (adv)	/faɪn/
teeth (n)	/tiθ/
tooth (n)	/tuθ/

Unit Vocabulary

arm (n)	/ɑrm/
backache (n)	/ˈbæˌkeɪk/
broken (n)	/ˈbroʊkən/
chest (n)	/tʃɛst/
ears (n)	/ɪrz/
elbow (n)	/ˈɛlˌboʊ/
eyeglasses (n)	/ˈaɪˌglæsɪz/
finger (n)	/ˈfɪŋgər/
flu (n)	/flu/
foot (n)	/fʊt/
head (n)	/hɛd/
healthy (adj)	/ˈhɛlθi/
high temperature (n)	/haɪ ˈtɛmprətʃər/

hospital (n) /ˈhɑspɪtəl/
illness (n) /ˈɪlnəs/
injury (n) /ˈɪnʤəri/
knee (n) /ni/
leg (n) /lɛg/
medicine (n) /ˈmɛdɪsən/
mouth (n) /maʊθ/
pain (n) /peɪn/
patient (n) /ˈpeɪʃənts/
seasickness (n) /ˈsiˌsɪknəs/
shoulder (n) /ˈʃoʊldər/
sick (n) /sɪk/
sports injuries (n) /spɔrts/ /ˈɪnʤəriz/
stomach (n) /ˈstʌmək/
unwell (adj) /ʌnˈwɛl/
virus (n) /ˈvaɪrəs/

Extension

accident (n) /ˈæksədənt/
ankle (n) /ˈæŋkəl/
blood (n) /blʌd/
bone (n) /boʊn/
brain (n) /breɪn/
cheek (n) /ʧik/
chin (n) /ʧɪn/
finger (n) /ˈfɪŋgər/
heart (n) /hɑrt/
lungs (n) /lʌŋz/
neck (n) /nɛk/
pump (v) /pʌmp/
recover (v) /rɪˈkʌvər/
toe (n) /toʊ/
wrist (n) /rɪst/

Vocabulary Building

attempt (v) /əˈtɛmpt/
believe (v) /bɪˈliv/
combine (v) /ˈkɑmbaɪn/
discover (v) /dɪˈskʌvər/
entire (v) /ɪnˈtaɪər/
find (v) /faɪnd/
mix (v) /mɪks/
normal (adj) /ˈnɔrməl/
sickness (n) /ˈsɪknəs/
think (v) /θɪŋk/
typical (adj) /ˈtɪpəkəl/
try (v) /traɪ/
well (adj) /wɛl/
whole (adj) /hoʊl/

Vocabulary in Context

institution (n) /ˌɪnstɪˈtuʃən/
hit the books (phrase) /hɪt/ /ðə/ /bʊks/
ignore (v) /ɪgˈnɔr/
passed out (v) /pæst/ /aʊt/
specialist (n) /ˈspɛʃəlɪsts/
take seriously (phrase) /teɪk/ /ˈsɪriəsli/

UNIT 4

Review

books (n) /bʊks/
class (n) /klæs/
classroom (n) /ˈklæsˌrum/
dictionary (n) /ˈdɪkʃəˌnɛri/
fail (v) /feɪl/
homework (n) /ˈhoʊmˌwɜrk/
lesson (n) /ˈlɛsən/
library (n) /ˈlaɪˌbrɛri/
map (n) /mæp/
pass (v) /pæs/
school bus (n) /skul/ /bʌs/
teach (v) /tiʧ/
teacher (n) /ˈtitʃər/
university (n) /ˌjunəˈvɜrsəti/

Unit Vocabulary

attend (v) /əˈtɛnd/
blackboard (n) /blækbɔrd/
class size (n) /klæs/ /saɪz/
creative (adj) /kriˈeɪtɪv/
desk (n) /dɛsk/
develop (v) /dɪˈvɛləp/
education (n) /ˌɛdʒəˈkeɪʃən/
elementary school (n) /ˌɛləˈmɛntri/ /ˌskul/
grade (n) /greɪd/
hard-working (adj) /ˌhɑrdˈwɜrkɪŋ/
high school (n) /ˈhaɪ/ /ˌskul/
notebook (n) /ˈnoʊtbʊk/
online learning (n) /ˈɔnˌlaɪn/ /ˈlɜrnɪŋ/
private school (n) /ˌpraɪvət/ /ˈskul/
public school (n) /ˌpʌblɪk/ /ˈskul/
skills (n) /skɪl/
student (n) /ˈstudənt/
study (v) /ˈstʌdi/
test (n) /tɛst/

Extension

after school activities (phrase) /ˈæftər/ /ˈskul/ /ækˈtɪvətiz/
algebra (n) /ˈældʒəbrə/
ancient history (n) /ˈeɪnʃənt/ /ˈhɪstəri/
bad grades (n) /ˈbæd/ /ˈgreɪdz/
band (n) /ˈbænd/
biology (n) /baɪˈɑlədʒi/
chemistry (n) /ˈkɛməstri/
chess (n) /ˈtʃɛs/
drama club (n) /ˈdrɑmə/ /ˈklʌb/
geography (n) /dʒiˈɑgrəfi/
geometry (n) /dʒiˈɑmətri/
history (n) /ˈhɪstəri/
math (n) /ˈmæθ/
orchestra (n) /ˈɔrkəstrə/
physics (n) /ˈfɪzɪks/
science (n) /ˈsaɪəns/
social studies (n) /ˈsoʊʃəl/ /ˈstʌdiz/
sports (n) /ˈspɔrts/
team (n) /ˈtim/

Vocabulary Building

beautiful (adj) /ˈbjutɪfəl/
careful (adj) /ˈkɛrfəl/
careless (adj) /ˈkɛrləs/
skillful (adj) /ˈskɪlfəl/
useful (adj) /ˈjusfəl/

Vocabulary in Context

100 percent (n) /wʌn/ /ˈhʌndrɪd/ /pərsent/
go into (phrase) /ˈgoʊ/ /ˈɪntu/
in other words (phrase) /ˈɪn/ /ˈʌðər/ /ˈwɜrdz/
make it to (phrase) /ˈmeɪk/ /ˈɪt/ /ˈtu/
producing (v) /prəˈdusɪŋ/
were in trouble (phrase) /ˈwɜr/ /ˈɪn/ /ˈtrʌbəl/

UNIT 5

Review

boy (n) /ˈbɔi/
children (n) /ˈtʃɪldrən/
cousin (n) /ˈkʌzɪn/
daughter (n) /ˈdɔtər/
divorced (adj) /dəˈvɔrst/
family (n) /ˈfæmli/
father (n) /ˈfɑðər/
friends (n) /frɛndz/
girl (n) /ˈgɜrl/
husband (n) /ˈhʌzbənd/
man (n) /ˈmæn/
men (n) /ˈmɛn/
married (n) /ˈmɛrid/
mother (n) /ˈmʌðər/
parents (n) /ˈpɛrənts/
single (n) /ˈsɪŋgəl/
son (n) /ˈsʌn/
wife (n) /ˈwaɪf/
woman (n) /ˈwʊmən/
women (n) /ˈwɪmən/

Unit Vocabulary

aunt (n) /ænt/
best friend (n) /bɛst/
brother (n) /ˈbrʌðər/
classmate (n) /ˈklæsmeɪt/
hug (v) /hʌg/
husband (n) /ˈhʌzbənd/
grandfather (n) /ˈgrændfɑðər/
grandmother (n) /ˈgrændmʌðər/
kiss (v) /kɪs/
mother (n) /ˈmʌðər/
partner (n) /ˈpɑrtnər/
say hello (v) /ˈsei/ /həˈloʊ/
shake hands (v) /ˈʃeɪk/ /ˈhændz/
sister (n) /ˈsɪstər/
son (n) /ˈsʌn/
stranger (n) /ˈstreɪndʒər/
teammate (n) /ˈtimmeɪt/
uncle (n) /ˈʌŋkəl/
wave (v) /weɪv/
wife (n) /ˈwaɪf/

Extension

acquaintance (n) /əˈkweɪntn̩s/
brother-in-law (n) /ˈbrʌðərənlɔ/
bow (v) /baʊ/
ex-husband (n) /ˈɛksˈhʌzbənd/
ex-wife (n) /ˈɛksˈwaɪf/
father-in-law (n) /ˈfɑðərənlɔ/
half-brother (n) /ˈhæfˈbrʌðər/
half-sisters (n) /ˈhæfˈsɪstərz/
kids (n) /ˈkɪdz/
mother-in-law (n) /ˈmʌðərənlɔ/
nephew (n) /ˈnɛfju/

niece (n)	/'nis/
stepbrothers (n)	/'stɛpbrʌðərz/
stepfather (n)	/'stɛpfɑðər/
stepmother (n)	/'stɛpmʌðər/
stepsister (n)	/'stɛpsɪstər/

Vocabulary Building

cultural (adj)	/'kʌltʃərəl/
emotional (adj)	/ɪ'moʊʃənl̩/
musical (adj)	/'mjuzɪkəl/
natural (adj)	/'nætʃərəl/
traditional (adj)	/trə'dɪʃənl̩/

Vocabulary in Context

odd (adj)	/ɑd/
origins (n)	/'ɔrədʒɪnz/
roots (n)	/ruts/
silly (adj)	/'sɪli/
weird (adj)	/wɪrd/

PHOTO CREDITS

002 (tl) Rawpixel.com/Shutterstock.com, **002** (tr) Nataliia Budianska/Shutterstock.com **002** (cl) Flashon Studio/Shutterstock.com, **002** (cr) Felix Mizioznikov/Shutterstock.com, **002** (bl) Look Studio/Shutterstock.com, **002** (br) alexandre zveiger/Shutterstock.com, **004** Rawpixel.com/Shutterstock.com, **007** Dudarev Mikhail/Shutterstock.com, **009** De Visu/Shutterstock.com, **013** Theo Wargo/Getty Images, **014** (tl) Africa Studio/Shutterstock.com, **014** (tr) Jeffrey M. Frank/Shutterstock.com, **014** (tcl) Africa Studio/Shutterstock.com, **014** (tcr) Petch A Ratana/Shutterstock.com, **014** (cl) Ljupco Smokovski/Shutterstock.com, **014** (cr) elena castaldi viora/Shutterstock.com, **014** (bcl) Photographee.eu/Shutterstock.com, **014** (bcr) kibri_ho/Shutterstock.com, **014** (bl) nexus 7/Shutterstock.com, **019** (l) Somphop/Shutterstock.com, **019** (r) Angela Harburn/Shutterstock.com, **020** snowturtle/Shutterstock.com, **021** Angela N Perryman/Shutterstock.com, **024** UTBP/Shutterstock.com, **026** (bcl) stihii/Shutterstock.com, **026** (bcr) Fotos593/Shutterstock.com, **026** (bl) Dragon Images/Shutterstock.com, **026** (br) Monkey Business Images/Shutterstock.com, **026** (tl) Dudarev Mikhail/Shutterstock.com, **026** (tr) Monkey Business Images/Shutterstock.com, **026** (tcl) Piotr Krzeslak/Shutterstock.com, **026** (tcr) Estrada Anton/Shutterstock.com, **026** (r) exopixel/Shutterstock.com, **026** Hero Images/Getty Images, **027** Alexander Kirch/Shutterstock.com, **031** Monkey Business Images/Shutterstock.com, **036** wavebreakmedia/Shutterstock.com, **038** (tl) Iulian Dragomir/Shutterstock.com, **038** (cl) Pavlin Plamenov Petkov/Shutterstock.com, **038** (cr) Jannis Tobias Werner/Shutterstock.com, **038** (bl) sirtravelalot/Shutterstock.com, **038** (br) Patricia Hofmeester/Shutterstock.com, **038** (b) maroke/Shutterstock.com, **038** (tr) nulinukas/Shutterstock.com, **039** Arlo Magicman/Shutterstock.com, **040** Africa Studio/Shutterstock.com, **043** Monkey Business Images/Shutterstock.com, **047** (tl) Mr. Luck/Shutterstock.com, **047** (tr) aliaksei kruhlenia/Shutterstock.com, **047** (bl) Ivana Milic/Shutterstock.com, **047** (br) elenabsl/Shutterstock.com, **050** (t) Golden Pixels LLC/Shutterstock.com, **050** (cl) Daniel M Ernst/Shutterstock.com, **050** (tr) CandyBox Images/Shutterstock.com, **050** (tl) leungchopan/Shutterstock.com, **050** (cr) sanjagrujic/Shutterstock.com, **050** (bl) Odua Images/Shutterstock.com, **050** (br) Jennifer Lam/Shutterstock.com, **052** (t) sirtravelalot/Shutterstock.com, **052** (tc) Dima Sidelnikov/Shutterstock.com, **052** (bc) Odua Images/Shutterstock.com, **052** (b) aslysun/Shutterstock.com, **055** pisaphotography/Shutterstock.com.